The Bishop and the Baptized

For Sarah

The Bishop and the Baptized

*Anglican episcopal ministry
through the lens of the ordinal*

Justin Pottinger

scm press

© Justin Pottinger 2025

Published in 2025 by SCM Press
Editorial office

3rd Floor, Invicta House,
110 Golden Lane,
London EC1Y 0TG, UK
www.scmpress.co.uk

SCM Press is an imprint of Hymns Ancient & Modern Ltd
(a registered charity)

Ancient & Modern

Hymns Ancient & Modern® is a registered trademark of
Hymns Ancient & Modern Ltd
13A Hellesdon Park Road, Norwich,
Norfolk NR6 5DR, UK

All rights reserved. No part of this publication may be reproduced,
stored in a retrieval system, or transmitted,
in any form or by any means, electronic, mechanical,
photocopying or otherwise, without the prior permission of
the publisher, SCM Press.

The Author has asserted their right under the Copyright, Designs and Patents Act
1988 to be identified as the Author of this Work

British Library Cataloguing in Publication data
A catalogue record for this book is available
from the British Library

ISBN: 978-0-334-06702-3

EU GPSR Authorized Representative
LOGOS EUROPE, 9 rue Nicolas Poussin, 17000, LA ROCHELLE, France
E-mail: Contact@logoseurope.eu

Scripture quotations are from the New Revised Standard Version Bible: Anglicized
Edition, copyright © 1989, 1995 National Council of the Churches of Christ in the
United States of America. Used by permission. All rights reserved worldwide.

No part of this book may be used or reproduced in any manner for the purpose of
training artificial intelligence technologies or systems.

Typeset by Natalie Quinn

Contents

Acknowledgements		ix
Abbreviations Used		xi
Introduction		1
1	The Church is an Institution Defined by Ecclesiology	12
2	The Significance of Baptismal Ecclesiology	24
3	Ordination: The Bishop's Hands Within the Church's Prayers	41
4	A Sacramental Ecclesiology for a Sacramental Ministry	54
5	Anglican Episcopal Ministry is Relational	68
6	Eschewing the Temptations to be Defined by Power and Institutional Demands	80
7	The Church Needs Foot Washers	91
8	The Use of Shepherd in the Anglican Ordinals of the British Isles	107
9	Shepherd in the Bible and Ancient Near Eastern Culture	118
10	The Pastoral Staff	130
11	Shepherd is the Defining Metaphor	141
12	Conclusions for Contemporary Episcopal Ministry	153
Bibliography		171
Index		183

Acknowledgements

As is often the case in matters theological, this book is not what I set out to write. It is the confluence of PhD study and my lived experience in the Church of England that spurred me into focusing my attention on the nature of episcopal ministry.

This book would not have come to pass without the help of Jo Lacy-Smith, Sally Dhruev, Dom Whitting, Stephen Conway, Dan Roberts, Belinda Marflitt, Edward Watkins and Julia Baldwin.

I couldn't have asked for a better doctorial supervisor than Simon Jones who calmly and authoritatively embodied that essential balance of critical friend and encourager. Mark Chapman's guidance and advice has been essential, as has that of James Woodward, Tim Thornton, William Price, David Stancliffe, Mary Marshall and Tomos Reed. Many conversations have been had; Lydia Cook, Jonathan Still, Daniel Inman and Lewis Pearson have been among those who have endured them most graciously.

The support of the Red Post Benefice, Sarum St Michael Trust and St George's Trust and the Lambeth Research Degrees in Theology made this research possible, and David Shervington and Rachel Edge at SCM Press have been key to bringing this book to life.

Thank you to all of you, my parents, and to my greatest supporters, my wife and children, who accompanied me through all of it. I am richly blessed and profoundly grateful.

Abbreviations Used

ASB   *Alternative Service Book*, the Church of England.

BCP 1662   *Ordering of Bishops, Priests and Deacons*, the Church of England.

BCP 1979   *Book of Common Prayer and Administration of the Sacraments and Other Rites and Ceremonies of the Church*, the Episcopal Church of the United States of America.

CW:OS   *Common Worship: Ordination Services*, the Church of England.

The Preface   The Preface to the Declaration of Assent.

Introduction

The hypothesis of this book is that *Common Worship: Ordination Services*,[1] the *de facto* ordinal of the Church of England and foundational document for the theology of ordained ministry, has a distinctive perspective on ordained ministry in England, and more widely for Anglicans globally.[2] Christian ministry is an integrated aspect of Christian discipleship, and the contemporary discussion is highly relevant to the challenges faced both internally and externally by Anglicans today. This book considers three key questions. What is the nature of the Church in which the bishop ministers? How does ecclesiology inform episcopal ministry? How do 'shepherd' and other key terms define and elucidate the bishop's ontology?[3] Throughout it will demonstrate that the basis for Anglican Christian ministry is an integrated sacramental ecclesiology, in which the minister, primarily the bishop, should have close pastoral connections with both lay and ordained members of the Church.

This is a work of liturgical theology, which sees the ordinal as a central articulation of the nature of the Church and of Christian ministry within the life of it. The focus will be the bishops of the Church of England as its principal ministers, and it will be demonstrated that the shape of episcopal ministry, as articulated in the ordinal, asks significant questions of the contemporary praxis of episcopal ministry in the Church.

The significance of the *Common Worship* ordinal

The liturgy of the Church both forms and reflects its ontology as a dynamic process of the Church creating, and being created by, its liturgy. Within the canon of liturgical texts, the ordinal is particularly significant for the study of ministry, as Stephen Platten explains:

> As each of the Common Worship ordination rites makes clear, the ministry of deacons, priests and bishops can only be understood in the

context of the Church – the company of all the baptized whom God forms into a royal priesthood. The ministries of deacon, priest and bishop are given by God to serve that royal priesthood and thereby to enable the Church to live out its calling. These ministries also represent to the Church the ministry of Christ. Thus, study of orders and ordination rites points beyond those subjects in two directions – to reflection on the Church as a whole, 'Christ's beloved bride, his own flock, bought by the shedding of his blood on the cross', and on Christ himself, 'the Apostle and High Priest of our faith and the Shepherd of our souls'.[4]

Discussion of the nature of Christian ministry is therefore an aspect of ecclesiology, which is itself an aspect of theology; to understand what it means to be a Christian minister requires articulation of the nature of the Church and of God.

Ecclesiology, being the study of the Church, has the additional complication of various possible approaches, with different perspectives and different primary evidence. The focus here is on the liturgy of the Church, specifically the ordinal, and dialogue with alternative approaches will elucidate the distinctiveness and benefits of this approach. Furthermore, while text is an important aspect of liturgical study, the study will draw on the work of David Fagerberg to describe liturgy as the enacted work of the Church.[5] It is in this holistic view that liturgy is best understood as being both the product of the Church and the Church as the product of the liturgy. The emphasis is on Church as lived experience: paradoxical, multi-faceted and beyond attempts to describe it in reductionist terms, whether that reductionism be historical, legal or doctrinal. This book seeks to be broad, engaging with the reality of the Church in its fullness, while being firmly rooted in the ordinal.

Ordination services, by their very nature, are self-consciously, confidently and explicitly ecclesiological. This significance is heightened in Anglicanism where the *lex orandi* is particularly prominent in the expression of the *lex credendi* both historically and doctrinally. Thus, the preface to the main volume of Common Worship states, 'The forms of worship authorized in the Church of England express our faith and help to create our identity.'[6] Platten draws particular attention to the role of the ordinal:

> [The historic Christian doctrinal tradition] is expressed in its liturgy; two of the three 'historic formularies', in which, according to Canon

A5, the doctrine of the Church of England is particularly to be found, are liturgical texts – *The Book of Common Prayer* and the Ordinal of 1662.[7]

Anglican ecclesiology, having an intentional lack of centralized dogma, is itself indicative of the dispersed authority characteristic of Anglicanism. Although legally only an alternative to the official 1662 *Ordering of Bishops, Priests and Deacons*,[8] CW:OS is the foundational liturgy for ecclesiology in the Church of England because it is the *de facto* ordinal, being the one that is most commonly, if not exclusively, used.[9] CW:OS has a significant role as an instrument of unity within the Church, with people from various traditions within it being ordained using a liturgy that carries a much higher degree of uniformity than other Common Worship rites. Although used less frequently than other rites, such as Holy Communion or Daily Prayer, the ordinal nevertheless carries significant authority in shaping the Church, giving it greater prominence in the corpus of liturgical rites.

The ordinal gives particular clarity and emphasis to ecclesiology because ordination is a key moment in the life of any Church. As well as conferring specific ministries on specific people, the celebration of ordination makes visible and reaffirms the ordered nature of the Church. This is as true for the laity as it is for the clergy, with the whole assembly self-consciously inhabiting their role as the body of Christ. The same is true for initiation services, where the Church is gathered in all its fullness. However, as will be shown below, ecclesiology in the ordinal is heightened and clarified to a greater degree as there is less perceived need to accommodate pastoral and accessibility concerns, which are prominent in the celebration of initiation services. The ordinal is therefore the prime locus for the expression of Anglican ecclesiology. Moreover, the ordinal is dependent on ecclesiology as the practical foundation and legitimacy for the Church's action in ordaining people. Paul Avis explains:

> Although ecclesiology clearly has a practical dimension and is nothing if it is not applied to the life of the Church, it is essentially a branch of Christian doctrine, concerned with what we believe about the Church and God's purpose for it and how that purpose is to be carried out in accordance with God's will revealed in scripture as interpreted in the light of tradition and reason.[10]

This book will therefore start by clearly establishing the ecclesiology of *CW:OS*. Ecclesiology requires nuance and careful articulation, and Anglican ecclesiology is especially complex and nuanced. Rather than suffering from a lack of ecclesiology, the challenge for the Anglican paradox is that there are numerous potential ecclesiologies, each reflecting the breadth of tradition within the Church. As Stephen Sykes has affirmed, 'there must be an *Anglican ecclesiology*; that is, that Anglicans cannot take their doctrine of the Church second-hand and unadapted from other sources'.[11] Careful articulation of Anglican ecclesiology is required to prevent collapse into tribalism, in particular where there is a desire to emphasize commonality with other denominations, such as the nineteenth-century 'branch theory'.[12]

Anglican ecclesiology is an aspect of the *via media*, the middle way, which although variously defined, has been an enduring aspect of Anglican self-understanding. It can run the risk of simply being a compromise between extremes but is more positively and more constructively understood as a creative and dynamic tension. David Stancliffe, former chair of the Church's Liturgical Commission, is particularly aware of this issue. With liturgical texts authored by committee, authorization by synod, and no single central authority to define ecclesiology, there is a danger that what results is something that is least offensive to the parties concerned, or even liturgy that has internal contradictions:

> Common Worship was conceived therefore not so much as a compromise between the crusaders in different camps as an inclusive book that contained what was actually in use in both contemporary and traditional language, built around a core that was theologically sound and ecclesiologically coherent.[13]

Differing ecclesiologies are indeed evident in *CW:OS*, but paradoxically it is their presence, rather than an attempt to suppress them under a *tertium quid* or lowest common denominator ecclesiology that enables *CW:OS* to express a distinctive, coherent and empowering ecclesiology.

The significance of bishops for Christian ministry

The Bishop and the Baptized focuses on Christian ministry as expressed through the role and relationships of bishops because episcopal ministry incorporates all aspects of Christian ministry. Anglican orders are cumulative, with each ordination being lifelong, and successive ordinations built on the continuing foundation of the previous ordination. Steven Croft offers a helpful analogy of dimensions, with deacon, presbyter and bishop each inhabiting a different dimension of ordained ministry. However, for Croft the dimensions are overly distinct. Thus, his chart of ministry unpacks each order as a distinct category.[14] The cumulative nature of orders is better understood as subsets in a Venn diagram. In this way, the whole people of God are represented by the outer set, which contains the set of deacons: to be a deacon is not to be removed from being among the baptized, but a way of being among the baptized. At the fundamental level, therefore, lay and ordained are not mutually exclusive groups, but rather the ordained are a distinctive aspect of the laity. Within the set of deacons are the presbyters or priests, and within that set are the bishops.

Although Croft recognizes the multi-faceted nature of ministry, rather than rooting this in the ontology of the orders, he places the emphasis on the practical needs of the role. He states:

> The vicar or minister needs to have a diaconal dimension to his or her ministry, so ministry proceeds from an attitude of service and Christian leadership can be seen to involve many basic and practical tasks; a presbyteral dimension focused around the service of the Word and sacraments; and the dimension of episcopal ministry – the need to guard and guide the unity of the pilgrim people of God in a particular place and to raise up, commission and nurture others in Christian service.[15]

This articulation of ministry raises two significant questions. The first is whether ministry in these terms is any different to other forms of leadership. For instance, the effective CEO of a charity would also have to offer leadership on several different levels. *The Bishop and the Baptized* asserts that cumulative orders speak of ontology rather than functionality. The bishop relates to the Church as one of the baptized, deacon, priest and bishop in each and every interaction. The orders therefore speak of a way of being and are not a toolkit of potential responses. Second, Croft's explanation reflects his fragmented approach to the three orders, as if they are each distinct aspects of Christian ministry that the minister draws on to carry out their tasks. The assertion of this book is far stronger; that the ministry of presbyters cannot be inhabited other than through diaconal ministry; the oversight of bishops can only be lived through a diaconal and presbyteral ministry; and that underlying all ministry is a rootedness in being a baptized child of God.

Cumulative orders, therefore, are fundamentally about connection rather than separation. Successive ordinations do not lead to further and further distance from the baptized and the world, but instead a greater and greater connection with the fullness of the life of the Church. The bishop who becomes a distanced manager or leader, as is often modelled by the demands of the institution placed on a diocesan bishop, who is rarely seen by the parishioners of the diocese, is therefore a distortion of the true vocation of those called to episcopal ministry. The bishop, rather, is someone who can identify with and embody the fullness of what it means to be baptized, deacon, priest and bishop. To speak of bishops' ministry as 3D is best understood as a fullness of relationship that encompasses the ministries of the laity, deacon and presbyter. The bishop does not act in a third dimension, distinct from other ministries, but inhabits a way of relating that is integrated in the Church and speaks sacramentally of the relationship that Christ has with the whole Church.

The *cursus honorum*, which suggests that each successive ordination should be seen as steps to greater power, privilege and status, is therefore not only undermined but also inverted. The most significant characteristic of the people of God is that they are baptized, and that relationship and ministry of prayer, service and connection with God through Jesus Christ in the power of the Spirit is the ongoing foundation of Christian life and therefore Christian ministry. There is no higher calling, and so the *cursus honorum* is inverted by recognizing and affirming baptized life as being at the heart of the matter, and each successive ordination as therefore in some way less significant than the former. No greater status should be afforded a bishop over a deacon; each is a fellow worker in Christ's service. Each order has a distinctive relationship with the Church, and the relationship between the bishop and the Church embodies both their baptism and their ordination as a deacon and priest.

It is important to emphasize at this early stage that the focus of this book is the ministry of bishops as expressed in *CW:OS*. A key aspect of the argument that is being advanced here is that the dualism of *authority* and *power*, as expressed by Paul Avis, whereby 'Anglicanism is called to pioneer a particular kind of salutary authority'[16] and *power* is defined 'as the ability to make people do what we want them to do'.[17] In this book, *power* is understood as coercive and *authority* is understood to be invitational, following Christ's own example and with a high regard for the importance of free will and obedience that is offered out of love.[18]

Richard Rohr describes this latter as an aspect of 'right relationship', which he identifies as a hallmark of the kingdom of God: '[Jesus] makes right relationship desirable, possible, and the philosopher's stone by which everything else is to be weighed and judged.'[19] Both *authority* and *power* involve obedience and vulnerability, but there is an ontological difference between that which is demanded by *power* and that which is offered freely in response to *authority*.

The prioritization of *authority* over *power* reflects the ideals of the kingdom of God, in which the ecclesiology of *CW:OS* is firmly rooted. It is important to note that the Church is always living with the tension of being in the world and in the kingdom:

> Remember this: There are always two worlds. The world as it operates is power; the world as it should be is love. The secret of Reign-of-God life is how we can live in both – simultaneously. The world as it is will always be built on power, ego, success. Yet, we also must keep our eyes intently on the world as it should be – what Jesus calls the Reign of God. Power apart from love leads to brutality, but love that does not engage with power is mere sentimentality. A lot of Christians today are still trapped in one or the other.[20]

This book reflects the priorities of the ordinal and seeks to reassert the importance of kingdom values in considering Anglican ecclesiology and ministry. Contemporary Anglicanism is experiencing crises on several fronts, including declining numbers[21] and safeguarding reviews[22] in the Church of England. There is a great temptation to *power*, but the assertion here is that the Christian call is to *authority*, not *power*. For some this will seem naïve, for others perhaps overly simplistic, but it is part of Christ's radical invitation to follow him. The bishop offers the fullest expression of Christian ministry, not because they have been freed from the mundane concerns of the 'lower' orders, but because they are called to express their ministry through their baptismal, diaconal and priestly life. Thus, in truth, the bishop is one who is deeply rooted in the life of the Church, serving through close relationship and example, the polar opposite of the distanced leader who rules by fiat.

Methodology

The juxtaposition of worldly concerns with kingdom values is rooted in both biblical narrative and liturgical praxis. Using the Road to Emmaus story, David Stancliffe sees the dialogue as between 'us and our self-centred story' and God's story which is set alongside it.[23] In the liturgical context, this is presented as the Gathering and Liturgy of the Word. It is in the dialogue between our story and the story of God in the liturgy of the sacrament that transformation and 'meaning making' is experienced: 'We receive the body and blood of Christ, and so are transformed from being broken individuals, isolated from each other and God by sin, into being members of the risen Christ.'[24] This theological reflection uses analysis of the ordinal to explore how the kingdom of God is inhabited by the Church (ecclesiology) and what sort of ministry bishops have within the Church. The source material is Anglican, but since the ordinal is rooted in Scripture and the tradition of the Church, and since Anglicans understand their orders as being kingdom-based, and not denominationally based, there are implications here for the ministry of all Christians.

Liturgy itself offers a useful example of the way in which a repeated spiral of reflection is constructed from linear progressions. Each celebration of the liturgy is linear, moving from a gathering through to a dismissal, and the repeated celebrations of the liturgy give a spiral in which recurring themes are explored, and there is a mutual interpenetration and integration of the elements of the rite. The dialogue that underlies my arguments is a spiral dialogue between texts, author and context, reflecting the pastoral cycle,[25] which offers a relevant model for describing the genesis and process of the study and is presented here as a linear argument. Other forms of practical theology and theological reflection are also present. *Habitus* is significant in liturgical study, as it describes the repeated discipline of lived existence and ongoing character formation and disposition.[26] Applied theology, with its linear direction and implied obedience to the command of God, is also significant in this study as the ordinal is used as the primary sources in responding to the contextual demands of the contemporary Church of England.[27]

The book is presented in linear form. However, the generation of that linear argument is spiral in nature, returning to themes within ecclesiology and Christian ministry. The product is therefore a record of an ongoing conversation, rather than a single interaction or even transcript of a debate. Questions are generated and earlier thoughts revisited as the landscape is opened up and the evidence honed and re-examined. The creative tension inherent in repeated liturgical celebrations is present in the research – a cyclical revisiting throughout the research, presented finally as a linear text, itself a snapshot of the ongoing process of theological reflection. This approach is therefore embedded in liturgical praxis. Moreover, the approach is theological – that is to say, it operates within a Christian worldview, seeking to discern the will of God, in the tradition of Anselm of Canterbury's *fides quaerens intellectum*, as a holistic expression of Christian discipleship.

It is also important to note the place of myself as author in the spiral of theological reflection, and how my own dealing with bishops, both nurturing and damaging, has helped focus my interest, fuelled my determination to articulate the insight contained here, and influenced the conclusions I have drawn. Much of the material in this book I submitted for my PhD thesis, which reflected on episcopal ministry in the Church through the lens of the ordinal and a contemporary reading of the Rule of St Benedict. This material has also been the basis of conversations with others who have an interest in this area: through being bishops, working with bishops, or having an academic background in leadership. This has helped broaden my understanding, and some of that is reflected in the final conclusions contained here. My hope is that this book sparks further conversations and reflection by all Christians on the shape of leadership in the kingdom of God.

Notes

1 Archbishops' Council, 2007, *Common Worship: Ordination Services*, London: Church House Publishing. This is hereafter referred to as 'CW:OS' followed by the page number.

2 The term 'Anglican' can refer to both the Church of England and the wider Anglican Communion. It is important to note that the Anglican Communion is not itself a Church, but a group of autonomous Churches. The member Churches, while maintaining mutual recognition, also tolerate a diversity of theology. The voice of *CW:OS*, and my thoughts here, seek to contribute to that discussion in the quest for greater mutual understanding.

3 'Ontology' is used in this book to describe the way of being established at ordination, affirming that the new relationship transcends functionality and permeates all aspects of the ordained person's life. There is therefore a character to episcopal life, and analogies will be drawn with the relationship between a couple established at a wedding ceremony.

4 Stephen Platten, 2007, 'Foreword' in Archbishops' Council, *Common Worship: Ordination Services*, p. 3.

5 David Fagerberg, 1992, *What Is Liturgical Theology?*, Collegeville, MN: Liturgical Press.

6 Archbishops' Council, 2000, *Common Worship: Services and Prayers for the Church of England*, London: Church House Publishing, p. ix.

7 Platten, 'Foreword', p. 2.

8 Church of England, 'Canon B2', <https://www.churchofengland.org/about/governance/legal-resources/canons-church-england/section-b>, accessed 11.09.2025.

9 That the 1662 ordinal is seldom used is evident in the address to General Synod by David Stancliffe, where he notes 'welcome and some relief' that permission to use the *Alternative Service Book* ordinal was to be extended, negating the need to revert to the 1662 ordinal. Archbishops' Council, *General Synod Report of Proceedings July 1999*, 30 (1), p. 449.

10 Paul Avis, 2018, *The Anglican Understanding of the Church*, London: SPCK, p. 3.

11 Stephen Sykes, 1994, 'Foundations of Anglican Ecclesiology' in Jeffrey John (ed.), *Living the Mystery: Affirming Catholicism and the Future of Anglicanism*, London: Darton, Longman and Todd, p. 29.

12 Sykes, 'Foundations of Anglican Ecclesiology', p. 43. '[Branch theory] has been soundly criticized ... and has no title to be regarded as more than one privately advanced theological proposal within an Anglican spectrum.' Branch theory was an attempt to affirm the authenticity of Anglican catholicity by describing the Church universal as being manifested in the Orthodox, Roman Catholic and Anglican traditions.

13 David Stancliffe, 2018, 'Making Common Worship: Securing Some Underlying Theologies' in Aidan Platten (ed.), *Grasping the Heel of Heaven*, Norwich: Canterbury Press, pp. 75–6.

14 Steven Croft, 2008, *Ministry in Three Dimensions*, second edition, London: Darton, Longman and Todd, p. 211.

15 Croft, *Ministry in Three Dimensions*, p. 41.

16 Paul Avis, 2015, *Becoming a Bishop: A Theological Handbook of Episcopal Ministry*, London: Bloomsbury/T&T Clark, p. 37.

17 Avis, *Becoming a Bishop*, p. 38.

18 A key verse here is Revelation 3.20, 'Listen! I am standing at the door, knocking'. In his painting *The Light of the World*, William Holman Hunt depicts this verse. Significantly, the door has no handle on the outside. Christ is powerless to enter; he can only invite a response from the person inside through his authority.

19 Richard Rohr, 2023, *Jesus' Alternative Plan*, London: SPCK, p. 13. He also expresses it more firmly: 'Every description Jesus offers of God's reign – of love, relationship, non-judgment, and forgiveness, where the last shall be first and the first shall be last – shows that any imposition on God's side is an impossibility!' Richard Rohr, 2024, 'An Attractive Alternative', *Centre for Action and Contemplation*, <https://cac.org/daily-meditations/an-attractive-alternative/>, accessed 02.08.2024.

20 Rohr, *Jesus' Alternative Plan*, p. 44.

21 See, for example, Emma Thompson, 2021, 'Holy relic: what will be left of the Church of England after the pandemic?', *The Spectator*, <https://www.spectator.co.uk/article/holy-relic-what-will-be-left-of-the-church-of-england-after-the-pandemic/>, accessed 11.09.2025.

22 For an overview of safeguarding reviews and reports in the Church of England, see 'Reviews and Reports', *Church of England*, <hhttps://www.churchofengland.org/safeguarding/reviews-and-reports>, accessed 11.09.2025.

23 David Stancliffe, 2003, *God's Pattern Shaping our Worship, Ministry and Life*, London: SPCK, especially pp. 15–18.

24 Stancliffe, *God's Pattern*, p. 20.
25 Paul H. Ballard and John Pritchard, 2006, *Practical Theology in Action*, London: SPCK, p. 85.
26 Ballard and Pritchard, *Practical Theology in Action*, p. 73.
27 Ballard and Pritchard, *Practical Theology in Action*, p. 60.

I

The Church is an Institution Defined by Ecclesiology

Christian ministry is contextual, and the primary aspect of that context is the nature of the Church in which that ministry is exercised. Ecclesiology is therefore a foundational consideration. The assertion here is that CW:OS forms a Church in which the bishop is an integrated member, and that the ontology of the Church is sacramental. Its sacramental nature is evident in its being constituted by the celebration of the sacraments, and that the Church, a visible sign of the kingdom of God, but which is yet to be fully realized, points beyond itself to the full realization of the kingdom of God and actively participates in the reality of the kingdom of God.[1] In this chapter, the ecclesiology of CW:OS will be established as the foundation for understanding the nature of Christian ministry within the institution of the Church.

CW:OS contains a creative tension between the authority of the bishop within the Church and the ontology of the Church as the gathering of the baptized. First, it will be demonstrated that the purpose of the institution of the Church is to manifest the kingdom of God, with particular emphasis on the distinctive interpretation of The Preface to the Declaration of Assent[2] in CW:OS. The lack of explicit, centralized dogma on Anglican ecclesiology has resulted in it being a notoriously complex and slippery concept. As Paul Avis notes:

> This analysis is not easy for Anglicans to undertake, because they have an innate reluctance to parade their deepest convictions of faith. Anglicans (not only in England) are diffident about making claims for their portion of the Christian Church and its tradition. They have an aversion to asserting a distinct ecclesial identity. Anglicans generally are allergic to making comparisons with other churches and to flaunting what they have. They find the sort of claims that are sometimes made by other churches – claims to enjoy a fullness that others lack – rather distasteful.[3]

THE CHURCH IS AN INSTITUTION DEFINED BY ECCLESIOLOGY

Although Anglican ecclesiology is subtle, almost to the point of obfuscation, it is nonetheless essential. The claim to be Church requires articulation if it is to have any meaning, even if the articulation is not given centrally or even explicitly. Moreover, the complexities and tensions within Anglican ecclesiology, specifically within the Church, need not be hidden. An accurate articulation of ecclesiology must reflect the lived reality of the Church if the ecclesiology is to be accurate, have integrity and make visible the grace of God on which the Church depends.

The Church is first and foremost the body of Christ, a spiritual community transcending geographical and historical boundaries, defined by a common relationship with God, and his creation, in Jesus Christ. Therefore, the foundation for the ontology and praxis of the Church is the kingdom of God. The Church of England, just as any Church, is a physical incarnation of the body of Christ, with an attendant polity and history. A key text in the Church's doctrinal inheritance is The Preface to the Declaration of Assent,[4] which is an expression of the Church's self-understanding both as an aspect of the body of Christ and as an institution. In this chapter, *The Preface* will be used as a text to explore the continuity and distinctive articulation of Anglican ecclesiology in *CW:OS*.

In Anglican ecclesiology, the Church is seen as a provisional but legitimate expression of the body of Christ, which also has other legitimate expressions, both in the wider Anglican Communion and other denominations. Anglican ecclesiology is therefore sacramental in asserting that the Church is a manifestation of the body of Christ while not claiming to be the totality of that manifestation, thereby pointing to that fullness which lies beyond itself. The most significant aspect of this ecclesiology is the acknowledgement of the authority of Christ himself as head of the Church, to whom the Church as a whole owes a duty of obedience.

As an institution, the Church of England transcends its current membership and new members are welcomed into a pre-existing reality. In a similar way, a school is not so much defined by its current pupils as the school defines the current cohort as being members of that institution. Emphasis is therefore placed on the institution's self-expression through laws and authority structures that transcend the particularity of any given post-holders. To this extent, the members accept and inhabit something already in existence, and which will be passed on to future generations in the same way that it has been passed down to the current generation. Given the established nature of the Church, this is particularly evident in the ecclesiastical role of the monarch, but it is also present in the Canons, the laws that regulate the life of the Church, parliamentary governance, mediated through the synodical framework, and the oaths of obedience required of the ordained clergy to the bishop and the monarch.

The structures of the institutional Church – for example the Canons – may therefore appear enticing material for articulating Anglican ecclesiology. However, the Canons are primarily related to temporal order and therefore any ecclesiology predicated upon them is inherently limited. If the body of Christ is the ontological foundation of the Church, and therefore essential in any adequate ecclesiology, an ecclesiology predicated primarily on the Canons is necessarily unsatisfactory. Rather, an articulation of the institutional aspect of ecclesiology is necessarily an aspect of an understanding of Church as the body of Christ. As Mark Chapman points out, 'Often [General Synod sessions] do not appear to be possessed of the great Christian virtues of faith, hope and love at all. And furthermore they seldom embody anything more than a modicum of unity or consensus.'[5]

Chapman also notes the varying degrees of authority enjoyed by General Synod, drawing on Paul Valliere's use of the term 'synodophobia'.[6] As he concludes, 'Synods may not be ideal but that is how the Church of England manages its conflicts this side of eternity.'[7] Thus, Chapman articulates both the need for an institutional aspect to a full ecclesiology and its subordination to the ecclesial ontology of the Church. Moreover, the Church is a *corpus permixtum*, both a visible sign of the grace of God and itself in need of redemption. Any full and honest account must therefore take account of both the Church's high calling and its share in the world's failings.

The Preface is the closest the Church comes to a succinct and regularly articulated theological justification of its legitimacy. Avis describes *The Preface* as 'a superb statement of the Anglican understanding of the Church on the part of one of the member churches of the Anglican Communion'.[8] It states:

> The Church of England is part of the one, holy catholic and apostolic Church worshipping the one true God, Father, Son and Holy Spirit. It professes the faith uniquely revealed in the Holy Scriptures and set forth in the catholic creeds, which faith the Church is called upon to proclaim afresh in each generation. Led by the Holy Spirit, it has born witness to Christian truth in its historic formularies, the Thirty-nine Articles of Religion, the Book of Common Prayer, and the Ordering of Bishops, Priests and Deacons. (CW:OS, 6)

THE CHURCH IS AN INSTITUTION DEFINED BY ECCLESIOLOGY

Although only candidates for ordination to the episcopate must publicly declare their assent, the declaration is a basic requirement for candidates to all orders,[9] and *The Preface* is referenced at all ordinations as part of the presentation, primarily to demonstrate that the candidates have been examined and found suitable for ordination.[10] While it would be sufficient for the registrar or archdeacon to simply reply 'They have' as others do earlier in the presentation (*CW:OS* 11, 33, 56), the opportunity is taken to rehearse a precis of the text, and the whole assembly hears this description of Anglican ecclesiology as a description of the Church in which the ministry of the newly ordained will be expressed:

> They have duly taken the oath of allegiance to the Sovereign and the oath of canonical obedience to the Bishop. They have affirmed and declared their belief in 'the faith which is revealed in the Holy Scriptures and set forth in the catholic creeds and to which the historic formularies of the Church of England bear witness'. (*CW:OS* 11, 33)

The Preface is therefore more than simply a preliminary to the service; the text is better seen as foundational, and particularly significant here is the interpretation given to *The Preface* by *CW:OS*. *The Preface* is the description of ecclesiology that is emphasized in the ordinal and on which *CW:OS* depends, but equally *CW:OS* proceeds to interpret and develop that ecclesiology in ways that are essential for the sacramental ecclesiology expounded here. *The Preface* and the ordinal are therefore in a dynamic relationship whereby *The Preface* provides the doctrinal context and legitimacy for the ordination and the ordinal reinterprets *The Preface* to give a distinctive articulation of Anglican ecclesiology.

The Preface starts by affirming that the Church is 'part' of the one Church and immediately the relationship between the institution and the body of Christ is brought to the fore. This is well expressed in The Dublin Agreed Statement of 1984, 'Anglicans are accustomed to seeing our divisions as within the Church: they do not believe that they alone are the one true Church, but they believe that they belong to it.'[11] Unlike other denominations, in particular those in the Orthodox tradition, Anglican ecclesiology makes a distinction between the institutional Church and the *body* of Christ. This is not a mutual-exclusivity, but an affirmation of sacramental ecclesiology, whereby the Church acknowledges its provisional nature as it points beyond the limitations of the institution towards the reality of the body of Christ: the Church of England is part of the Church and at the same time points beyond itself to the fullness of it, which lies beyond the confines of the Church of England, or even the Anglican Communion. Paul Avis explains this paradox thus:

> The one, holy, catholic and apostolic Church of Christ is both an empirical reality in the world and an object of faith, affirmed in the Creed. As such it transcends its empirical manifestation, while being concretely expressed in it.[12]

This forms the basis for the insistence of *CW:OS* that those ordained are not just ordained to an office in the Church but one in the 'Church of God' (*CW:OS* 11, 33, 56).

On the same basis, *CW:OS* asserts that the Church's unity, that which connects the various Churches into the body of Christ, is theologically rooted in the unity of God. The presiding bishop introduces the rite by explaining, 'The Church is the Body of Christ, the people of God and the dwelling-place of the Holy Spirit' (*CW:OS* 10).[13] While the Church is not synonymous with, or encompassing of, the body of Christ, the definite article (as opposed to 'this Church' or 'the Churches') affirms its status as being a legitimate expression of the Church catholic. Alongside this mystical or spiritual understanding of the Church, the Church is also placed alongside other denominations as part of the temporal Church 'formed throughout the world' (*CW:OS* 20, 42, 66) in the opening words of the ordination prayer.[14] While this could refer to the worldwide Anglican Communion, the intent here is clear: the Church is a legitimate expression of the body of Christ, and it ordains, therefore, as an expression of the Church of God, and not just as the Church of England.

There is therefore a significant question about how the relationship between the mystical and institutional is constituted: what is it that makes the Church a legitimate expression of the body of Christ? The 1662 ordinal for priests places its emphasis on the ordained ministry, constituted by bishops in historical succession, as a direct continuation of the apostolic ministry established by Christ himself.[15] Indeed, bishops in historical episcopal succession are clearly an integral element of the ordinal, being the only legitimate presiding ministers at the ordination. However, Paul Avis questions whether this need be seen in purely mechanical terms, with the bishop acting in isolation, and as sole validator of the apostolicity and legitimacy of the Church:

> Historical episcopal succession, together with the ordination of presbyters by those bishops only, is a sign of God's faithfulness to the

Church through history. It is also a sign of the Church's intention to remain faithful to the teaching and mission of the apostles. It assures the faithful of that intention. It is, so to speak, a sacramental link with the Church of the Apostles who were called, taught and commissioned by Jesus Christ himself and were chosen witnesses of his resurrection. It demonstrates that the Church does not feel free to cut loose from the authority of the apostolic Church, but on the contrary, believes that it is called above all to faithfulness to the gospel and to the community of the gospel with its sacraments and ministries.[16]

Bishops in historical succession ordaining bishops, priests and deacons speak of the apostolic nature of the Church. However, it is not in the bishops alone that the apostolicity is held. Rather, it is the Church corporately, which lives in continuity with the apostolic faith, of which the bishops are the guardians.[17] As Avis affirms, 'The whole Church shares in Christ's apostolate'[18] and thus the ordinal draws not only on the apostolic succession, but on the Christ as being 'the Apostle and High Priest of our faith' (*CW:OS* 66). In so doing, 'in terms of the current ecumenical consensus, [episcopacy in historical succession] is a sign but not a guarantee of the apostolicity and catholicity of the Church'.[19] What is therefore evident in *CW:OS* is a development of the 1662 ordinal, placing bishops in historical succession within the wider context of the apostolicity of the whole Church.

This is congruent with the Church's ecumenical dialogue, whereby Churches without an episcopate in historical succession can be recognized as sharing in episcopacy through other ways, but that bishops in historical succession are required for full communion between denominations, as in the Porvoo agreement.[20] While episcopacy is therefore significant, it is neither a mechanical means transmitting legitimacy, nor all-encompassing of the Church's legitimacy. *CW:OS* asserts that the catholicity, apostolicity and the holiness of the Church are held in common by the Church, lay and ordained, as a present reality of the lived expression of the mystical body of Christ.

Having asserted the Church's apostolicity, *The Preface* turns to historical and theological anchors of the realized Church, primarily the place of Scripture, as essential to the distinctiveness of the Church.[21] Although the scriptural foundations of *CW:OS* may not be immediately evident to the assembly, the annotations of the text make clear the importance of Scripture and the Liturgical Commission affirms, 'The best liturgical texts are a fabric woven chiefly from Scripture' (*CW:OS* 10). In the tradition of Richard Hooker, Scripture is used in a dynamic relationship with tradition and reason. On occasion, Scripture is used literally, as when ordinands to the episcopate are asked whether they will 'make your home a place of hospitality and welcome' (*CW:OS* 62).[22] But in the main it is scriptural analogy and imagery that is drawn together and alluded to. This is a further development of the 1662 ordinal which, in places, uses simplistic, direct use of Scripture – for example, in the words of the archbishop at the ordination of bishops, 'Brethren, it is written in the Gospel of Saint Luke ... Let us therefore ...' (*BCP 1662* 105). Scripture in *CW:OS* is not seen as something imposed upon the Church, to dictate to the Church in fundamentalist terms, but closer to the description offered by John Barton: 'The relation of the faith which Christians profess to the Scripture which informs and nourishes that faith is not just accidentally or occasionally but essentially and inherently one of tension.'[23] The Scriptures are a given, and the Church, not just bishops alone but the Church corporate, has authority to interpret and use them.

Scripture also has a ritual function in the ordination, where a Bible is given as the reduced form of the *traditio instrumentorum*, the giving of the tools necessary for the ministry conferred at ordination. Deriving from the 1550 ordinal, this is a subtle yet significant shift away from the pre-Reformation practice of both symbolically and practically giving the tools required for the ministry conferred.[24] The giving of a Bible becomes 'a sign of the authority given by God to preach the Word of God and to administer the sacraments of the New Covenant, and it gives vivid liturgical expression to the truth that all Christian ministers are under the authority of that Word'.[25] The gift of the Bible therefore places the bishop among the baptized, which as a whole is under the authority of Christ. Scripture therefore is seen as balancing the authority of the bishop, as an authority that is over the whole Church. The threefold order is not explicit in Scripture and the title 'Reverend Father in God' for the presiding bishop (*CW:OS* 11)[26] requires a defence from the Liturgical Commission, for not literally adhering to Jesus' prohibition on calling anyone, other than God, 'Father' (*CW:OS* 125). Once again Scripture is seen as foundational, but not in a literalistic or fundamentalist way. It is rather the Church's use of Scripture that is significant. By grace, Scripture is given to the Church, and by grace the Church must discern how best to use and interpret Scripture.

It is unsurprising therefore that *CW:OS* emphasizes analogy and poetry in Scripture, and Scripture itself as symbolic, rather than attempting a literalistic application of Scripture that would be doomed to failure through the paucity of biblical evidence about ordination. Ecclesiologically, therefore, it remains the Church that has the primacy over Scripture and how it is used, rather than Scripture having primacy over the Church. Without a centralized authority structure to define doctrine, interpretation is an inherently collective activity, as evidenced by General Synod's role, including the house of laity, in agreeing liturgical reform. The use of Scripture in *CW:OS* is therefore symptomatic of the integrated sacramental nature of the Church, both emphasizing the grace of the gift of Scripture and the need for additional grace, mediated through the community of the Church, to interpret that Scripture.

The Church's role in interpreting Scripture includes the ability to develop and grow beyond the literal confines of it. For the Church of England, this is particularly expressed in the distinctive approach of *quinquesecularism*, 'the doctrine that the unanimous consent of the first five centuries contains all the Churches need to know about the faith, with neither deviation nor accretion'.[27] However, it should not be inferred that doctrinal development halted at this point: alongside Scripture, the Creed forms one of the foundations from which doctrine and praxis can develop, as seen in the Church's decision to ordain women to all three orders, and for doctrine to be expressed in new ways, as in the Lambeth Quadrilateral.[28]

The ordinals of the Church reveal a clear development: each ordinal is a culturally relative document and a product of a changing society. In *CW:OS* there is a significant movement away from an 'Erastian paradigm' towards a missional focus. The Liturgical Commission notes the need to develop more explicit reference to mission 'as a central concept for speaking about the life of the Church and the ministry of the ordained'[29] than was found in the *Alternative Service Book*[30] which it replaced. This therefore becomes a key theme for *CW:OS*[31] and is particularly seen in the introduction, common to all three rites, where the Church's purpose is defined by the presiding bishop as '[to] declare the wonderful deeds [of God]', 'to witness to God's love and to work for the coming of his kingdom' (*CW:OS* 10, 32, 54). Thus 'proclaiming afresh in each generation' has taken on a new importance and practical purpose, as the Church seeks to re-emphasize its place in the life of the people of England and, in particular, this fresh proclamation places significant emphasis on the importance of all the baptized.

Fresh proclamation requires more than a new vocabulary and expression. It entails development of doctrine to engage with the developing society. The juxtaposition of the two ordinals emphasizes the assertion here that CW:OS, in a legitimate development, has given new expression to the life of the Church. David Stancliffe identifies three interlocking factors in this development from the ASB:

> First, the developing set of relationships with other Churches; second, a renewed understanding of the distinctiveness of the Order of Deacons; and, third, a growing awareness of the place of a distinctively ministerial vocation in relation to the vocation of all the baptized.[32]

The fresh proclamation in CW:OS, although unrealized in some of its potential, is nonetheless a distinctive and constructive synthesis. It is an Anglican ecclesiology that embraces the *via media* as described by the Episcopal Church of the United States of America as 'a happy mean between too much stiffness in refusing, and too much easiness in admitting variations in things once advisedly established'.[33] This is further evidence of the integrated sacramental nature of the ecclesiology of CW:OS, as the dynamic tensions within the institution of the Church are balanced and evident with the synthesis articulated.

This dynamic tension is maintained in large part by the intentionally dispersed nature of authority within the Church. The hierarchy, although significant and necessary, is unable to dominate the Church as a whole, but must work with and within the community of the Church. A committee report from the 1948 Lambeth Conference explains:

> Authority is single in that it is derived from a single Divine source ... [but] is distributed among Scripture, Tradition, Creeds, the Ministry of Word and Sacraments, the witness of the saints, and the *consensus fidelium*, which is the continuing experience of the Holy Spirit through His faithful people in the Church. It is thus a dispersed rather than a centralized authority having many elements which combine, interact with, and check each other.[34]

This evolutionary, accommodating approach depends on what Paul Avis describes as having 'fairly light doctrinal baggage'[35] – in other words, a doctrinal nimbleness. Virtue can also be made of having an 'ecclesiological instinct' which is 'much clearer and more persuasive than we sometimes give ourselves credit for'.[36] Significantly, this instinct is not the preserve of the bishops but is a culture held by the Church as a whole. In response to Victoria Miller's question as to whether authority in the Church of England is 'dispersed to the point of dissolution and ineffectiveness'[37] the sacramental nature of the Church points beyond itself to the person of Christ. The locus of authority for the Church lies outside of the institution, dependent as it is on the grace that comes from Christ himself to form the baptized into the body of Christ. Although potentially frustrating, there is a fundamental truth and integrity in the Church of England's polity, perhaps a permissive one, that has little room for legal discipline and sees communion with the Archbishop of Canterbury not as a guarantor of apostolicity or catholicity but rather a sign of allegiance and loyalty. Once again integrity and sacramentality are therefore at the core of Anglican ecclesiology with its emphasis on the need for dependency on the grace of God, rather than strong institutional leadership.

The interpretation of *The Preface* by *CW:OS* demonstrates the way in which Anglican ecclesiology has been shaped, developed and proclaimed afresh. This development is in the 'spirit of restraint, balance and moderation that is indeed characteristic of much in the Anglican heritage'.[38] It has been shown that the institution is significant as a tool for making the body of Christ manifest in the world. The maxim 'in the world but not of the world' is particularly evident and the primacy of the ecclesial reality is the foundation for the institution and its structures, which are shaped and reshaped in the light of that ontology. It has been shown that authority is dispersed within the Church, and not restricted to those ordained bishop. This is particularly evident in the emphasis that *CW:OS* places on baptismal ecclesiology, as an aspect of the sacramental ecclesiology that the ordinal avows. The next chapter will demonstrate and explore the influence of baptismal ecclesiology in *CW:OS*.

Notes

1 For a different explanation of the Church as sacramental according to F. D. Maurice, see, for example, Jeremy Morris, 2013, 'Building Community' in Julie Gittoes, Brutus Green and James Head, *Generous Ecclesiology: Church, World and the Kingdom of God*, London: SCM Press, pp. 42–6. See also Karl Rahner's description of the Church as 'the fundamental sacrament' in Gerald A. McCool, 1975, *A Rahner Reader*, London: Darton, Longman and Todd, p. 281.

2 A historical articulation of Anglican ecclesiology which is common to all three ordination rites in *CW:OS*.

3 Paul Avis, 2008, *The Identity of Anglicanism*, London: T&T Clark, p. 82.

4 This is hereafter referred to as '*The Preface*'.

5 Mark Chapman, 2013, 'Does the Church of England have a Theology of General Synod?', *Journal of Anglican Studies*, 11 (1), pp. 15–31, p. 18.

6 Chapman, 'Does the Church of England have a theology of General Synod?', p. 26.

7 Chapman, 'Does the Church of England have a theology of General Synod?', p. 31.

8 Paul Avis, 2018, *The Anglican Understanding of the Church*, London: SPCK, p. 13.

9 Church of England, Cf. Canon C15.1(1). Cited in *CW:OS*, p. 57.

10 *The Preface* is voiced in response to the Bishop's invitation, 'I invite the archdeacon/registrar to confirm that the ordinands have taken the necessary oaths and made the Declaration of Assent' (*CW:OS* 11, 33).

11 Anglican-Orthodox Dialogue Joint Doctrinal Commission, 1984, *The Dublin Agreed Statement of 1984*, <https://www.anglicancommunion.org/media/103812/the_dublin_statement.pdf>, accessed 11.09.2025. The statement was issued by the Anglican-Orthodox Joint Doctrinal Commission in response to the Episcopal Church of the United States of America's move to ordain women. It offers an insight into Anglican ecclesiology through dialogue with Orthodoxy. The distinctiveness of this understanding is then elucidated in comparison with the Orthodox: 'Orthodox, however, believe that the Orthodox Church is the one true Church of Christ, which as his Body is not and cannot be divided.'

12 Avis, *The Identity of Anglicanism*, p. 100.

13 Cf. John Macquarrie, Christian Unity, cited in Victoria C. Miller, 1993, 'Ecclesiology, Scripture, and Tradition in the "Dublin Agreed Statement"', *Harvard Theological Review*, 86 (1), pp. 105–34, p. 133.

14 For a wider discussion of the levels of ecclesiology, cf. Avis, *The Anglican Understanding of the Church*, p. 2.

15 'You have heard, brethren, as well in your private examination, as in the exhortation which was now made to you, and in the holy Lesson taken out of the Gospel and writings of the Apostles, of what dignity and of how great importance this office is, whereunto ye are called (*BCP 1662* 94). It is clear here that the 1662 ordinal views the bishop as being in direct historical succession to the Apostles.

16 Avis, *The Anglican Understanding of the Church*, p. 71.

17 'Bishops are ordained to be shepherds of Christ's flock and guardians of the faith of the apostles, proclaiming the gospel of God's kingdom and leading his people in mission' (*CW:OS* 55).

18 Paul Avis, 1990, *Christians in Communion*, London: Geoffrey Chapman Mowbray, p. 93.

19 Avis, *The Anglican Understanding of the Church*, p. 70.

20 Cf. The Porvoo Communion, 'Porvoo Communion – A Communion of Churches', <http://porvoocommunion.org/>, accessed 11.09.2025.

21 It is worth noting here that the eucharistic context for ordination ensures that ordination is always in response to the proclamation of Scripture in the Liturgy of the Word.

22 The reference is to 1 Timothy 3.2, 'Now a bishop must be above reproach, married only once, temperate, sensible, respectable, hospitable, an apt teacher'.

23 John Barton, 1988, *People of the Book*, London: SPCK, p. 8.

24 Paul Bradshaw, 1971, *The Anglican Ordinal*, London: SPCK, p. 2.

25 The Liturgical Commission, 2007, 'Commentary' in the Archbishops' Council, *Common Worship: Ordination Services*, London: Church House Publishing (*CW:OS* 135).

26 Cf. *CW:OS* 80.

27 Stephen Sykes, 1994, 'Foundations of Anglican Ecclesiology' in Jeffrey John (ed.), *Living the Mystery: Affirming Catholicism and the Future of Anglicanism*, London: Darton, Longman and Todd, p. 39.

28 Cf. Avis, *Anglican Understanding of the Church*, pp. 56–7.

29 Avis, *Anglican Understanding of the Church*, p. 120.

30 The Central Board of the Church of England, 1980, *The Alternative Service Book*, London: SPCK, 1980. This is hereafter referred to as '*ASB*' followed by the page number.

31 Cf. *CW:OS* 140.

32 David Stancliffe, 1998, 'Extended Authorisation for the Ordinal in the Alternative Service Book 1980', GS 1319, London: General Synod, p. 449.

33 The Episcopal Church of the United States of America, 1979, *The Book of Common Prayer and Administration of the Sacraments and Other Rites and Ceremonies of the Church*, New York: Seabury Press, pp. 9–10. This is hereafter referred to as '*BCP 1979*' followed by the page number.

34 Anglican Communion, 1948, 'Committee Report on the Anglican Communion' in *The Lambeth Conference 1948 – The Encyclical Letter from the Bishops: Together with Resolutions and Reports*, London: SPCK, pp. 84–5, cited in Miller, 'Ecclesiology, Scripture and Tradition in the "Dublin Agreed Statement"', p. 120.

35 Avis, *The Anglican Understanding of the Church*, pp. 12–13.

36 Sykes, 'Foundations of an Anglican Ecclesiology', p. 32.

37 Miller, 'Ecclesiology, Scripture, and Tradition in the "Dublin Agreed Statement"', p. 121.

38 Avis, *The Identity of Anglicanism*, p. 85.

2

The Significance of Baptismal Ecclesiology

The influence of baptismal ecclesiology on *CW:OS* is clear when it is compared in detail with the ordinal of the Episcopal Church of the United States of America contained in the *Book of Common Prayer* of 1979.[1] While the differences between Churches within the Anglican Communion can be over-emphasized, it would be rash to assume that there is a common and clearly defined ecclesiology across the Anglican Communion. Although a 'lowest common denominator' ecclesiology can be established, these being the matters on which the member Churches can agree, this falls a long way short of an accurate description of the Churches and their self-perception. Rather, the differences, often in emphasis (as evidenced in their liturgies) offer helpful insights and deepen the ecclesiological discussion.

After exploring the ecclesiological field of baptismal ecclesiology through a consideration of the work of Louis Weil and the debate between Colin Podmore and Pierre Whalon, this chapter demonstrates that baptismal ecclesiology has had a significant influence on *CW:OS* itself. *CW:OS* will be described as a culturally relative document, drawing on the work of Martyn Percy to demonstrate the reality and importance of not regarding the Church in isolation from factors that are an inherent aspect of worldwide Anglicanism. The integrity of *CW:OS* will be further explored in the integration of baptismal and eucharistic ecclesiology within the liturgy. Thus, *CW:OS* will be shown to make a distinctive contribution to the ecclesiology of the Church, primarily in its emphasis on the importance of relationship within the Church, in particular through the collaboration of lay and ordained in the ministry of the Church.

It is taken as read that baptism plays a role in the ordinal. As Paul Avis asserts, 'The Church is given birth by the sacrament of baptism, because that sacrament is what unites the Church to the baptism of Christ, which symbolizes the paschal mystery of the cross and resurrection.'[2] Baptism therefore performs a practical, unifying and theological function in the life of the whole Church and it is not surprising that baptism has been a major focus for ecumenical attempts at Christian unity.[3]

The assertion here is that *CW:OS* has a highly developed baptismal ecclesiology, but not in such a way that it promulgates individualism, or undermines the institutional ecclesiology that has already been established. In seeking to establish baptismal ecclesiology as a common foundation for an Anglican theology of ordination, *The Berkeley Statement* states:

> understanding baptism as the foundation of the life and ministry of the church (that is, having a baptismal ecclesiology) leads us to see ordained ministers as integral members of the body of Christ, called by God and discerned by the body to be signs and animators of Christ's self-giving life and ministry, to which all people are called by God and for which we are empowered by the Spirit.[4]

The significance of baptism for ministry within the Church is both in understanding the nature of the Church into whose offices the candidates are being ordained, and in terms of the nature of ordained ministry as servants and representatives of the Church. So far, this is uncontroversial. However, *The Berkeley Statement* glosses over the nuances of baptismal ecclesiology, which has several different expressions and is the cause of some debate, particularly regarding baptism's relationship with the Eucharist, ordained ministry and the process of initiation. Baptismal ecclesiology is not a singularity but rather a coverall for a range of understandings of the Church, which share a common focus on the importance of baptism. While efforts in some quarters have been fruitful in fostering aspects of mutual recognition between denominations, others have sparked much controversy and threaten to open controversy and disunity within the Anglican Communion itself.

This diversity is highlighted by Louis Weil, one of the chief protagonists for baptismal ecclesiology in the US Episcopal Church, who states, 'we recognise that others are using a word in a sense quite different from our own meaning'.[5] For Weil, baptismal ecclesiology is not an attempt to separate baptism, or even pit it against the Eucharist as an alternative foundation for ecclesiology: 'When I speak of baptismal ecclesiology, the totality of Initiation is presumed to include both baptism and the eucharist.'[6] Rather, baptism is the foundation on which the life of the Church rests: 'It seems reasonable to suggest that a baptismal ecclesiology offers us the most adequate theological context for an affirmation of the "one Lord, one faith" which all Christians share through the one baptism.'[7]

Therefore, for Weil, baptismal ecclesiology does not refer exclusively to the water rite that inaugurates the Christian journey. It encompasses the whole Christian journey, with baptism being a common denominator in the life of each Christian. Therefore, it is not a claim that baptism is the sole and complete basis for the life of the Church, rendering each individual as a full manifestation of the Church in their own right, but a claim to greater unity, by emphasizing the shared foundation for Christian discipleship.

Weil is making a political, cultural and theological statement about the nature of the Church. It is theological because it articulates the primacy of God's action, with baptism being the active acceptance of God's call by people who respond by accepting baptism and are thereby being incorporated into the life of the Church; it is cultural in as much as Weil is seeking to emphasize commonality within Churches and between denominations; and it is political in his deliberate attempt to establish an ecclesiology that is not dependent on hierarchical and clerical models of the Church. He prefers the term 'baptismal ecclesiology', because it has fewer hierarchical and ecumenical complications than, for example, eucharistic ecclesiology, which has attendant issues around admission to eucharistic fellowship, eucharistic hospitality between denominations, and the relationship between the ordained president and the lay community. Not all these aspects are necessarily the case for baptismal ecclesiology; in particular, for the purposes of my argument, baptismal ecclesiology need not connote contra-distinction and competition with institutional ecclesiology, but rather creative tension.

However, it is with these characteristics in mind that Colin Podmore has argued forcefully that the US Episcopal Church has a distinctly different ecclesiology from that of the Church of England, portraying the *BCP 1979* ordinal as both a symptom and a tool for the promulgation of a particular understanding of baptismal ecclesiology, which he terms a 'Baptismal Revolution'. He states:

> The Episcopal Church has come to espouse a developed form of baptismal ecclesiology, in which all laypersons are believed to be ministers by virtue of their baptism and the ordained ministry is understood as a particular form of the ministry of all the baptized.[8]

Drawing on the work of Ruth Meyers and focusing his attention on the theology of Louis Weil, Podmore narrates the development of baptism within the West from being

> previously often regarded as a rite affecting the status of the individual, it was increasingly viewed as a sacrament which constitutes the Church (understood as the community of the baptized) ... However, the American Episcopalian understanding of 'baptismal ecclesiology' goes beyond this, seeing baptism not only as constitutive of the Church but also as the fount of all ministry within it lay and ordained.[9]

Quoting Bruce Kaye's *An Introduction to World Anglicanism*, Podmore explains this development in terms of cultural relativism: 'The 1979 changes to the prayer book and the new baptismal ecclesiology it provided are significant in that they gave a theological framework within which the underlying democratic and individual rights instinct could be expressed.'[10] Podmore suggests that the form of baptismal ecclesiology adopted by the US Episcopal Church is individualistic: that in baptism each individual is given the gifts required for any ministry in the Church. Additionally, the discernment of that vocation is down to the individual: the baptismal covenant, as between the individual believer and God, celebrated in baptism, becomes the complete and controlling source of ecclesial reality. He cites Louis Weil's *A Theology of Worship*, which envisages ordained ministry as 'how people have chosen to exercise their baptismal gifts of ministry'.[11] However, elsewhere, Weil is clear that ordination is a 'radical particularity, not merely different degrees of the same gift, but different kinds, manifesting the rich diversity of the gifts of the Holy Spirit.'[12]

Podmore, most notably in his essay entitled 'A Tale of Two Churches', characterizes the US Episcopal Church's baptismal ecclesiology and understanding of episcopacy as being quasi congregationalist, while the Church of England maintains pre-Reformation Catholicism in an Anglican, non-papal expression:

> It is easy to see why, in a church in which the clergy are appointed and paid by their parishes, in which the bishop is a superintendent without there being a clear sense of the priest ministering and presiding on his or her behalf, in which the bishop has the right to preside at parochial worship only at the beginning of a new ministry and during a visitation, and in which the bishop may have no involvement in

the ordination to the priesthood of a deacon ministering in his or her diocese, one frequently encounters the opinion (at least among priests ministering in America who have also ministered in England) that The Episcopal Church is essentially a congregational church with bishops, rather than an episcopal church as that term is understood in the Church of England – a church which has 'taken episcopacy into its system' but perhaps not fully digested it.[13]

However, this assertion has been rebutted by Pierre Whalon, who asserts that, like the Church of England, the US Episcopal Church's polity is one of 'catholic episcopacy within a synodical framework'.[14] Whalon directly negates Podmore's assertion about baptismal ecclesiology in the US Episcopal Church, and questions his underlying assertion that the Church represents an individualistic, congregationalist ecclesiology. Podmore himself recognizes that there is distinction between how polity is derived and how it is exercised,[15] and Whalon's critique points to the complexity of articulating culture. It is highly questionable whether Podmore's narrow, legalistic and historical approach is sufficient to give a full account of the nature of either the US Episcopal Church or the Church of England specifically to the extent of defining them in contra-distinction.

Podmore is not alone in identifying distinctions between the ecclesiologies within the Anglican Communion. Martyn Percy also raises the question about a distinction between the US Episcopal Church and the Church of England, focusing on the latter being distinct from 'the Church *in* England'.[16] However, rather than suggesting that the US Episcopal Church is peculiar within the Anglican Communion, it is the established Church of England that Percy sees as having a distinctive character, in which the monarch rather than the episcopate holds the earthly role of supreme governor of the Church. Thus, the cultural relativism identified by Podmore and Kaye applies equally to both Churches, with English society shaping the Church of England. Indeed, if its self-understanding is to have a basis in reality and not retreat into the realms of fantasy, it is entirely likely that the Church of England will have to reimagine its own relationship with the state as multiculturalism grows and a smaller percentage of the population identify with the Church.

Although Podmore recognizes the developments within the Church of England as well as within the US Episcopal Church, he fails to comprehend the possibility that the medieval episcopal model that he identifies as normative for the Church is itself a culturally relative manifestation of episcopal government that would have been alien in earlier eras:

> And, of course, the temptation to be conformed to this world has always been present in England as it has been in America. The mediaeval conformity of English episcopacy to English feudalism, or a twentieth-century assumption of a modern public-service ethos and mentality, is different from, but may not be much better or worse than, assimilation to the Enlightenment philosophy of the American Revolution or to the culture of corporate America.[17]

For example, Michael Northcott sees this expression of episcopacy as an example of how 'centrist tendencies in ecclesiastical polity emerged in fourth-century accounts of the universal church'.[18] Further, he suggests that the role of the bishop should not be separated from the eucharistic assembly, and hence the Church, including the laity: 'If the Eucharist is the Incarnation in each particular place, and this Eucharist is episcopal in essence, then the bishop is in each particular place the head of the church in that place.'[19] Moreover, Podmore declines to note that the 'rapprochement'[20] between the US Episcopal Church and the Church of England is due to the changing nature of secular polity within the UK. He points to the effective veto of the bishops over synod in the Church and suggests that it would be 'inconceivable that any member of an English diocesan synod would move a motion purporting to "direct" the bishop to do anything'.[21] However, surely these powers and deference must be seen in the same light as the role of the monarch in British government, whereby the monarch's assent must be sought, but there is little or no expectation that the monarch would do otherwise, and a keen awareness that the refusal by the monarch would be met with outrage. The financial climate of the Church means that payment by parishes of financial contributions towards diocesan costs of ministry has become a powerful tool in the hands of the laity, and is increasingly threatened and invoked, as is eloquently expressed in the words 'not with our money you don't'[22] and 'no taxation without representation'.[23] This of course does not undermine Podmore's assertion of the distinctive foundations on which the US Episcopal Church and the Church of England have been built, but it does significantly narrow the gulf that he is seeking to portray as lying between the two Churches.

In context, baptismal ecclesiology is here understood as connoting the belief that the Church is primarily constituted by people whose relationship to Christ and to other Christians forms the Church as a dynamic community of people each with an active role to play. In investigating the text, the primary quest is to look for evidence of this and compare the way in which this is presented in the two ordinals. A secondary, and confirmatory, investigation will now demonstrate that the texts themselves do not support Podmore's suggestion of individualism, and his characterization of a division between the ecclesiologies of the US Episcopal Church and the Church of England. *CW:OS* will be seen to have a highly developed baptismal ecclesiology, especially in relation to the *BCP 1979*, and one that is congruent with the relational anthropology and theology which encompasses both baptismal and eucharistic ecclesiology.

The order in which the rites for the ordaining of bishops, priests and deacons is presented is interesting: *CW:OS* presents them in the order deacon, priest, bishop, which maintains the order of the 1662 ordinal. However, the *BCP 1979* inverts the order. While it is easy to read too much into the way in which the texts are arranged, nevertheless if there were to be any suggestion of focusing on the individual and the potential for reflecting concerns around the *cursus honorum*, as the candidates progress through the ranks, it is surely indicated more strongly by the arrangement in *CW:OS*. In contrast, the *BCP 1979*, in moving away from the *BCP 1662* sequence of services, indicates support for an ecclesiology in which the Church is gathered around the bishop, as key pastor and instrument of unity within the community.

In the opening responses, *CW:OS* has the presiding bishop boldly affirm unity grounded in a common baptism, clearly demonstrating from the outset the rite's indebtedness to baptismal ecclesiology:

> There is one body and one Spirit.
> **There is one hope to which we were called.**
> One Lord, one faith, one baptism,
> **One God and Father of all.**
> (*CW:OS* 10, 31, 54)

By comparison, the *BCP 1979* opens with:

> Blessed be God: Father, Son and Holy Spirit.
> And blessed be his kingdom, now and for ever. Amen.
> (*BCP 1979* 512)[24]

THE SIGNIFICANCE OF BAPTISMAL ECCLESIOLOGY

Paul Bradshaw highlights the opening dialogue of *CW:OS* as a manifestation of the International Anglican Liturgical Consultation (IALC)'s proposal that the gathering rite should 'convey the sense that the whole church is coming together to order its life for ministry' and that this brief dialogue sets 'the context by celebrating the ministerial gifts of the whole church'.[25] So, baptismal ecclesiology and the genesis of its influence is clear in *CW:OS* from the opening dialogue.

Although the *BCP 1979* has no equivalent to the introduction by the presiding bishop in *CW:OS*,[26] the preface to the ordination rites makes no mention of the ministry of the laity. Rather, it asserts the importance of ordained ministry: 'Those persons who are chosen and recognized by God to the ordained ministry are admitted to these sacred orders by solemn prayer and the laying on of episcopal hands' (*BCP 1979* 510). Podmore's characterization of the US Episcopal Church's ecclesiology is therefore not substantiated in this preface. Rather it is *CW:OS*, in the bishop's introduction, which states:

> The Church is the Body of Christ, the people of God and the dwelling-place of the Holy Spirit. In baptism the whole Church is summoned to witness to God's love and to work for the coming of his kingdom. (*CW:OS* 10, 32, 55)

In the introduction, therefore, *CW:OS* articulates an integrated ecclesiology in which lay and ordained belong together as distinctive, collaborative constituents of the Church.

When collaboration in ministry is being expounded, it is unsurprising that the declaration in *CW:OS* that concerns collaborative ministry makes no distinction between ordained and lay: 'Will you work with your fellow servants in the gospel for the kingdom of God?' (*CW:OS* 26, 38, 62). Although 'servants in the gospel' could be a technical term for ordained ministry, this is not borne out by the biblical texts referenced. The inference in 1 Corinthians 3.9[27] is that the phrase refers to leaders or influencers within the Church, but not apostolic ministry exclusively; similarly, 1 Thessalonians 3.2[28] implies that there is a leadership role for Timothy but it is not defined further; Colossians 4.11[29] clearly has a specific group in focus, but it is not clear whether this group's ministry is as a result of holding a particular office within the life of the Church, or is the common ministry shared by all servants of Jesus Christ, which is the implication of verse 12;[30] Philippians 1.5[31] is a clear reference to the whole Church in Philippi, including the bishops and deacons mentioned in verse 1,[32] as articulated in verse 4 with 'prayers for all of you'. It is clear therefore that collaboration within the Church as a whole is the intention of CW:OS.

The annotations from the Liturgical Commission do not identify the 'servants in the gospel' with the ordained, but rather with a more nebulous concept of leadership which necessarily encompasses both lay and ordained. Moreover, in *The Welcome* in the deacons' rite the 'servants in the gospel' are explicitly identified as the whole people of God: 'We welcome you as fellow servants in the gospel' (*CW:OS* 22). The fellowship here is clearly with the congregation as a whole, who – as the Church – are a mixture of lay and ordained.

In stark contrast, the equivalent declaration in the *BCP 1979* has a clear emphasis on collaboration among those set aside for leadership within the Church, rather than with the Church as a whole. The candidate for episcopal ministry is asked:

> Will you share with your fellow bishops in the government of the whole Church; will you sustain your fellow presbyters and take counsel with them; will you guide and strengthen the deacons and all others who minister in the Church? (*BCP 1979* 518)

While 'all others' may refer to lay ministers, this is clearly not a reference to the baptized but to those who undertake specific ministry within the life of the Church. In the priests' rite, it could be possible to suggest that the fellow ministers are lay, but the implication is that they are other ordained people: the 'and' implying that the 'fellow ministers' are distinct from those whom the priest will be pastoring: 'Will you undertake to be a faithful pastor to all whom you are called to serve, laboring together with them and with your fellow ministers to build up the family of God?' (*BCP 1979* 532).

For deacons, there is no equivalent declaration about collaborative ministry. It is clear therefore that *CW:OS* has a much stronger emphasis on the ministry of the Church as a whole, lay and ordained alike, founded upon its strong commitment to baptismal ecclesiology.

This distinction between the understanding of collaborative ministry as between lay and ordained and a product of baptismal ecclesiology, on the part of *CW:OS*, and as referring to the ordained and certain lay leaders, on the part of the *BCP 1979*, is also clear in the dismissal. Whereas the *BCP 1979* has an unprefixed, generic dismissal, common to all three rites, to 'go forth into the world, rejoicing in the power of the Spirit'

(*BCP 1979* 535), *CW:OS* has a specific fourfold blessing, common to all three rites, including the element: 'May the Holy Spirit, the comforter, equip you and strengthen you in your ministry' (*CW:OS* 25, 47, 71). Addressed to the whole assembly, the bishop is clearly affirming the ministry of the laity alongside that of the ordained.

Within the rite itself, the role of the baptized as the whole people of God is markedly less prominent in the *BCP 1979* than in *CW:OS*. The placing of the litany before the readings in the *BCP 1979* separates the prayers of the people from the act of ordination, giving a heightened sense of the ordination being a specific point in the service, administered by the bishop.[33] The result is that the laity's role is fulfilled in bringing the candidate to the bishop for ordination. In contrast, *CW:OS* places the litany alongside the ordination prayer, giving a sense of the laity's active involvement in the ordination which is itself an act involving the whole Church, over which the bishop presides. This is the praxis commended by Richard Geoffrey Leggett, where:

> 'Ordination prayer' describes a liturgical unit not a liturgical element. A liturgical unit brings together various elements intimately related to each other by juxtaposition and the complementary actions of presider and assembly. In so doing the corporate action of the church in ordination is made more evident.[34]

The inclusion of the laity in the ordination is cemented by *The Welcome* in *CW:OS*, where the laity have an active role in accepting the newly ordained.[35] Although the notes in the *BCP 1979* assign a similar role to the Peace,[36] it is in no way as powerful and mutual as *The Welcome* in *CW:OS*, which has a specific welcome for each order, and is most balanced in the deacons' rite, which affirms the common servanthood of the laity with the diaconate. Even where there is a greater distinction between lay and ordained in the identification of priests as 'ambassadors' and bishops as 'shepherds', the role of the laity in actively welcoming the newly ordained remains clear.

The final nail in the coffin, as far as the ordinals are concerned, of Podmore's assertion that the US Episcopal Church's understanding of ordination is rooted exclusively in baptism is the explicit invocation of the Holy Spirit in all three rites in the *BCP 1979*. Not only is the *Veni Creator Spiritus* or *Veni Sancte Spiritus* sung, the ordination prayer is that the Father will 'make' the candidate the order to be conferred.[37] It is clear that the petition is not simply for grace to fulfil the specific task, common to all the baptized, but rather for a new relationship established at ordination between the ordained and the rest of the Church.

Neither *CW:OS* nor the *BCP 1979* endorses an individualistic description of baptismal ecclesiology which would see it in isolation from the corporate life of the Church. They both set ordination within the eucharistic context as the foundational act of Christian worship, in which the corporate life of the Church is most clearly articulated. It is in response to the individualistic potential within some descriptions of baptismal ecclesiology that Paul Gibson emphasizes the importance of the relational nature of the Eucharist: 'An ecclesiology built on the table demands not only that there are servants (ministers) but also that others accept their service.'[38] However, this need not demand a unidirectional service of the laity by the ordained: lay and ordained are called to serve the world and to serve one another in a dynamic response which is a sacramental sign of the service offered to the Church by Christ and by Christ to the Church. While some may wish to pit eucharistic ecclesiology against baptismal ecclesiology,[39] such a portrayal depends on a version of baptismal ecclesiology that is not substantiated by the ordinals. Rather, the Eucharist is the natural gathering of the baptized, where the Church is most clearly seen to be 'the Body of Christ, the people of God and the dwelling-place of the Holy Spirit' (*CW:OS* 10).

Ordinations are in the name of the Church because of the collective petition of the baptized, presided over by the bishop, as a full realization of the Church. The catholicity of the Church in *CW:OS* is therefore not expressed through the optional rituals that are also practised by the Roman Catholic Church – such as the anointing and distinctive clerical vestments. Rather, it is in the presiding bishop's legitimacy in acting on behalf of the Church of God, as manifested by the gathered Church. This is the Church fully manifested with the full diversity of God's people, all three orders and laity, celebrating together as the local Church,[40] invoking the Holy Spirit in the name of Christ. The significance of both lay and ordained sharing the same baptism, as the foundation of their common life in Christ, does not negate the subsequent distinction between lay and ordained. Rather, their common baptism affirms the need for both lay and ordained to be integrated into the Church, so that the Church can be a sacrament of Christ's presence in the world.

The primary purpose of the eucharistic assembly in *CW:OS* is therefore to be a manifestation of the full expression of the Church. This is clear when comparing the emphasis on the diocese and parish in other Anglican ordinals. While all ordinands must be ordained to a particular place, the involvement in and ownership of the process by the people where they will minister is minimal in *CW:OS*, compared with the communal celebrations in other parts of the Anglican Communion. In the Episcopal Church of the Philippines, for example, not only are all diocesan clergy expected to attend, but the candidate enters the service, which is not necessarily held in the cathedral, in procession with key laity and clergy from their locality.[41] A similar scenario is referenced for the ordination of a Torres Strait Islander as bishop.[42] Although *CW:OS* does make provision in the notes for ordinands to be seated in the congregation initially,[43] it is only a suggestion and, particularly in the case of those ordained to the diaconate, the congregation of the parish where the person is to serve has no specific role to play in the ordination as a whole, not even in the presentation.[44] While the Liturgical Commission emphasizes the importance of the symbolism of ordinands moving from being seated with the congregation at the beginning of the service, several practical reasons are also given as excuses for not doing so.[45] There is thus a distinctive nuance to the role of the congregation in *CW:OS*. Rather than an oversight or omission, the congregation are deliberately generalized: they represent neither the parish nor the diocese, but the Church in its fullest sense.

This explains the lack of theological attention that is given to whether the ordination happens in a cathedral or parish church. The setting can significantly change the ecclesiological focus: the bishop coming to the parish emphasizes the importance of the local context and the ministry of the newly ordained in that locality; the ordination in the cathedral emphasizes the unity of the diocese and the bishop as one who draws the diocesan Church together, rather than the one who reflects the diocese to the parish. Such differences may speak to many in the congregation more strongly than the careful weaving of scriptural allusion into the text, because liturgy is more than text. It is concerned with 'the reality and "guts" of a people doing their thinking about what the relationship between God and themselves might be.'[46] This is significant because the parish remains the key ecclesial experience for most Anglicans, who will rarely see their bishop, and there is considerably more scope for active involvement in the service by the laity of the community in which the newly ordained will serve.[47] It is only when the laity are seen as representative of the whole Church, rather than of the parish or diocese, that such nuances are re-contextualized and reduced in significance. For *CW:OS*, such nuances are insignificant because the focus is on the Church gathered to invoke the Holy Spirit to establish a new relationship at ordination.

While the ordinals of both the US Episcopal Church and the Church of England are indebted to baptismal ecclesiology, it is *CW:OS* in which baptismal ecclesiology has a fuller expression, emphasized by the lack of attention to parochial or even diocesan significance. The laity are representative of the apostolicity of the Church as much as the presiding bishop. Although a case could be made for the downplaying of parish involvement as a significant statement of the diocese rather than the parish being the base ecclesial reality, it is clear from the example of the Episcopal Church of the Philippines that both parish and diocese can be in focus. Moreover, there is significant scope for a greater role and prominence for the people of the diocese; for example, in having the expectation that the diocesan clergy will attend, as many dioceses expect for the Chrism Eucharist on Maundy Thursday.[48]

There may be a pragmatic reason for the underdeveloped significance of the parish and diocese in *CW:OS* – for example, the realization that the congregation present are often more akin to a wedding congregation than the weekly eucharistic congregation with a predominance of supporters, friends and family of the candidates rather than a conscious gathering of the body of Christ. Equally, it could simply be a demonstration of vestigial clericalism that sees the laity as passive observers rather than active participants. However, equally possible, and entirely congruent with what has thus far been established, is the transcendence of these categorizations of the laity, by identifying them with the catholicity of the Church, rather than the specificity of geographical location.

It has been clearly demonstrated that Colin Podmore's assertion that the US Episcopal Church has developed a radical form of baptismal ecclesiology, incongruent with the Church of England, is not substantiated by a comparison of the ordinals of the *BCP 1979* and *CW:OS*. Largely this is due to the theological developments that are an integral part of *CW:OS*. Podmore helpfully uses the imagery of two streams mingling to depict the Anglican Communion as the product of two diverse ecclesiologies: 'the traditional western catholic ecclesiology of England and Ireland and the more democratic, egalitarian ecclesiology of the American Episcopal Church'.[49] However, what the metaphor fails to articulate is the way in which both the US Episcopal Church and the Church of England are evolving, and thus are not 'pristine head waters' but more like the brackish waters of a river meeting the sea, where the rising tide increases the salinity of the river. This book is not suggesting that Podmore has misunderstood or misrepresented his sources, but that *CW:OS* portrays another side of the story: an alternative lens through which a different, arguably fuller, Anglican ecclesiology is projected.

In conclusion, therefore, baptismal ecclesiology in *CW:OS* is highly developed and explicit, shaping the text and referred to throughout the text. It is expressed in a way that is consistent with Paul Avis' holistic view of baptismal ecclesiology, drawing on the breadth of what it means to be part of the body of Christ, and whose relational focus expects the members of the Church to work together in building the kingdom of God. This collaborative ministry is an essential part of what it means to be Church, not an optional *modus operandi*. It speaks of the integrated sacramental nature of the Church, which as a whole ministers in the name of Christ. This is particularly clear in the eucharistic assembly, which is therefore the essential context for the celebration of the ordination rite. In the next chapter, the relationship between bishop as presiding minister and the rest of the Church, represented by the congregation, will be explored further.

Notes

1 This is hereafter referred to as '*BCP 1979*' followed by the page number.

2 Paul Avis, 2008, *The Identity of Anglicanism*, London: T&T Clark, p. 109.

3 Cf. The World Council of Churches, 1982, *Baptism, Eucharist and Ministry*, Faith and order paper no. 111, Geneva: World Council of Churches.

4 International Anglican Liturgical Consultation, 2006, *The Berkeley Statement: To Equip the Saints: Ordination in Anglicanism Today*, in Ronald L. Dowling and David R. Holeton (eds), Blackrock: Columba Press, pp. 219–43, p. 220.

5 Louis Weil, 2006, 'Baptismal Ecclesiology: Uncovering a Paradigm', in Ronald L. Dowling and David R. Holeton (eds), *Equipping the Saints: Ordination in Anglicanism Today*, Blackrock: Columba Press, pp. 18–34, p. 18.

6 Weil, 'Baptismal Ecclesiology: Uncovering a Paradigm', p. 21.

7 Weil, 'Baptismal Ecclesiology: Uncovering a Paradigm', pp. 33–4.

8 Colin Podmore, 2010, 'The Baptismal Revolution in the American Episcopal Church: Baptismal Ecclesiology and the Baptismal Covenant', *Ecclesiology*, 6, pp. 8–38, p. 8.

9 Podmore, 'The Baptismal Revolution in the American Episcopal Church, pp. 14–15.

10 Podmore, 'The Baptismal Revolution in the American Episcopal Church, p. 15, citing B. Kaye, 2008, *An Introduction to World Anglicanism*, Cambridge: Cambridge University Press, p. 226.

11 Podmore, 'The Baptismal Revolution in the American Episcopal Church', p. 23.

12 Weil, 'Baptismal Ecclesiology: Uncovering a Paradigm', p. 25.

13 Colin Podmore, 2008, 'A Tale of Two Churches: The Ecclesiologies of the

Episcopal Church and the Church of England Compared', *Ecclesiastical Law Journal*, 10 (1), pp. 34–70, reprinted in *International Journal for the Study of the Christian Church*, 8, pp. 124–54, p. 143.

14 Pierre Whalon, 2000, 'The Tale Needs Re-telling: A Reply to Colin Podmore's "A Tale of Two Churches"', *Theology*, 114 (1), pp. 3–12, p. 8.

15 Colin Podmore, 2000, 'Re-telling the Tale', *Theology*, 114 (1), pp. 13–22, p. 20.

16 Martyn Percy, 1998, *Power and the Church: Ecclesiology in an Age of Transition*, London: Cassell, p. 125.

17 Podmore, 'Podmore, 'The Baptismal Revolution in the American Episcopal Church', p. 151.

18 Michael Northcott, 2011, 'Parochial Ecology on St Briavels Common: Rebalancing the Local and Universal in Anglican Ecclesiology and Practice', *Journal of Anglican Studies*, 10 (1), pp. 68–93, p. 68.

19 Northcott, 'Parochial Ecology on St Briavels Common: Rebalancing the Local and Universal in Anglican Ecclesiology and Practice', p. 88.

20 Podmore, 'The Baptismal Revolution in the American Episcopal Church', p. 151.

21 Podmore, 'The Baptismal Revolution in the American Episcopal Church', p. 144.

22 David Holloway, *Finance, Centrism and the Quota*, <https://www.churchsociety.org/wp-content/uploads/2021/05/finance_centralism_quota.pdf>, p. 7, accessed 11.09.2025.

23 Mark Chapman, 2013, 'Does the Church of England have a Theology of General Synod?', *Journal of Anglican Studies*, 11 (1), pp. 15–31, p. 17.

24 This is the standard opening for Holy Baptism, Holy Eucharist: Rite One, Holy Eucharist: Rite Two, and Confirmation in the BCP 1979.

25 Paul Bradshaw, 'The Church of England' in Ronald L. Dowling and David R. Holeton (eds), *Equipping the Saints*, pp. 146–9, p. 146.

26 There is a printed text, but this is not read publicly in the rite.

27 'For we are God's servants, working together; you are God's field, God's building' (1 Cor. 3.9).

28 'and we sent Timothy, our brother and co-worker for God in proclaiming the gospel of Christ, to strengthen and encourage you for the sake of your faith' (1 Thess. 3.2).

29 'And Jesus who is called Justus greets you. These are the only ones of the circumcision among my co-workers for the kingdom of God, and they have been a comfort to me' (Col. 4.11).

30 'Epaphras, who is one of you, a servant of Christ Jesus, greets you. He is always wrestling in his prayers on your behalf, so that you may stand mature and fully assured in everything that God wills' (Col. 4.12).

31 'because of your sharing in the gospel from the first day until now' (Phil. 1.5).

32 'To all the saints in Christ Jesus who are in Philippi, with the bishops and deacons' (Phil 1.1).

33 For example, the *BCP 1979* 527.

34 Richard Leggett, 'By Public Prayer and the Imposition of Hands: The Prayer of the People and the Ordination Prayer' in Dowling and Holeton (eds), *Equipping the Saints*, 71–84, p. 84.

35 For example, from the deacons' rite: 'We preach not ourselves but Christ Jesus as Lord and ourselves as your servants for Jesus' sake. We welcome you as fellow servants in the gospel: may Christ dwell in your hearts through faith, that you may be rooted and grounded in love' (*CW:OS* 22). See also priests' and bishops' rites (*CW:OS* 44, 68).

36 The inclusion of the laity here is non-verbal, and the rubric is markedly hierarchical, especially in the bishops' rite: 'The Presiding Bishop and other Bishops greet the new bishop. The people greet one another. The new Bishop also greets other members of the clergy, family members, and the congregation' (*BCP 1979* 522). Cf. the priests' rite (*BCP 1979* 534) and deacons' rite (*BCP 1979* 546).

37 For example, 'Therefore, Father, make N. a bishop in your Church' (*BCP 1979* 521); see also priests' and deacons' rites (*BCP 1979* 533 and 545).

38 Paul A. Gibson, 2006, 'A Baptismal Ecclesiology: Some Questions' in Dowling and Holeton (eds), *Equipping the Saints*, pp. 35–44, p. 42.

39 Cf. Alexander Irving, 2019, 'Baptismal Ecclesiology and the Ordination Rites of the Church of England in the 2005 Common Worship Ordinal', *Churchman*, 133 (3), pp. 203–23, p. 209: 'While The Episcopal Church's identification of baptism as "full initiation by water and the Holy Spirit into Christ's body the Church" is consistent with Anglican formularies with regards to the centrality of baptism to inclusion into the church, its absolutizing of baptism as the one initiatory event is not the view of the CofE ... For the CofE, baptism is the sacrament through which believers are incorporated into the Body of Christ in conjunction with confirmation and Holy Communion.'

40 There is a perennial discussion in Anglican ecclesiology as to whether the 'local' is constituted by the diocese or the parish. This is a result of the split between the bishop and the regular worshipping community, due to the size of the diocese. Since a bishop must preside, the ordinal transcends this dichotomy.

41 Tomos S. Maddela, 2006, 'The Episcopal Church in the Philippines' in Dowling and Holeton (eds), *Equipping the Saints*, pp. 153–9, pp. 154–5.

42 Ronald L. Dowling, 2006, 'The Presentation of Candidates' in Dowling and Holeton (eds), *Equipping the Saints*, pp. 136–7.

43 'If the ordinands are to begin the service seated among the congregation with those who are to present them, they take their places before the entry of the ministers' (*CW:OS* 26); see also priests' rite notes (*CW:OS* 48) and bishops' notes (*CW:OS* 72).

44 There is a growing awareness of place through the three rites, from no contribution in the deacons' rite (*CW:OS* 27), to the involvement of the training incumbent, albeit couched in terms of vouching for the candidate's development (*CW:OS* 49), to the bishops' rite where only in the presentation of a candidate who has been elected for a diocesan see is there the suggestion to involve a local lay person. Suffragan bishops are to be presented by their receiving diocesan (*CW:OS* 73).

45 The Liturgical Commission, 2007, 'Celebrating Ordinations: A Practical Guide' in Archbishops' Council, Common Worship: Ordination Services, London: Church House Publishing (*CW:OS* 159–60).

46 Tom Clammer, 2018, '"Be Born in Our Hearts": Being Transported and Transformed by the Liturgy' in Aiden Platten (ed.), *Grasping the Heel of Heaven*, Norwich: Canterbury Press, p. 98.

47 For a detailed treatment of the place of the parish in the Church of England,

see Andrew Rumsey, 2017, *Parish: An Anglican Theology of Place*, London: SCM Press.

48 The expectation and inclusion of the whole diocese in an ordination would give a much clearer sense that the ordination is something significant in the life of the whole Church, and not simply for the ordinands and their supporters.

49 Colin Podmore, 2008, 'A Tale of Two Churches', pp. 34–70, p. 12.

3

Ordination: The Bishop's Hands Within the Church's Prayers

In the previous chapter the significance of baptismal ecclesiology for *CW:OS* was clearly established. In this chapter, the relationship between those being ordained and the baptized will be explored, with particular reference to their roles in the rite of ordination. The relationship between bishop and the Church will be established through a consideration of agency within the ordination rite, demonstrating it is the Church that celebrates the ordination rite at which the bishop presides. Together with the preceding chapters, these discussions will collectively demonstrate that sacramental ecclesiology is the most appropriate term to encapsulate the distinctive ecclesiology of *CW:OS*. The evolution of *CW:OS* and the distinctive emphasis it places on the active role of the Church as a whole in the rite of ordination will be demonstrated through a careful analysis of the ordinals of the Church, specifically the 1662 *Ordering of Bishops, Priests and Deacons*,[1] and the *Alternative Service Book* of 1980.[2] Although the bishop has a distinctive role in the ordination, the assembly is an essential aspect of the ordination because it is not the bishop alone who ordains; the bishop's role in the liturgy is to preside over the eucharistic assembly. The question of who the active participants are in an ordination was brought into specific focus on the 15 July 2020, when Covid-19 restrictions impacted the ordinations of the Bishops of St Germans and Horsham[3] and, separately, the Bishop of Lewes.[4] This attracted much debate and mirrored the arrangements being made in dioceses across the Church concerning suitable Covid-specific restrictions for the ordination of priests and deacons.

Of particular significance here is David Fagerberg's concept of *leitourgia* in which the liturgy is identified as a relational encounter with God. This active engagement in the rite will underpin the identification of the active participation of the whole body of Christ in *CW:OS*. The distinctive contribution of *CW:OS* is clear when compared with the *BCP 1662* in both the text and rubrics of the rites. Most significant is the role of the whole congregation in invoking the Holy Spirit both at the ordination and for the continued relationship that has been established at ordination. Comparisons with the *Common Worship* marriage and baptism rites will demonstrate that the distinctive contribution of *CW:OS* to Anglican ecclesiology is part of a wider integrated sacramental ecclesiology of the Church.

At the heart of the rite is the invocation of the Holy Spirit by the congregation, both lay and ordained, in the *veni creator* sung by the whole eucharistic assembly and the ordination prayer articulated by the bishop on behalf of the Church. For Fagerberg, it is the involvement of the Holy Spirit in the rite that enables *leitourgia*, the defining characteristic of the Church: 'Leitourgia creates a people, a people called ekklesia. The Church might develop liturgy, leitourgia creates Church ... leitourgia as encounter with God is the source for the ekklesia's life.'[5] Fagerberg defines *leitourgia* as the means 'by which a group of people become something corporately which they had not been as a mere collection of individuals. In this case, believers become Christ's body.'[6]

Fagerberg's statements relate to liturgical worship in general, but are given particular emphasis in ordination rites, where the Church is self-consciously being created and ministry procreated though the assembly and the future assemblies in which the newly ordained will play a significant role.

The implication of Fagerberg's assertion is that:

> The liturgy symbolizes the kingdom of God, but if liturgy's symbolic intelligibility is lost then liturgy has no theological muscle and it is replaced by flabby sentimentalism or rationalism. The service becomes a mystical, other-worldly, symbolism; or hieratic pageantry which might not even require a congregation's presence much less their participation; or audio-visual technique to set the mood for speech.[7]

Fagerberg is clear that the creation of *leitourgia* is not the product of academic endeavour, but rather is elicited through the rite itself, expressed theologically in response to the question 'What happened?'[8]

Although the approach of asking this question is vulnerable to reduction to individual emotivism, to be investigated as an aspect of congregational studies, there remains the intent and expectation of the rite that it is an encounter with God. This is not to say that the rite need necessarily be successful in its intent, could that be measured, but that this is the expectation of the rite and therefore the context for understanding the role of the bishop, and the wider assembly. That the rite facilitates encounter with God not only gives a context for those in the congregation, but also an expectation of an active role for everyone involved in the rite. Moreover, if the ordination is to be *leitourgia*, it must not only be an act in which those present are caught up into the kingdom of God but it must be something that speaks to the world:

> Theology used only microcosmically, within the Church and for Church business alone, becomes the rational version of cult, perpetuating isolation from an allegedly profane world. The body of Christ does not assemble to do Church, it assembles to do the world, redeemed.[9]

The aim of the rite cannot therefore be confined to those who are present in the assembly; it is 'macrocosmic'. Those who are engaged in the *leitourgia* of ordination are therefore actively representing the totality of redeemed creation on behalf of others. Thus *CW:OS* does not limit the assembly to the diocese or parish, with their attendant potential for introspection, but as the body of Christ, looking to redemption of all creation.

In this view, therefore, the involvement of the whole Church is more than simply having a specific role to play or words to say in the rite; they are an integral part of the assembly, with a more fundamental and essential role in creating the necessary context for the ordination. There is no 'moment of ordination', as was evidenced by Leggett earlier; rather, it is a process of ordination that itself is dependent on the context undergirding the whole. The ordination takes part in the *leitourgia* of the Church, which can be neither individualistic, concerning the bishop or the candidate in isolation, nor cultic, in isolation from the world. It is personal, and therefore at its heart relational: the action of the people is an expression of their relationship with Christ and the world, both as diverse persons, and as a community.

With this view in mind, the question of who is ordaining is reframed: no longer is there a polarization between episcopal and congregational authority. Instead, the question is one of appropriate agency and how that agency is expressed, with both the Church as a whole, and the bishop in particular, acting on behalf of Christ. In comparing the development of the ordinal in the Church, it will be demonstrated that while episcopal ordination is required, the role of the presiding bishop in *CW:OS* is not separated from the communal work of the assembly.

This is most clearly seen in the words 'whom we ordain in your name', which *CW:OS* inherits from the *ASB* (*CW:OS* 152–3), and is a common aspect of all three ordination prayers, the only modification being the substitution of 'ordain' for 'consecrate' in the bishops' rite. While it is possible that this is a use of the royal 'we' as used by diocesan bishops when issuing licences,[10] the context of the ordination prayer makes it clear that the bishop is speaking on behalf of the Church, as they do in the Eucharistic Preface.[11] This is in marked contrast with the *BCP 1662*, whose ordination prayers lack this corporate emphasis. Direct comparison with the deacons' rite is complicated by the omission of an ordination prayer, which appears to be deemed unnecessary for this 'inferior office' (*BCP 1662* 52). The ordination prayer in the bishops' rite is unclear, with the use of the passive 'given' meaning that there is no clear subject:

> Grant, we beseech thee, to this thy servant such grace, that he may evermore be ready to spread abroad thy Gospel, the glad tidings of reconciliation with thee; and use the authority given him, not to destruction, but to salvation; not to hurt, but to help.

It might be that it is God himself who has given the authority, set in the context of God's empowering and equipping for various offices within the Church, 'making some Apostles, some Prophets …' (*BCP 1662* 108). Alternatively, it may be a reference to the authority that was given at ordination to the priesthood. In the priests' rite the ordination prayer makes it explicit that this is a direct call by God, thanking him 'for these so great benefits of thy eternal goodness, and for that thou hast vouchsafed to call these thy servants here present to the same office and ministry, appointed for the salvation of mankind' (*BCP 1662* 99). In contrast with the *BCP 1662*, the active participation of the whole assembly in *CW:OS* is clearly evident and emphasized.

The bishop in *CW:OS* is not acting alone but within the active assembly. As Alexander Irving has identified, *CW:OS* emphasizes ordination as both an act of God and an act of the Church:

> In stressing the agency of the church through the bishop, the CW Ordinal displays the impact of baptismal ecclesiology in the emphasis it gives to the fact that ordination is both an act of God and an act of the church.
>
> Unmistakably, the ecclesial dimension of ordination is accentuated

in the CW Ordinal. The gathering of the people is underscored because ordination takes place in the context of the whole church coming together to order its common ministry.[12]

Here, therefore, *CW:OS* is clearly expecting and espousing *leitourgia*, as expressed by Fagerberg, in a development of the *BCP 1662* rite, which it has inherited from the *ASB*.

While a congregation is expected in the *BCP 1662* rites, nevertheless their role is minimal, focused on the preliminary verification of the candidate's suitability. A helpful analogy may be drawn with the role of the congregation at a wedding: in the *BCP 1662* rites for both deacons and priests, the opportunity is given for the congregation to raise objection to a candidate being ordained,[13] in a similar vein to the final calling of banns for a wedding ceremony.[14] Interestingly, even this minimal, but important, role is omitted from the rite for bishops; the inference being that the priests are beyond reproach by the laity. The *ASB* maintains the theme of suitability in the questioning, but it is modified by the inclusion of the bishop enquiring: 'Is it therefore your will that they should be ordained?' and 'Will you uphold them in their ministry?'[15] The effect of the change is twofold: first, requiring the congregation to give their active consent, rather than passively failing to raise sufficient objection; and second, giving the congregation an ongoing active role in supporting the candidates throughout their ministry.

Irving suggests that the relocation of the affirmation to after the declarations subsumes ecclesial election into an emphasis on the personal vocation of the candidate, and undermines the ecclesial focus of *CW:OS*:

> In this structural change, the CW Ordinal could be taken as implicitly undermining the very point that it is trying to convey: that ordained ministry arises out from the common priesthood on behalf of the common priesthood. As ordination is an act of God in calling and equipping ministers for the threefold ministry of ordained service that takes place through the church, it is by the election of the church to ordained ministry that the call of God is discerned ... Certainly, while the personal sense of call should not be diminished, it should not be advanced ahead of ecclesial election, as is implicitly the case in the CW Ordinal's relocation of the affirmation of the assembly after the declarations.[16]

However, this interpretation is unsubstantiated, and seems to be more of an interpolation, aided by Irving's overly individualized reading of baptismal ecclesiology. The explicit purpose of the declarations is to give the congregation a stronger and more affirmative voice, rather than simply an opportunity to raise objections as in the *BCP 1662*. It is clear that the declarations give greater emphasis to ecclesial election, as an integral part of the emphasis placed on the active participation of the whole Church in *CW:OS*.

In all three rites the bishop enquires of the congregation, 'Brothers and sisters, you have heard how great is the charge that these ordinands are ready to undertake, and you have heard their declarations. Is it now your will that they should be ordained?' (*CW:OS* 17, 39).[17] Thus there is a significant change in emphasis; it is less a question about the suitability of the candidates and more about the weight of the responsibility that is to be placed on them. This shift in emphasis is strengthened by the question being moved from the introductory elements of the rite to following the declarations. The candidates' acceptance of the declarations therefore forms the basis of the congregation's support of them: the foundation for the ordination is therefore the coming together of the active willingness on the part of the candidate, the bishop and the Church as a whole eucharistic assembly. This collaboration is confirmed by the bishop further enquiring: 'Will you continually pray for them?' and 'Will you uphold and encourage them in their ministry?' (*CW:OS* 17, 39). The ordination is therefore affirmed by the Church, who are actively involved both in the rite and in the ongoing ministry of the ordained.[18]

The active involvement of the whole assembly has therefore been well established, and it is on this basis that the role of the bishop in the rite is best understood. Although the presidency of the bishop over the whole rite and at the laying on of hands in particular is common to the *BCP 1662*, the *ASB* and *CW:OS*, the role of the bishop is clearly different, as highlighted by the posture of the bishop at the laying on of hands. Most significant is the *BCP 1662*'s rubric that the bishop be seated for the deacon's ordination.[19] Accompanied by the lack of an ordination prayer, the choreography, with the candidates kneeling before the seated bishop, speaks of the authority vested in the bishop to preside over the ordination, without any visible connection with the rest of the Church. It is close to a situation in which the bishop acts in isolation from the rest of the Church, who appear incidental to this aspect of the rite.

For the ordination of priests and bishops in the *BCP 1662*, the inference is that the bishop is standing,[20] as it is with the *ASB* deacons' rite

(*ASB* 348); the rubric's earlier direction that the bishop should stand (*ASB* 378) having not been rescinded. However, when priests and deacons are ordained in the same *ASB* rite, there is a rubric for the bishop to stand after they have ordained the deacons and prior to ordaining the priests, implying that the bishop sits for the ordination of deacons (*ASB* 378). In the priests' and bishops' rites in the *ASB*, the rubric is explicit in directing the bishop to stand for the ordination (*ASB* 362). There is no explanation for the change away from the bishop speaking *ex cathedra*, which emphasizes the authority vested in the bishop, akin to a monarch speaking from their throne. However, the rubric of *CW:OS* clarifies the intention: 'the bishop stands to pray' (*CW:OS* 20, 42, 66). The emphasis here, therefore, is on the role that the bishop has within the Church as a community dependent on God's grace. The bishop is praying as part of the prayerful assembly, presiding over and leading the people in prayer.[21]

This is reflected in the words that accompany the laying on of hands. The authority of the bishop is emphasized in the *BCP 1662*. The deacons' rite lacks an epiclesis, invocation of the Holy Spirit, other than a benediction given in the name of the Trinity: 'Take thou authority to execute the office of a Deacon in the Church of God committed unto thee; In the name of the Father, and of the Son, and of the Holy Ghost. Amen' (*BCP 1662* 89). Interestingly, this 'Amen', as in all three rites of the *BCP 1662*, is not intended to be congregational, but instead said by the bishop alone, further suggesting a passive role for the congregation in the rite. This is strengthened in the priests' rite:

> Receive the Holy Ghost for the office and work of a Priest in the Church of God, now committed unto thee by the imposition of our hands. Whose sins thou dost forgive, they are forgiven; and whose sins thou dost retain, they are retained. And be thou a faithful dispenser of the Word of God, and of his holy Sacraments; In the Name of the Father and of the Son, and of the Holy Ghost. Amen. (*BCP 1662* 99)

Although there is mention of the Holy Ghost, it appears to be given as a gift of God through the bishop, who confers the gift of the Holy Ghost, by virtue of his or her office rather than through invocation by the bishop on behalf of the Church.[22] The same is true in the bishops' rite, but with an additional admonition:

> Receive the Holy Ghost for the office and work of a Bishop in the Church of God, now committed unto thee by the imposition of our

hands; In the Name of the Father, and of the Son, and of the Holy Ghost. Amen. And remember that thou stir up the grace of God which is given thee by this imposition of our hands: for God hath not given us the spirit of fear, but of power, and love, and soberness. (*BCP 1662* 108)

A significant change comes in the *ASB*, which shortens the words at the laying on of hands and includes an explicit epiclesis: 'Send down the Holy Spirit upon your servant N for the office and work of a deacon/priest/bishop in your Church' (*ASB* 349, 362, 394). This is maintained in *CW:OS* with the minor substitution of 'on' for 'upon'.[23] What is clear is that the bishop, standing in prayer as a focal minister for the prayers of the whole assembly, is here asking the Holy Spirit to be sent on behalf of the Church as a whole. *CW:OS*, therefore, envisages ordination to be a collaboration of the congregation as a whole, presided over by the bishop,[24] collectively calling on God to send the Holy Spirit to establish the new relationship between the candidate and the other members of the body of Christ.

The ordination prayer in *CW:OS* therefore echoes the eucharistic prayer, and the eucharistic context for ordination is presented as essential rather than merely appropriate. The Eucharist is a consistent element in the ordination rites; however, its emphasis in *CW:OS* is clearly on the eucharistic assembly as the active participants, in contrast to the *BCP 1662* where the emphasis is placed on the new relationship between the newly ordained deacon and the bishop, without reference to the rest of the Church: 'Then shall the Bishop proceed in the Communion: and all that are Ordered shall tarry, and receive the Holy Communion the same day with the Bishop'[25] (*BCP 1662* 89). In a further contrast with the *BCP 1662*, where the ordination rite is sandwiched between morning prayer and the communion, the eucharistic context of *CW:OS* is a marked development, with the bishop presiding over the assembly which is mutually and actively involved in both the prayer of consecration and the celebration of the Eucharist, as an integrated whole.

This move away from the individual, emphasizing the personal authority of the bishop, towards the relational, emphasizing the bishop's role within the active church community, is also evidenced by the change in focus from the candidate to the ministry that the newly ordained will undertake. In the ordination prayers of both the *BCP 1662* and the *ASB* the focus is very much on the candidates and the support and development they will need. In the rite for deacons, the *BCP 1662* petition that they 'may so well behave themselves in this inferior office, that they may be found worthy to be called unto the higher ministries in thy Church' (*BCP 1662* 90),[26] although amended to give a higher value to diaconal ministry by the *ASB*, maintains the focus on the candidate; that 'they may continue strong and steadfast in your Son' (*ASB* 349). It is in *CW:OS* that a significant shift comes, with a focus on those who will benefit from the ministry of the candidates rather than the candidates themselves: 'that your people may walk with them in the way of truth and be made ready for the coming of our Lord Jesus Christ' (*CW:OS* 21). The newly ordained are therefore, from the very outset, set within the body of Christ among whom they will minister, actively journeying together.

This petition for eternal glory being made on behalf of the whole Church, re-emphasizes the corporate nature of the Church. It is therefore all the more jarring that the rite for bishops in *CW:OS* reverses this emphasis that had been present in the *ASB*, removing the inclusion of 'with all your servants' in the promise of glory. The final petition becomes a request on behalf of the bishop personally that he or she 'enter your eternal joy' (*CW:OS* 154). This change is the exception that proves the rule in terms of the argument being advanced here, in giving an individualistic focus at the expense of the communal. Although it is possible that this is because of the distinct office of the bishop, this assertion is not substantiated elsewhere by *CW:OS*, and the change remains a strange anomaly.

Overall, *CW:OS* demonstrates a clear and decisive move to the active participation of the whole Church in the ordination rites, with the bishop and the congregation invoking the Holy Spirit. The fullness of the ecclesial expression creates the necessary context for ordination. This fundamental intention of the rite is in marked contrast with the way in which some bishops have chosen to carry out ordinations while restrictions on public gathering were enforced during the Covid-19 pandemic. Although the restrictions were significant, the clear liturgical emphasis of *CW:OS* was ignored at the consecration of the bishops of St Germans and Horsham[27] and subsequently the Bishop of Lewes[28] on 15 July 2020.

Particularly notable were the omission of the presentation before the declaration of assent; the choice of venue;[29] the prioritizing of the number of bishops over representation of the laity; the prioritizing of the candidates' familial bubbles over representatives from the receiving dioceses;[30] and the choice of online media. While live-streaming the event opened it up to potentially a wider audience, it failed to enable active participation by a full expression of the Church. The viewers were passively watching rather than taking an active part. Had a virtual conference platform such as Zoom been used, participation at key points – including the presentation, prayers and welcome – could have been enabled. The choice of media relegated the vast majority of the congregation, or audience, to the same state of passivity allocated them in the *BCP 1662*. The significance of the development of active participation by the Church in all its fullness in *CW:OS* was therefore lost. The ignorance of this loss was evident in the Archbishop of Canterbury's introductory words, which concerned the accommodations made to enable the ordination of a 'traditionalist', rather than those that had alienated the wider Church.[31]

In conclusion, *CW:OS* presents and expects full active participation by the whole assembly as a manifestation of the Church. This gives a context in which there is *leitourgia*, in which the Church is formed through the Holy Spirit in response to God's call and seeks to enable the work of the Holy Spirit in creating the body of Christ. There is a dynamic inter-relationship and collegiality between the congregation and the bishop, as an ordered ecclesial reality formed and empowered by the Holy Spirit. Ordination is therefore an act of the body of Christ, constituted temporally by the congregation and presided over by the bishop, empowered by the Holy Spirit. The emphasis on the Holy Spirit as the foundation for ordination, enabling the assembly to subvert their separateness and be a sacrament of the redeemed creation – a divine society that is ordered by having bishops, priests, deacons and laity integrated within the Church. It is the people of God, the body of Christ, who in the power of the Holy Spirit presents and welcomes the candidate in the persons of the congregation, and presides and lays hands on the candidate through the person of the bishop.

A useful comparison here is the administration of Holy Baptism, where a similar fullness of expression of the life of the Church is expected. The notes in *Common Worship: Initiation Services* set the context for baptisms: 'Holy Baptism is normally administered by the parish priest in the course of public worship on Sunday "when the most number of people come together" (Canon B 21).'[32] Pastoral concerns are the only rationale for foregoing a full expression of the Church as the necessary context for baptism. A reductionist approach, which seeks to define the minimum efficacious requirement, leads not to greater understanding but rather a skewed view, defined by a hermeneutic of poverty rather than one of fullness. Thus, Louis Weil's comments on baptism that 'it is an act of the Church, and its celebration must normatively manifest that meaning'[33] and 'minimal representation of the community is appropriate only by way of exception as in the case of emergency baptism',[34] are equally applicable to ordinations, although with less demand for emergency ordinations.

The bishop presides over the Church, not on behalf of himself or herself, neither on behalf of the college of bishops, but as an aspect of the fullness of the life of the Church. Equally, the congregation acts on behalf of the Church catholic neither as particular supporters of the candidate, nor on behalf of their local church. Even the candidates offer themselves to be ordained by, on behalf of, and for the benefit of, the Church, which includes those who will be drawn into the body of Christ through their ministrations. Active and communal participation, dependent on people in right relationship, lies at the heart of *CW:OS*. It is through the Church as community that the Holy Spirit works and in which the Holy Spirit dwells.

Notes

1 This is hereafter referred to as the '*BCP 1662*'; the page numbers given refer to the text as produced in *CW:OS*.

2 The Central Board of the Church of England, 1980, *The Alternative Service Book 1980*, London: SPCK. This is hereafter referred to as the '*ASB*' followed by the page number.

3 The Archbishop of Canterbury, 2020, 'Lambeth Palace Chapel – 15th of July 2020 11:30am', <https://www.youtube.com/watch?v=r7zIK5ojkgI&feature=youtu.be>, accessed 11.09.2025.

4 The Archbishop of Canterbury, 2020, 'Lambeth Palace Chapel – 15th of July 2020 2:30pm', <https://www.youtube.com/watch?v=NUpxLoJCCWc&feature=youtu.be>, accessed 11.09.2025.

5 David Fagerberg, 1992, *What is Liturgical Theology?*, Collegeville, MN: Liturgical Press, p. 187.

6 Fagerberg, *What is Liturgical Theology?*, p. 288.

7 Fagerberg, *What is Liturgical Theology?*, p. 293.

8 Fagerberg, *What is Liturgical Theology?*, p. 289.

9 Fagerberg, *What is Liturgical Theology?*, p. 297.

10 See also the use of the royal 'we' in a prayer following confirmation, 'upon whom we have now laid our hands'. Archbishops' Council, 2006, *Common Worship: Initiation Services*, London: Church House Publishing, p. 126. The royal 'we' is more evident in the ASB, for example, at the declarations: 'In order that we may know your purpose, and that you may be strengthened in your resolve to fulfil your ministry, you must make the declarations we now put to you' (*ASB* 373).

11 See, for example, the proper prefaces for the deacons' rite (*CW:OS* 52).

12 Alexander Irving, 2019, 'Baptismal Ecclesiology and the Ordination Rites of the Church of England in the 2005 Common Worship Ordinal', *Churchman*, 133 (3), pp. 203–23, p. 220.

13 See, for example, from the deacons' rite p. 80: 'BRETHREN, if there be any of you who knoweth any impediment or notable crime in any of these persons presented to be ordered Deacons, for the which he ought not to be admitted to that office; Let him come forth in the Name of God, and shew what the crime or imped-

iment is' (*BCP 1662* 80). In the priests' rite: GOOD people, these are they whom we purpose, God willing, to receive this day unto the holy office of Priesthood: For after due examination we find not to the contrary, but that they be lawfully called to their function and ministry, and that they be persons meet for the same. But yet if there be any of you, who knoweth any impediment or notable crime in any of them, for the which he ought not to be received into this holy ministry; let him come forth in the Name of God, and shew what the crime or impediment is' (*BCP 1662* 91).

14 At a wedding, the officiating minister asks, 'First, I am required to ask anyone present who knows a reason why these persons may not lawfully marry, to declare it now.' Archbishops' Council, 2000, *Common Worship: Pastoral Services*, London: Church House Publishing, p. 106.

15 The questions are the same in all three rites (*ASB* 344, 356, 387).

16 Irving, 'Baptismal Ecclesiology and the Ordination Rites of the Church of England, pp. 222–3.

17 Note in the bishops' rite the assumption is that there is a solitary candidate, and the wording reflects this: 'Brothers and sisters, you have heard how great is the charge that N is ready to undertake, and you have heard his declarations. Is it now your will that he should be ordained?' (*CW:OS* 63). However, it is adapted when multiple bishops are consecrated in the same service.

18 The role of the laity as an active aspect of the Church emphasized here is significantly more than the confirmatory 'Axios!' of the Orthodox tradition, where their refusal to affirm the worthiness of the candidate by shouting 'Anaxios!' is ineffective. See Timothy Ware, 1997, *The Orthodox Church*, new edition, London: Penguin Books, p. 291.

19 '*And before the Gospel, the Bishop, sitting in his Chair, shall examine every one of them that are to be ordained, in the presence of the people, after this manner following*' there is then no change in the bishop's posture before the next rubric: '*Then the Bishop, laying his hands severally upon the head of every one of them, humbly kneeling before him, shall say*' (*BCP 1662* 88–9).

20 In the priests' rite the previous mention of the bishop's posture is at the prayer preceding the *Veni, Creator Spiritus*: '*Then shall the Bishop, standing up say*' (*BCP 1662* 96); there is no direction before the ordination prayer (*BCP 1662* 99). The same pattern is followed in the bishops' rite (*BCP 1662* 107, 108).

21 This could be made clearer if the congregation too were to be standing in prayer at this point.

22 The assertion here is that the imposition of the bishop's hands, as a necessary aspect of the ordination, is more firmly rooted in the context of the Church community in *CW:OS* than in the *BCP 1662*, where the congregation appears incidental to the rite. The focus in the *BCP 1662* could even be expressed as being on the bishop in isolation.

23 'Upon' and 'on' are synonymous. Cf. J. M. Sinclair et al., 2000, 'Upon' in *Collins Dictionary and Thesaurus*, Glasgow: HarperCollins, p. 1313.

24 See, for example, Paul Bradshaw, 2006, *A Companion to Common Worship*, London: SPCK, pp. 232–3. 'The way an ordination is celebrated can sometimes make it look as if the bishop is setting some persons apart from the community of faith and transmitting to them a distinct "power". But an ordination is an act of the whole community presided over by the bishop.'

25 It is noteworthy here that the rubrics feel it necessary to instruct the newly ordained to stay and make their communion with their bishop, as if it were not something that could be assumed.

26 With no ordination prayer, these words are taken from the post-communion prayer.

27 The Archbishop of Canterbury, 'Lambeth Palace Chapel 15th of July 2020 11:30am'.

28 The Archbishop of Canterbury, 'Lambeth Palace Chapel 15th of July 2020 2:30pm'.

29 At the consecration of the Bishop of Lewes, the archbishop did seek to add historical legitimacy to the choice of venue, but the case is insufficient to outweigh the concerns raised here about the restriction that the venue places on the expression of Church.

30 This was particularly evident at the Peace, where the unintended result of the bubbles was that the Peace was shared much more fully within the two family units than among the congregation, giving added weight to the impression that rather than the Church receiving the newly ordained, the candidates' families were congratulating them, as one might celebrate with those who have received some personal accolade.

31 The Archbishop of Canterbury, 'Lambeth Palace Chapel 15th of July 2020 2:30pm', from 4 mins 15 seconds to 8 minutes 5 seconds.

32 Archbishops' Council, *Common Worship: Initiation Services*, p. 98.

33 Louis Weil, 1983, *Sacraments and Liturgy: The Outward Signs*, Oxford: Blackwell, p. 104.

34 Louis Weil, 2002, *A Theology of Worship*, Cambridge, MA: Cowley Publications, p. 41.

4

A Sacramental Ecclesiology for a Sacramental Ministry

The integrated sacramental ecclesiology of CW:OS is primarily relational. CW:OS articulates an active participatory relationship between the members of the Church, which itself speaks of a relational anthropology and is grounded in the relational theology of the Trinity. The basis and paradigm for episcopal ministry is therefore relational; it is ontologically and practically dependent on the relationships that establish the Church as the body of Christ. The relationships within the Church also establish the sacramental, or missional, aspect of the Church in the world, as it is the relationships themselves that make visible the invisible grace of God.

Sacramental ecclesiology seeks to emphasize the commonality of baptismal[1] and eucharistic[2] ecclesiologies and undermines attempts to polarize these approaches. It also looks to the Augustinian definition of 'an outward and visible sign of an inward and invisible grace', depicting the Church as a physical manifestation of the work of God in the world. The primary role of Christians and of the Church is to be oriented towards God and, in so doing, to make God known in the world. Within an Anglican context the term also acknowledges the importance of holding paradox as the route to deeper truth. This approach is most clearly evident in the 1662 *Order for the Administration of The Lord's Supper or Holy Communion*, where the words for the distribution juxtapose both realist and memorialist descriptions of the elements[3] without seeking to resolve the evident paradox.

In the previous chapter it was argued that the congregation is actively engaged in the ordination rite and the importance of baptismal ecclesiology for CW:OS has been clearly established. In this chapter, these threads will be drawn together in the assertion that sacramental ecclesiology is the most helpful way to describe CW:OS ecclesiology. CW:OS will be shown to have a collaborative and corporate ecclesiology in which people are admitted through baptism, fed at the Eucharist, and share in ministry and mission. With particular reference to Ellen T. Charry, CW:OS will be shown to incorporate the dominical sacraments in an ecclesiology that articulates the essence of the Church and thereby the ontology of the Church. Grounded in the significance of the eucharistic assembly as an expression of the *koinonia* of the Church, relationship within the body of Christ will be shown to be the key aspect of the ecclesiology of *CW:OS*, and therefore fundamental to Christian ministry, particularly the ministry of the bishop.

Charry defines 'sacramental ecclesiology' as

> the idea that the body of Christ is that community of persons whose identity, vision and mission are constituted by being made part of the community created by the redeeming and reconciling work of God in Israel and in Jesus Christ. Her members are grafted into that symbolic identity by the Holy Spirit in baptism and, by being sealed as Christ's own forever, are co-opted into that identity, vision and mission in all that they are, all that they do, and all that they have. The baptized do not create their own identity because they are under orders to be faithful to the one they have from God. Their belonging is not a matter of choice but of willingness to accept and grow into who they are by God's grace.[4]

There remains within this ecclesiology a distinctive place for the ordained, within the dynamic and active communal life of the Church, which comprises both ordained and lay. Here Charry addresses the introspective view of Gibson's table analogy, cited above,[5] which curtails the role of the ordained to caring for the laity. Liturgically, the dismissal gives fullest expression to this outward action of the Church as the assembly is sent out in mission into the world, a mission that applies as much, if not more, to the laity whose primary locus for service is the world. Moreover, Charry emphasizes the communal aspect of the life of the Church, in which each person has a role to play complementing and belonging with the other people within the body of Christ.

Sacramental ecclesiology emphasizes the relatedness of baptism and eucharist in unifying the Church. For *CW:OS*, these two dominical sacraments are two sides of the same coin, each depending on, and expectant of, the other, as has been evidenced by the significance of the eucharistic context for the ordination and the emphasis in the liturgy on baptismal ecclesiology. As Paul Avis wisely notes:

> A baptismal ecclesiology is needed alongside a eucharistic ecclesiology because baptism and the Eucharist are the two foundational and

generative moments in the Church's life. They should not be played off, one against another, in ecclesiology, as though they were alternative approaches, but they need to be brought together in an ecclesiology that reflects and embodies the unified totality of Christian initiation that begins in baptism and is completed in the Eucharist.[6]

Sacramental ecclesiology therefore draws together the dominical sacraments that lie at the heart of the life of the Church and that underpin the ordinal. The Anglican emphasis on the dominical sacraments is an emphasis on the sacramental nature of the Church, since it is these rites in which the body of Christ is most clearly established. Ordination is the next most significant rite, explicitly dependent on the dominical sacraments and establishing the relationships within the Church that will facilitate future celebrations of the Eucharist and baptism. In this way, *CW:OS* integrates the dominical sacraments and points forward to their centrality within the life of the Church.

The foundation for these relationships is the relationship that the Church enjoys with Christ. As this relationship is therefore the primary ontology for the Church, it is nonsensical to make distinctions between mutual recognition of baptism, eucharistic hospitality and recognition of ordination, whether ecumenically or within the Church, as seen in the ordinations on 15 July 2020, segregated because of irreconcilable beliefs around the ordination of women. While the Archbishop of Canterbury's desire and commitment to maintaining some semblance of mutual acceptance within the process is admirable, and perhaps institutionally necessary, it does so at the expense of the fundamental sacramental ecclesiology that underpins *CW:OS*. The Archbishop's retreat from laying on hands and the provision of separate services speaks of a church that is fundamentally not in a good relationship with itself, and which is so divided that the sacramental unity of the Church can no longer be expressed through the sacramental ministrations of its Archbishop. The accommodation, therefore, while attempting to demonstrate the breadth within the Church, made visible the fact that if this approach is to become acceptable because communion within the Church is impossible, a schism has *de facto* already happened.

Here again the significance of sacramental ecclesiology in emphasizing relationship is important. Mutual recognition of baptism while refusing to share communion is a fundamentally individualistic approach, creating false separation not only between the sacraments but also in relation to specific persons. Moreover, John Zizioulas states:

A SACRAMENTAL ECCLESIOLOGY FOR A SACRAMENTAL MINISTRY

Arguably the most important aspect of the mystery of *koinonia* – of all *koinonia* in the true sense of the term – is linked to the notion of the *person*. To be a person is to be in communion. Without this communion, one is an *individual*, but not a *person* ... This applies not only to humanity, but to God himself, at least the triune God, whose existence is characterized precisely by personal communion. And the Eucharist, as it transcends in itself the antinomy between the 'one' and the 'many', reveals and accomplishes the very meaning of the person and the community.[7]

The term 'sacramental ecclesiology' does significantly more than transcend the false distinctions between baptism and the Eucharist; it articulates the nature of the Church as a community that is in relationship with itself and in which identity is formed through relationship. In so doing it is not creating a cult, separated from the world, but rather a conscious expression of the world as it is intended to be, making visible what is already fundamentally the case: that the creation is interconnected and dependent on God and making this visible is an integral aspect of the Church's sacramental ontology. It is in this context that *CW:OS* places ordination as an outworking of the relational nature of the Church, and the ordination itself is therefore sacramental in making that ordering conscious and visible. The significance of the eucharistic context is therefore more than just a suitable setting; it is an inherent part of the ordination, in which the Church, in its fullest expression, ordains the candidates.

The full expression of the Church is the basis for the inclusive nature of the it. While the Church's diversity creates the potential for power dynamics and partisan interests, as portrayed by Stancliffe's 'crusading camps', the relational ontology of sacramental ecclesiology affirms the potential for the ordinal to facilitate a liturgy of dynamic and creative relationship. In this context, liturgy is far more than an institutional attempt to create an uneasy peace or a lowest common denominator bland compromise. Sacramental ecclesiology requires that this potential is turned to an opportunity to make visible God's grace, through the *corpus permixtum* that is the Church. Martyn Percy and Anthony Bash address this sacramental way of being which takes seriously the realities of both the fallen and redeemed natures of the Church:

> Ecclesiologically speaking, the Church stands in the gap between power and the powerless, between strength and weakness, between

absolutism and outright vacuity. As the social transcendent community, a particular kind of body, it has knowledge but not certainty, boundaries but not limit, is discerning but open, is for the other and others but not for itself.[8]

The liturgical unity envisaged in *CW:OS*,[9] is the open and accommodating space that Anglican ecclesiology requires. Percy takes this further by suggesting that, 'The fourfold relationship between scripture, tradition, reason and experience (or culture) is sacred to the ecclesiology of Anglican identity.'[10] This is the positive, creative context that has been identified in *CW:OS*; an integrated sacramental ecclesiology in which the Church's lack of self-sufficiency speaks of its dependence on God and its readiness to move into greater truth through the incorporation of difference which is sacramental of the diversity of the body of Christ.

Alongside the confident assertion that *CW:OS* is a legitimate expression of the continuity of the faith of the Apostles, and therefore an outward sign of the presence of the body of Christ in the world, is the assertion that the diversity of institutional expression within the Church points beyond the institution to the Church catholic. As Michael Ramsey states:

> For while the Anglican church is vindicated by its place in history, with a strikingly balanced witness to Gospel and Church and sound learning, its greater vindication lies in its pointing through its own history to something of which it is a fragment. Its credentials are its incompleteness, with the tension and the travail in its soul. It is clumsy and untidy, it baffles neatness and logic. For it is sent not to commend itself as the 'best type of Christianity', but by its very brokenness to point to the universal church.[11]

CW:OS, in claiming that the Church ordains ministers 'in the Church of God', relies on both continuity with Christ's apostles and a recognition that the Church universal is spread across several denominations. The Anglican *via media* is the result of a creative tension, and is in continuity with the key thinkers, including Richard Hooker and Michael Ramsey. Within this creative tension, which is essential to Anglicanism, there is an inherent dynamism and development, in which doctrine, including ecclesiology, evolves and is reformed. It is about 'becoming as well as being',[12] legitimate but provisional, seeking to express an ecclesiology that is relevant, comprehensible and developing. The Church does not do this in an ideological vacuum, but with a basis in tradition, which Fagerberg describes as the 'grammar' of ecclesiology,[13] and it is therefore to be expected that each new expression has both continuity and newness. Explicitly articulating its provisionality, development and learning is therefore indicative of a Church that is self-consciously seeking to express its sacramental nature.

For *CW:OS*, Christ is the head of the Church and therefore head of the Church of England. This is a development from Hooker's understanding of the monarch as the Head of the Church.[14] No longer is the role of Christ's Vicar to be vested in an individual, but rather in the Church corporately. The view is of a society that is ordered both for the benefit of the members of the Church and, more significantly, for the benefit of the wider world, of which the Church is a part. In being a sacramental sign, the Church is a legitimate partaker in that which it points to, being fully worldly and fully part of the body of Christ, a true *corpus permixtum*.

Sacramental ecclesiology, therefore, emphasizes the sacramental nature of the Church as being the Church, the body of Christ in the world as is most clearly evident in the eucharistic assembly. *CW:OS* portrays ordination within this dynamic community by emphasizing that the Holy Spirit is invoked both for establishing the new relationship at ordination, and in the living out of that new relationship that the ordained will have within the Church and thereby with the world.

In particular, this is reflected in the renewed emphasis on the importance of the collaboration between lay and ordained. All three rites ask the ordinands: 'Will you work with your fellow servants in the gospel for the sake of the kingdom of God?' (*CW:OS* 16, 38, 62). As the Liturgical Commission explains:

> The new services try also to be attentive to the contemporary rediscovery in the Church of England of the centrality of mission in the life of the Church, of the importance of collegiality and collaboration in the Church's structured ministry, and of the foundational place of baptism as the beginning of all ministry.[15]

This balance has also been demonstrated to be present in the role of the congregation within the rite itself; not only in prayer, through silence, singing and the litany, but also in the congregational responses at the end of the decisions (presenting the candidate) and in the Peace (welcoming the newly ordained and establishing their new relationship with the rest of the Church).

The Church acts as a sign of God's order in creating persons in communion, rather than individuals in a group or jobs with functions, as the world redeemed in which people are drawn to own and be renewed in the image of God, awaiting the resurrection. Theologically this relational ontology is grounded in the relational nature of the Trinity. Thus the opening to all three rites sets the Trinitarian context for the rite and for the wider life of the Church (CW:OS 10, 31, 54). Just as the unity of God is constituted by the relationship between the persons of the Trinity, so lay, deacon, priest and bishop are unified in a relationship founded on their relationship with Christ. The ordination liturgy in which the Church is ordered requires that the fullness of the Church is present, so that the rite is sacramental of the relationship that defines the Church – that is, the kingship of Christ.

The nature of episcopal ministry is defined by being integrated within the sacramental nature of the Church, and the Church is constituted by its relationship with Christ. The bishops inhabit a relationship that points beyond themselves to the primacy of Christ's relationship with the Church. This is the focus of the ordinal's teaching about the ministry of bishops; their ordination establishes a new relationship between the person ordained as bishop and the rest of the Church, including all other clergy as well as the laity.

Key to the assertions made here is the distinction between the bishop's ordination as bishop and their installation in a particular role. Making this distinction is crucial to articulating the ontology of the bishop. Ordination confers a lifelong, sacramental way of being that is both personal to the bishop and constitutes the relational nature of the Church. This transcends any specific role that the bishop may have. The nature of the role – for example, being bishop of a given see – is dependent upon the relationship that was established at ordination. The ordination continues to define their ministry in the same way that the wedding liturgy should shape the lifelong relationship between husband and wife. In making this distinction between the ecclesial and institutional role of the bishop, the suggestion is not that they are unconnected; rather, it is the understanding of episcopal ministry having become somewhat muddled, with ecclesial and institutional concerns becoming tangled: a situation in which the primary purpose and ontology can all too easily be subsumed beneath practical pressures.

The process here is therefore to highlight the primary significance of the relationship established at ordination and to affirm this as both the ontological basis and as primary *habitus*, or way of being, with the bishops inhabiting their distinctive relationship with the rest of the Church in every aspect of their ministry. The New Testament gives little detailed evidence on which to base episcopal ministry, but that there is clear evidence for episcopal ministry and that the nature of that ministry is relational. This is corroborated by the development of the role in the Early Church, providing a scriptural and historical basis for the relational nature of episcopal ministry in the Church today.

The New Testament is the natural place to start a theological reflection on the foundations for episcopal ministry. However, *episkopos* is not a term used in the Gospels,[16] and there is no direct teaching from Jesus about ordained ministry within the Church, let alone the role and nature of episcopal ministry.[17] The only time that *episkope* is mentioned in the Gospels is Luke 19.44, where it refers to divine rather than human oversight, in terms of God's visitation.[18] God's own oversight is the primary context for the sacramental oversight offered by the bishop, which places the bishop firmly within, rather than distinct from, the community of the Church.

The verb *episkopeo* refers to human oversight in 1 Peter 5.2,[19] which is one of the key texts for the ordinal.[20] It describes episcopal oversight in terms of shepherding and emphasizes the importance of pastoral care. The emphasis in Acts 1.20,[21] where Peter recognizes the need to find an apostle to replace Judas Iscariot, is placed on someone who can witness to the ministry and resurrection of Jesus. This gives a distinctive missional aspect to the description of the role of the Apostles, notably with no indication that the Apostles' ministry will continue beyond those who shared Jesus' earthly life. Although the numerical emphasis on the need for having 12 apostles is lost as the Church grows,[22] the missional focus is maintained in the ordinal as a descriptor of bishops, allied to the primary description of the bishop as 'shepherd'.

It is in the epistles that the role of the *episkopos* takes a fuller shape. However, even here there are only a handful of references with no uniform or even clear understanding of bishop that could be easily identified with episcopal ministry today. Particularly unclear is Philippians 1.1,[23] which Sean F. Winter describes as 'so oblique as to be almost indecipherable'.[24] Although Winter is more fulsome about the description in 1 Timothy 3.1–7[25] and Titus 1.7,[26] these passages give little insight into either the ontology or role of the bishop, although some inference may be drawn from the description of the qualifying characteristics of potential bishops. It is unclear whether they are ordained in any way that might be recognizable to the contemporary Church, whether it is a lifelong vocation, or even whether there is any sort of relationship with the Apostles. What is clear is that there is some form of responsibility for stewardship, which resonates with the pastoral leadership described in 1 Peter 5.2. Whether the bishop has local or translocal leadership is not clear; the prefix *epi-* could equally refer to a greater depth of oversight, as to a greater geographical responsibility. As Winter concludes, '"Bishops", it seems, were locally appointed and locally accountable leaders'.[27] Whether responsibilities were spiritual or practical[28] is also lost to history, but the emphasis on the relationship being one that is for the good of the whole Church is clearly evident.

The New Testament mandate for episcopal ministry is therefore thin. That is not to say it is non-existent, but that the connection between the episcopal ministry described in the New Testament and the episcopal ministry exercised within the contemporary Church cannot be taken for granted. The strands of oversight, as pastoral care and responsibility for those in their care, are established, as is the importance of the bishop embodying Christian faith for and on behalf of the Christian community, and being witnesses of Jesus' ministry and resurrection, in common with Jesus' apostles. While not systematized or explicitly connected, these themes are the key descriptors in the ordinal for bishops in the Church today.

Development around ordained ministry and ecclesiology in the Church through history is inevitable, given the lack of detail and explicit teaching on the nature of episcopal oversight in the New Testament. However, the continuity and essence of the ecclesial relationship are clear: it might look very different and the responsibilities may have morphed, but the essential relationship between the bishop and the rest of the Church is still discernible. The potential for variety in the institutional relationship is made clear by Winter, who defines three possible forms this ministry might have taken in the Early Church: as itinerant; envoy; and as local governance,[29] none of which necessarily relates to the institutional requirements placed upon a contemporary diocesan bishop. As Roger Standing describes, 'there are a variety of things happening, out of which the future shape of the Church emerges'.[30] It is not until the third century that the role of the '*monepiscopos*, now ruling over multiple assemblies within a broader geographical region'[31] appears to take precedence within the life of the Church. It is important to note, especially when considering the contemporary Church, that the *monepiscopos* is a significant but later development. While the Church maintains *monepiscopacy* in its dioceses, in the person of the diocesan bishop, the relationship between bishop and the rest of the Church is not grounded in the diocesan bishop, but in the ontology of the relationship established at ordination, which all bishops, whether in a diocesan role or not, share equally. There is no sense, for the ordinal, that diocesan bishops are in some way more fully bishops than other bishops. The model of the *monepiscopos* is a particular manifestation of the episcopal role which, through its geographical boundaries, seeks to promote both unity and unifying pastoral care within the Church; the territorial aspect fosters the relational.

Although the New Testament does not give a uniform, definitive account of the shape of Christian ministry, the Church of England is not alone in emphasizing the importance and even necessity of bishops as indicators of the authenticity of the Church. Many other denominations share this theological conviction. As Joe Aldred states, for the Church of God of Prophecy, 'oversight by bishops is foundational to the life of the Church, as it is for Roman Catholics.'[32] For the Church of England, bishops are a part of the developed life of the Church, as Rowan Williams explains:

> In the first Christian centuries, the bishop became the visible sign of continuity in teaching, guaranteeing that the Church remained accountable to the primary creative witness of the apostles. Like the canon of Scripture, the existence of ministerial presence connecting the congregation here and now to the beginnings of the faith was a reminder that the congregation did not set its own standards of belief but needed to be guided back towards the mystery at its origins, to the Word made flesh, crucified and risen.[33]

It is in this context of the Anglican tripod of scriptural basis, development through the history of the Church and reasoned reflection, that Standing describes the Anglican ecclesiology, of which bishops are an integral part, as 'the mature fruit of the theological dialogue of Scripture, tradition and reason'.[34]

The importance of bishops for the life of the Church is rooted in their relational ministry. This was made clear at the Council of Nicaea in AD 325, where Canon 4 describes the relationship between the bishop and their diocese as a marriage.[35] However, over time, the responsibilities given to bishops have evolved. For instance, the medieval practice of the bishops leading their knights into armed battle, is not one that the contemporary Church expects or would feel is acceptable.[36] While a detailed analysis of the growth in use of secular power falls to others, it suffices to note here that there is a corollary with the growth of Christendom – for example, in Constantine's granting of *episcopale iudicium*, the power to adjudicate in civil cases.[37] As Lenski notes, 'Constantine had taken a giant step down the road converting the bishop and his clergy into a new class of civic leader separate from and much more powerful than the traditional curial order.'[38] While the role of bishops has evolved over time, the New Testament witness and Christ's own praxis in leadership are the ideals by which this evolution is to be compared. Moreover, in a post-Christendom age, the accretions of secular power become more anachronistic. The power of the bishops has evolved over time, and the suggestion here is that this is a time when episcopal ministry needs to re-inhabit its biblical and early church roots. Understanding the evolution of episcopal ministry both helps understand what needs to be reclaimed from the past[39] and what is no longer helpful in furthering the life of the Church.

It is clear from the New Testament evidence that the Church ordaining people to be bishops is a legitimate expression of continuity with the praxis of Jesus and the Early Church. The nature of the ministry has been shown to be the relationship between the bishop and the rest of the Church as members of the body of Christ. This is the ontology of episcopal ministry which, though expressed in various ways through history, is the essence that the contemporary Church needs to reclaim today both as an ideal and as facilitated by the Church's institutional structures. Fundamental to this is the Church's self-understanding of sacramental ecclesiology, making the kingdom of God visible, and shaping all aspects of Church life in the light of this paradigm.

Notes

1 Baptismal theology defines the Church in terms of a shared initiation rite. See, for example, Martyn Percy's summary and critique of Paul Avis' description of baptism as the 'supreme ecclesial fundament'. Paul Avis, 1989, *Anglicanism and the Christian Church*, Edinburgh: T&T Clark, pp. 300f, cited in Martyn Percy, 1998, *Power and the Church: Ecclesiology in an Age of Transition*, London: Cassell, p. 177.

2 Eucharistic theology defines the Church as the people who celebrate the rite of Holy Communion. See for example, Julie Gittoes, Brutus Green and James Head, 'Introduction' in their book *Generous Ecclesiology: Church, World and the Kingdom of God*, London: SCM Press, p. 9: 'The Eucharist is central to the way in which the Church proclaims the gospel; it is central to its very being as the body of Christ in and for the world.'

3 Church of England, 2004 [1662], *The Book of Common Prayer and Administration of the Sacraments and other Rites and Ceremonies of the Church according*

to the Use of the Church of England together with the Psalter or Psalms of David pointed as they are to be sung or said in Churches and the form or manner of making, ordaining and consecrating of Bishops, Priests and Deacons, Cambridge: Cambridge University Press, pp. 256–7: 'The Body of our Lord Jesus Christ, which was given for thee, preserve thy body and soul unto everlasting life: Take and eat this in remembrance that Christ died for thee, and feed on him in thy heart by faith with thanksgiving'; 'The Blood of our Lord Jesus Christ, which was shed for thee, preserve thy body and soul unto everlasting life: Drink this in remembrance that Christ's Blood was shed for thee, and be thankful.' While this could be dismissed as an historical accommodation of irreconcilable difference, it is also clear liturgical evidence of Anglican readiness, even rejoicing, in paradox as an articulation of a truth that cannot be encompassed by simplistic explanations.

4 Ellen T. Charry, 2005, 'Sacramental Ecclesiology' in Mark Husbands and Daniel T. Treier (eds), *The Community of the Word: Towards an Evangelical Ecclesiology*, Leicester: Apollos, p. 216.

5 Paul Gibson, 2006, 'A Baptismal Ecclesiology: Some Questions' in Ronald L. Dowling and David R. Holeton (eds), *Equipping the Saints: Ordination in Anglicanism Today*, Blackrock: Columba Press, pp. 35–44, p. 42.

6 Paul Avis, 2008, *The Identity of Anglicanism*, London: T&T Clark, p. 116.

7 John D. Zizioulas, 2011, *The Eucharistic Community and the World*, edited by Luke Ben, London: T&T Clark, p. 21, n. 35.

8 Martyn Percy and Anthony Bash, 1998, 'Wisdom and Weakness in Ministerial Formation: "Ambassadors" as a Paradigm for the Early Church' in Martyn Percy, *Power and the Church: Ecclesiology in an Age of Transition*, London: Cassell, pp. 40–58, p. 42.

9 The lack of options in *CW:OS* is in marked contrast to the plethora of options in the other *Common Worship* services.

10 Percy, 1998, *Power and the Church*, p. 125.

11 Michael Ramsey, 1956, *The Gospel and the Catholic Church*, second edition, London: Longmans, Green & Co., p. 220.

12 Douglas Dales, 2005, 'One Body: The Ecclesiology of Michael Ramsey' in Douglas Dales et al. (eds), *Glory Descending*, Norwich: Canterbury Press, p. 237.

13 David Fagerberg, 1992, *What is Liturgical Theology?*, Collegeville, MN: Liturgical Press, p. 295.

14 Percy, *Power and the Church*, p. 124.

15 The Liturgical Commission, 'Commentary' in Archbishops' Council, 2007, *Common Worship: Ordination Services*, London: Church House Publishing, p. 140.

16 Cf. G. Abbott-Smith, 1922, *A Manual Greek Lexicon of the New Testament*, London: T&T Clark, pp. 171–2.

17 Hence the importance attached historically to the gathering of the Twelve Disciples and the commissioning of the Twelve Apostles.

18 'They will crush you to the ground, you and your children within you, and they will not leave within you one stone upon another; because you did not recognize the time of your visitation from God' (Luke 19.44).

19 'to tend the flock of God that is in your charge, exercising the oversight, not under compulsion but willingly, as God would have you do it – not for sordid gain but eagerly' (1 Pet. 5.2).

20 See, for example, the ordination prayer and welcome (*CW:OS* 67, 68).

21 '"Let another take his position of overseer." So one of the men who have accompanied us throughout the time that the Lord Jesus went in and out among us, beginning from the baptism of John until the day when he was taken up from us – one of these must become a witness with us to his resurrection' (Acts 1.20–2). The verse quotes Psalm 109.8.

22 The use of drawing lots has also been forsaken as an aspect of the discernment process. It is beyond the scope of this book to explore the relative merits of its reintroduction.

23 'Paul and Timothy, servants of Christ Jesus, To all the saints in Christ Jesus who are in Philippi, with the bishops and deacons' (Phil. 1.1).

24 Sean F. Winter, 2020, 'Beyond the Household: The Emergence of Translocal Ministry in the New Testament' in Roger Standing and Paul Goodliff (eds), *Episkope: The Theory and Practice of Translocal Oversight*, London: SCM Press, pp. 3–13, p. 9.

25 'The saying is sure: whoever aspires to the office of bishop desires a noble task. Now a bishop must be above reproach, married only once, temperate, sensible, respectable, hospitable, an apt teacher, not a drunkard, not violent but gentle, not quarrelsome, and not a lover of money. He must manage his own household well, keeping his children submissive and respectful in every way – for if someone does not know how to manage his own household, how can he take care of God's church? He must not be a recent convert, or he may be puffed up with conceit and fall into the condemnation of the devil. Moreover, he must be well thought of by outsiders, so that he may not fall into disgrace and the snare of the devil.'

26 'For a bishop, as God's steward, must be blameless; he must not be arrogant or quick-tempered or addicted to wine or violent or greedy for gain' (Titus 1.7).

27 Winter, 'Beyond the Household: The Emergence of Translocal Ministry in the New Testament', p. 9.

28 See Alistair C. Stewart, 2014, *The Original Bishops: Office and Order in the First Christian Community*, Grand Rapids, MI: Baker Academic.

29 Winter, 'Beyond the Household: The Emergence of Translocal Ministry in the New Testament', pp. 5–7.

30 Roger Standing, 2020, 'Theological Issues: Constants in Context' in Standing and Goodliff (eds), *Episkope*, pp. 14–43, p. 23.

31 Winter, 'Beyond the Household: The emergence of Translocal Ministry in the New Testament', p. 9.

32 Joe Aldred, 2020, 'Foreword' in Standing and Goodliff (eds), *Episkope*, pp. xix–xx, p. xix.

33 Rowan Williams, 2020, 'Foreword' in Standing and Goodliff (eds), *Episkope*, pp. xxi–xxii, p. xxi.

34 Standing, 'Theological Issues: Constants in Context', p. 25.

35 Colin Podmore, 2001, 'The Choosing of Bishops in the Early Church and in the Church of England: An Historical Survey' in Archbishops' Council, *Working with the Spirit: Choosing Diocesan Bishops*, GS 1405, London: Church House Publishing, pp. 113–38, p. 113.

36 Cf. Jonathan Sneddon, 2013, 'Mitres and Maces – The Medieval Clergy at War', *Medieval Warfare*, 3 (2), pp. 6–8.

37 Noel Lenski, 2016, *Constantine and the Cities: Imperial Authority and Civic*

Politics, Philadelphia, PA: University of Pennsylvania Press, p. 197.

38 Lenski, *Constantine and the Cities*, p. 206.

39 For instance, Podmore suggests the removal of the laity from the election process has pragmatic origins in addressing riotous behaviour. Given that such behaviour is less likely now, or could be controlled by other means, there is no longer a rationale for removing the laity from the election process. Cf. Podmore, 'The Choosing of Bishops in the Early Church and in the Church of England, An Historical Survey', p. 113.

5

Anglican Episcopal Ministry is Relational

In the previous chapter, the scriptural and historical basis for the relational nature of episcopal ministry was established. In this chapter, it will be shown that this relational ontology is as significant for episcopal ministry today. Based on the cumulative nature of orders, episcopal ministry will be firmly rooted in diaconal ministry and a review of whether bishops are 'ordained' or 'consecrated' will demonstrate that the essence of the ordination is the establishment of the relationship between the Church and the newly ordained bishop. It is this relationship, rather than any specific institutional role that a bishop may take up, which defines the nature of episcopal ministry in the Church.

The ministry of the baptized has already been established as significant in understanding episcopal ministry. So too are presbyteral and diaconal ministry integral to episcopal ministry. Ordinations are cumulative, and permanent, so any attributes of a deacon and priest are also ontologically attributes of a bishop. As Paul Avis explains, 'Because the order of bishop includes and embraces, so to speak, the orders of deacon and priest, episcopacy can be seen as the most fully representative ministry of the Church.'[1] It is also the foundational ministry of the Church of England, and a prerequisite for any denomination before full communion, with interchangeable ministry, can be considered. Unlike 'Church' and 'ecclesiastical' there is no significant distinction in derivation to be made between 'bishop' and 'episcopal', as the former is merely an Anglo-Saxon corruption of the latter.[2]

A significant debate surrounding the writing of *CW:OS* was whether bishops are 'ordained' or 'consecrated'. For the ordinal, which uses both words in the title of the rite, a detailed analysis of the relative merits of 'ordained *and* consecrated' and/or 'ordained *or* consecrated' as an appropriate conjunction is also relevant here in addressing the foundational question of whether a new relationship is being established, or a specific aspect of the existing presbyteral relationship is being celebrated. A careful analysis of the terms will demonstrate that bishops are indeed ordained, establishing a new relationship with the rest of the Church. This ecclesial relationship is then compared with the dangers of the institutional relationship through a consideration of Church reports and the concept of 'shared episcopacy'.

The notes to all three ordination rites in *CW:OS* commence by affirming the threefold ministry:

> The Church of England maintains the historic threefold ministry of bishops, priests and deacons. Its ministers are ordained by bishops according to authorized forms of service, with prayer and the laying on of hands (see Canons C1–C4). (*CW:OS* 26, 48, 72)

Moreover, put in stronger terms than the ordinal, Canon C1 asserts that, 'The Church of England holds and teaches that from the apostles' time there have been these orders in Christ's Church: bishops, priests, and deacons.'[3] However, Canon C2 speaks not of the ordination of bishops but of their consecration;[4] so both ordination and consecration have contemporary usage outside of the ordinal, as they do within the liturgical text.

The genesis for the *Common Worship* usage of both terms is the *BCP 1662*, which also uses both words in the title: 'The form of ordaining or consecrating of an archbishop or bishop' (*BCP 1662* 101). Given the theological weight attached to each term, there were significant discussions around the use of either term (or both) in *CW:OS*, which finally resulted in the title 'The ordination and consecration of a bishop' (*CW:OS* 54). Significant discussion is reported from the Revision Committee in both January and May 2005, where it was established that there was relatively widespread acceptance that 'ordering' is simply an archaic term for 'ordination'.[5] However, the difference between, or synonymity of, ordination and consecration was still contested, and the attempt in the 2004 draft of *CW:OS* to do away with 'consecration' did not survive in the final version.

The desire to site the ontology of episcopacy solely within the existing presbyteral relationship was expressed by General Synod in 2004. The Revision Committee noted:

> Advocating continued use of the term 'consecration' in respect of bishops, members of the Synod argued that 'Bishops are not a separate order of ministry from Presbyters', that it 'is not right to ordain them for a second time, they should be consecrated (i.e. set aside) for a new

aspect of ministry with new responsibilities', that 'our formularies do not imply, never mind require, that bishops are a separate order', and that the distinction is one of function rather than order.'[6]

The Revision Committee attempted to downplay the ontological issues of the nature of episcopal ordination by suggesting that, 'The draft Ordination Services are very clear as to the distinctive *functions* of bishops, while not making explicit statements about ontology.'[7] However, the Committee was also concerned not to encourage ambiguity and personal interpretation: 'The majority of members of the Committee were, however, concerned about the possibility of the title implying that the order of bishop is not a distinct order to which people are ordained (albeit one which is closely related to the presbyterate).'[8] The Committee's response to Synod, albeit a muted one, was nevertheless to affirm that bishops are ordained.

The preference for 'consecrate' in the debate connotes a distinct meaning from what is meant by 'ordain'. However, this is not clear in its historical usages by Anglican ordinals. The 1662 ordinal contains three distinct gerunds for the three ordination rites: making of deacons, ordering of priests and consecrating of bishops (*CW:OS* 77). It isn't clear whether the distinction between 'making', 'ordering' and 'consecrating' is significant; for example, focusing on the presbyterate as those ordained, with a preliminary diaconate and subset of presbyters given oversight in episcopal ministry, or whether this is just historical usage. There is still a threefold order, all are ordained, and the bishops are both ordained and consecrated. The potential of 'consecration' to connote a reformed model of ministry, of the presbyterate, with deacons as apprentices and bishops as senior colleagues, is not substantiated by the text. Moreover, in *CW:OS* deacons are 'ordained' and so the maintenance of consecration over ordination for bishops lacks consistency; if 'ordination' is suitable for deacons then it is also suitable for bishops. Consecration does not exclude ordination, but both terms are used alongside each other. On this basis, it is difficult to see the merits of including 'consecration' alongside 'ordination' as a term that adds any meaning not already contained within 'ordination'. The inclusion of 'ordination' clearly establishes that a new relationship is being created.

There was widespread support for a motion at General Synod by David Banting favouring a return to the use of 'or' instead of 'and' and this was discussed at the May 2005 Revision Committee. Its merits lie in its historicity as part of the 1662 ordinal and its ability to encompass a breadth of interpretation. The members of the committee

> reject[ed] the argument that the title was meant to allow room for two alternative understandings of the same event (which has been described by some as an exercise in 'studied ambiguity'), pointing out that the word 'ordained' was introduced into the rite as well as into the title in 1662 precisely in order to make clear that the order of bishop is an order of ministry to which people are ordained.[9]

In the January report, the argument is stronger, explicitly rejecting the possibility that the two terms might have legitimately different interpretations regarding the purpose of the rite:

> They noted that in the sixteenth and seventeenth centuries (and notably in the Book of Common Prayer) several synonyms were often employed in a single sentence to refer to the same thing, and these might be conjoined by 'or' rather than 'and. Today, however, the phrase 'ordination or consecration' might be heard as implying alternative understandings of the same event, rather than merely alternative names for that event.[10]

However, 'and' lacks the clarity that the Committee are seeking: 'and' also has a sequential meaning, as when new incumbents are 'licensed and installed', indicating that there are two distinct, albeit related, actions. Moreover, this is the natural reading of 'consecration and ordination'. Therefore, it is impossible to infer from the rite anything other than that bishops are ordained into a new relationship with the rest of the Church.

The use of 'and' means that bishops are ordained, and it remains unexplained what 'consecrated' adds to this term: had consecration been used instead of ordination, then the import for the nature of the relationship between the bishop and the rest of the Church would be significant. Bishops, instead of being a distinct order within the Church, would be more akin to archdeacons who are presbyters set apart for a specific purpose. However, alongside ordination, the merits of consecration in connoting a reformed model of ministry are lost, and the term is essentially superfluous in describing the nature of the relationship between bishop and Church. This is evidenced by the rite itself, which only has a single mention of 'consecrated' in the text of the liturgy – when it is used in conjunction with 'ordained' – at the presentation (*CW:OS* 56). The text has nine further references to 'ordain' in the rubrics and so the balance within the text is clearly in favour of 'ordain'.[11]

The difference in terms is best understood as similar to that between 'christening' and 'baptism': while there is a preference for one over the other, and there may be certain circles in which one term is preferable to another, essentially they are synonymous. There is no greater meaning in the use of 'consecrate' over 'ordain' for bishops than there is for 'making' over 'ordain' for deacons. The ontological relationship that the bishop has with the rest of the Church is the focus of *CW:OS*. Who God is and, therefore, what the Church is as the body of Christ, must be the defining factor in the institutional rights and responsibilities of a bishop, particularly the diocesan bishop, as an office holder within the Church. The institutional aspects are secondary, and should be a response to, and facilitation of, the Church as the body of Christ. The legal and institutional aspects of the Church only have any value while they prosper the kingdom of God, the spiritual union of all the children of God.

It is important to note, therefore, not just the distinction between the ecclesial and institutional but also the potential for tension. This is brought to light when comparing the ordinal with several of the Canons of the Church. While the ordinal looks to the Canons for legal legitimacy, there is a tension between the institutionally predicated Canons where the focus is on the legal rights and responsibilities of the diocesan bishops, and the ordinal, which concerns itself with the ontology of being and having bishops. Thus, Canon C18.1 seems to imply that all bishops are diocesan bishops or at least that the diocesan bishop is the full or archetypal expression of episcopal ministry:

> Every bishop is the chief pastor of all that are within his diocese, as well laity as clergy, and their father in God; it appertains to his office to teach and to uphold sound and wholesome doctrine, and to banish and drive away all erroneous and strange opinions; and, himself an example of righteous and godly living, it is his duty to set forward and maintain quietness, love, and peace among all men.[12]

Canon C18.4 therefore goes on to further define the role of the bishop in terms of their rights and responsibilities:

> Every bishop is, within his diocese, the principal minister, and to him belongs the right, save in places and over persons exempt by law or custom, of celebrating the rites of ordination and confirmation;

of conducting, ordering, controlling, and authorizing all services in churches ...[13]

This is not to say that the ordinal and Canons are in opposition, which would be a significant issue for the Church, but that the emphasis, aims and terms of reference are different. The ordinal is of primary importance to the nature of the Church and the Canons seek to put in place safeguards on how ministry is exercised, in particular by diocesan bishops. To define the nature of episcopal ministry in terms of the legal rights and responsibilities of the diocesan bishop would therefore be a category error.

The ecclesial relationship between bishop and Church is particularly significant in consideration of episcopal ministry as 'translocal oversight', a transliteration of the Greek derivation of *episkopos*. Joe Aldred emphasizes the importance of a shift in function and institutional relationship when taking up episcopal ministry: 'Preparing for such a translocal role, and then serving effectively and faithfully in it, requires significant adjustments for those whose experience hitherto has been confined to parish or congregational life.'[14] While this may be a recognizable experience of diocesan bishops, not all Church bishops minister in geographical translocal contexts,[15] or hold posts that ordinarily require episcopal ordination.[16] Two insights can be gained from these roles. The first is that the institution of the Church in certain quarters equates episcopal ordination with institutional hierarchy, thus the archbishop cannot have a priest as a chaplain but requires a bishop. This is also reflected in leaked 'proposals that some senior bishops could be detached from geographical regions to serve as spokesmen and women on political matters'[17] and the suggestion in 2015 by the then Bishop of London that the see of Islington could be as follows: 'The role is inherently episcopal but not territorial; thoroughly collegial but with an independent sphere of responsibility.'[18] This approach to bishops equates them with 'senior leaders', rather than rooting their ministry in the pastoral relationship established at ordination. Second, the existence of bishops without a see, although a small minority of bishops, elicits a distinction between the ordination and the role held in the life of the Church, similar to that which is commonly understood for those ordained to the priesthood, where priests in secular employment, chaplaincy or with permission to officiate are no less a priest than an incumbent. It would seem that it is only the hierarchical association noted above that is preventing there being self-supporting or

House for Duty bishops, to mirror the variety of roles held by priests in the contemporary Church.

Discerning in Obedience, a theological review of the Crown Nominations Commission, states, 'all bishops are bishops *of* somewhere'.[19] As has been established, this is factually incorrect, all bishoprics are bishoprics of somewhere but there are many bishops who hold neither diocesan nor suffragan posts and are therefore not 'bishops of somewhere'. Moreover, the existence of suffragan bishops raises questions for the review about the place of *monepiscopacy*: 'Are there two bishops, then? Not strictly speaking. There is one coordinated ministry of oversight, with two people exercising episcopal duties within it. The unity of the bishop's diocese is not a purely personal unity.'[20] Not only is there potential for confusion when there is clearly a suffragan bishop in the diocese, hence the question, but also the articulation of the response by the review is confused: there are two bishops, but only one diocesan bishop.

When there is more than one bishop in the diocese, as when there is a diocesan and one or more suffragans, the relative authority and responsibility of each is an institutional rather than ecclesial distinction: all bishops are fully bishops. Throughout, the review seems to conflate bishops with diocesan bishops. Thus, in the conclusions it states: 'A community with much life will have many leaders, but it needs just one bishop, to help the leaders work with one another.'[21] However, unlike dioceses in the Church in Wales,[22] for example, it is usual for Church of England dioceses to have suffragan or area bishops in addition to the diocesan bishop. While there may be an institutional difference in their seniority, both diocesan and suffragan bishops are fully bishops in terms of their ordination. Ecclesially, therefore, there are two bishops although there is only one diocesan bishop, which should shape the role of the suffragan such that there is a clear unity within the diocese. This is the only approach that can be countenanced by the ordinal, and which reflects the relationship between the bishops and the rest of the Church established at ordination.

The report reflects wider confusion within the Church between the essence of being a bishop, and the role of the diocesan bishop, with the tacit assumption that the diocesan bishop is the fullest expression of being a bishop. However, to suggest this renders suffragan and other bishops a second class of bishop, in a distinction that would not be recognized between parish incumbents and those ordained to the priesthood who do not have incumbent status: all priests are equally priests, and the essence of priesthood is distinct from, and not defined by, the role that the priest has within the Church. In the same way, all those ordained as bishops, whatever role they hold, continue to be fully bishops, inhabiting the bishop's relationship with the rest of the Church.

Discerning in Obedience expresses the distinction between the ecclesial and institutional role in terms of 'powers':

> An ancient Christian tradition spoke of bishops as having two distinct 'powers', of 'order' and 'jurisdiction', which roughly amount to a spiritual authority exercised in the word and sacrament and an authority to make decisions. Since the church as the body of Christ exists in two ways, as the spiritual communion of the faithful in Christ and as an organised body with institutional structures within the world, so the authority of the bishop's office must serve it in both these respects.[23]

Although it is understandable that the review focuses on the role of the diocesan bishop, as it is appointments to diocesan posts that concern the Crown Nomination Commission, the ministry of bishops is once again reduced to that of the diocesan. Moreover, the review seems to make no attempt to prioritize one power over the other. As has been noted above, a bishop in the Church need not have any specifically episcopal power of jurisdiction. However, all bishops share in the spiritual power, or ecclesial relationship. Moreover, the report goes on to state: 'There need in principle be no tension between spiritual leadership and administrative qualifications.'[24] However, in practice often there is a tension, most notably surrounding the role of bishops in disciplinary matters and pastoral reorganization, and the report would have benefited from an emphasis on the foundational order of bishops as a bishop, rather than their jurisdictional responsibilities, which may be associated with a specific bishopric.

The diocesan bishop's role is not exhaustive of episcopal ministry, and from the ordinal's perspective neither is it definitive of episcopal ministry. Therefore, the ministry of a bishop cannot be defined by the institutional aspects of the diocesan bishop role any more than the institutional demands on an incumbent should define the nature of being a priest. Many priests minister as associate priests, assistant curates, chaplains and in various other contexts, as has been widely recognized in the literature around priestly and diaconal ordination.[25] The diocesan bishop must be a bishop in the Church duly ordained, but not all those who are ordained bishop will minister as diocesan bishops. Indeed, given that many dioceses have more than one suffragan and many retired bishops, the diocesan bishops are therefore in a minority among the bishops of the Church.[26]

Making a clear distinction between the ontology of episcopal ministry and certain institutional roles that require episcopal ordination is therefore significant for bishops and the ecclesiology of the Church. It also has a significance in discussions around 'shared episcopacy' in the Church. Primarily, there is a significant and essential distinction between sharing in the burdens of the institution and the way that institution is inhabited by those ordained to the episcopate. A variety of ministers are drawn into translocal oversight both through ecclesial and institutional demands for 'shared episcopacy'. These include deans of cathedrals, archdeacons, rural or area deans and, increasingly, incumbents of multi-parish benefices.[27] The bishop no more contains the totality of episcopal ministry than the deacon inhabits the totality of diaconal ministry. Rather, the ordained embody aspects of the life of the Church in which all the members share, being, as they are, members of the royal priesthood. It is only by having ministers integrated within the Church as a sacramental presence that ministries can be shared and not devolved.

Shared episcopacy does not mean that all Christians can carry out the traditional ministries of confirmation and ordination, but that all have a responsibility to the wider Church beyond their own needs and personal discipleship, living out a life shaped by the gospel in their own lives and contexts. The institution also has a need for 'shared episcopacy', with reducing numbers of clergy and increasing administrative burden, which is a euphemism for a need for more middle managers. A clear distinction between these two needs is important, both in terms of clarifying the primary ontology of episcopal ministry, as expressed in the ordinal, as opposed to shared managerialism, but also in terms of transparency: the needs must be clearly articulated as an expression of the truth and so ecclesial and institutional needs are not confused. The ecclesial relationship is always primary and is the foundation for the institutional structures put in place to resource and support the body of Christ.

In affirming the primacy of relational ontology over role and function, the ordinal is not blind to the roles that a bishop might undertake. It uses a variety of characteristics and virtues to describe the sort of lifelong ministry that the bishop will have within the worldwide Church. It is these characteristics that will benefit the institution of the Church in their holding episcopal office. Ontology and office are therefore clearly related; no bishop is ordained in the Church without having a vacant office that they will fill (*CW:OS* 56),[28] and the representatives of the vacant see play a significant role in the rite. However, the ordination is not to be Bishop of 'X', but rather to be a bishop in the Church of God, who, in the case of a diocesan bishop, is subsequently taken to the cathedral of the vacant see and enthroned. Hence, when a bishop is translated from one see to another, no further ordination is required.

Although the relationship between episcopal ordination and the requirements of a given office in the Church are connected, it is vital to remember which is primary and rightly influential of the other.[29] It is not the needs of the institution that define the nature of episcopal ministry. Rather, it is the nature of episcopal ministry that defines both the personal ministry of a bishop, the way in which they inhabit a given role, and the relationship they have with the wider Church. As Rowan Williams states, it is when this dependency is reversed that problems arise for the Church both as a community of faith and as an institution:

> When episcopal ministry fails, as it does, it is when the needs of an abstract institution prevail over this kind of faithful attention – whether in the shameful confusions and collusions around abuse that have come unmercifully to light in recent years, or in a bureaucratic and insensitive implementing of discipline, or in a preoccupied distance from the pressures and anxieties and hopes of actual believers.[30]

The relationship between the bishop and the rest of the Church established at ordination must be primary both in theory and in daily praxis.

Notes

1 Paul Avis, 2015, *Becoming a Bishop: A Theological Handbook of Episcopal Ministry*, London: Bloomsbury/T&T Clark, p. 20.

2 F. L. Cross and E. A. Livingstone, 2005, *The Oxford Dictionary of the Christian Church*, third edition, Oxford: Oxford University Press, p. 210.

3 Church of England, 'Canon C1.1', <https://www.churchofengland.org/about/governance/legal-resources/canons-church-england/section-c#b59>, accessed 11.09.2025.

4 Church of England, 'Canon C1.1'.

5 Church of England, 2005, GS 1535Y, *Report of the Revision Committee*, p. 5, n. 14.

6 Church of England, *Report of the Revision Committee*, p. 5, n. 13.

7 Church of England, *Report of the Revision Committee*, p. 5.

8 Church of England, *Report of the Revision Committee*, p. 6.

9 Church of England, 2005, GS 1535Z, *Second Report of the Revision Committee*, p. 10, n. 49

10 Church of England, *Report of the Revision Committee*, p. 6, n. 18.

11 This movement is taken further in the Scottish ordinal, which makes no mention of 'consecration,' and the Irish ordinal has a variation between the two possible rites. The first order has 'ordained and consecrated' once; the second has 'ordained' five times and 'consecrated' twice. In the notes, the preference is for 'consecration', with no mention of 'ordained'. It is only the Church in Wales that omits the word 'ordain' from the title of the rite. However, in the text of the rite, 'ordain' is used widely both distinctly and in conjunction with 'consecrate'. The omission of 'ordain' in the title of the Welsh rite is therefore not indicative of a theological difference so much as a linguistic one. This is not to say that there is not a legitimate discussion to be had about the relationship between bishops and presbyters; the term 'consecration' gives voice to those within the Church of England who would wish to emphasize a reformed ecclesiology.

12 Church of England, 'Canon C 18.1' <https://www.churchofengland.org/about/leadership-and-governance/legal-services/canons-church-england/section-c>, accessed 11.09.2025.

13 Church of England, 'Canon C 18.4', <https://www.churchofengland.org/about/leadership-and-governance/legal-services/canons-church-england/section-c>, accessed 11.09.2025.

14 Joe Aldred, 2020, 'Foreword' in Roger Standing and Paul Goodliff, *Episkope: The Theory and Practice of Translocal Oversight*, London: SCM Press, pp. xix–xx.

15 For example, the Rt Revd Tim Thornton, Bishop at Lambeth 2017–21: 'Bishop Tim Thornton to retire as Bishop of Lambeth', *The Archbishop of Canterbury*, <https://www.archbishopofcanterbury.org/news/news-and-statements/bishop-tim-thornton-retire-bishop-lambeth>, accessed 11.09.2025. The position became less connected to place by his successor, the Rt Revd Emma Ineson, who became 'Bishop to the Archbishops of Canterbury and York' on 1 June 2021: 'Bishop Emma Ineson to be Bishop to the Archbishops of Canterbury and York', *The Archbishop of Canterbury*, <https://www.archbishopofcanterbury.org/news/news-and-statements/bishop-emma-ineson-be-bishop-archbishops-canterbury-and-york>, accessed 11.09.2025. Bishops who do not hold translocal posts have normally held a suffragan or diocesan post previously, and it would be an interesting question as to whether the Church of England would contemplate ordaining someone bishop with the specific purpose of taking up these roles, in particular for the role of 'Bishop to the Archbishops'.

16 For example, the Rt Revd Jonathan Frost became Dean of York Minster on 2 February 2019: 'Jonathan Frost installed as 76th Dean of York', *York Minster*, <https://yorkminster.org/latest/jonathan-frost-installed-as-76th-dean-of-york/>, accessed 11.09.2025, and the Rt Revd Humphrey Southern became Principal of Ripon College Cuddeson in 2015: Cuddesdon, 'Principal', <https://www.rcc.ac.uk/about-us/our-staff/rt-revd-humphrey-southern>, accessed 11.09.2025.

17 Kaya Burgess, 2022, 'Behold the Bishop of Brexit as church models itself on politics', *The Times*, <https://www.thetimes.co.uk/article/bishop-of-brexit-church-models-itself-politics-vd8mv2fgg>, accessed 11.09.2025.

18 Richard Chartres, 2015, 'Islington 2015', https://www.thinkinganglicans.org.uk/wp-content/uploads/2015/03/20150101-London-Bishops-Council-item-9-Revival-of-The-See-of-Islington-2015.pdf>, accessed 11.09.2025.

19 Church of England, 2017, 'Discerning in Obedience: A Theological Review of

the Crown Nominations Commission', <https://www.churchofengland.org/sites/default/files/2018-01/gs-misc-1171-discerning-in-obedience-report-on-the-review-of-the-cnc.pdf>, p. 13, accessed 23.03.2025.

20 Church of England, 'Discerning in Obedience', p. 13.

21 Church of England, 'Discerning in Obedience', p. 37.

22 Although it should be noted that Bangor now has an assistant bishop following the appointment of the Bishop of Bangor as Archbishop of Wales.

23 Church of England, 'Discerning in Obedience', p. 17.

24 Church of England, 'Discerning in Obedience', p. 7.

25 See, for example, Michael Ramsey, 2009, *The Christian Priest Today*, reissue, London: SPCK, or Rosalind Brown, *Being a Deacon Today*, 2008, Norwich: Canterbury Press, among many others.

26 The constitution of the House of Bishops therefore is somewhat swayed in not necessarily representing the view of the bishops of the Church of England, but more properly the view of the diocesan bishops.

27 For incumbents of multi-parish benefices, there is a significant question as to whether theirs is a local or translocal ministry, and whether their ministry should be focused on an episcopacy that comes from realizing and empowering local ministry or whether their role is increasingly institutionalized and separated from the local as they pick up the legal requirements of their parishes. See *From Anecdote to Evidence*, especially p. 12, for a discussion of the laity as local leadership in rural benefices: *From Anecdote to Evidence: Findings for the Church Growth Research Programme 2011–2013*, <https://www.churchofengland.org/sites/default/files/2019-06/from_anecdote_to_evidence_-_the_report.pdf>, accessed 11.09.2025.

28 'Reverend Father in God, N has been chosen to be Bishop of X [in the Diocese of Y].'

29 Here it is worth noting that the confirmation of election of a new bishop muddies the clarity of the process: even when the bishop elect is not yet consecrated, they appear at the confirmation vested as a bishop. However, it is important to note that the primary role of this act is legal, confirming the election and identity of the candidate, rather than ecclesial. The significant change in relationship with the rest of the Church is therefore not affected until the consecration. The vesture of the candidate is therefore somewhat anomalous and does not significantly undermine the argument advanced here. Cf., for example, the confirmation of Rachael Treweek as Bishop of Gloucester: Diocese of Gloucester, 2015, 'Confirmation of Election', <https://www.gloucester.anglican.org/2015/confirmation-of-election/>, accessed 11.09.2025. Note, for example, the Welsh bishops elect who wear priestly choir dress at the Sacred Synod.

30 Rowan Williams, 2020, 'Foreword' in Standing and Goodliff (eds), *Episkope*, London: SCM Press, pp. xxi–xxii, p. xxii.

6

Eschewing the Temptations to be Defined by Power and Institutional Demands

The relational nature of episcopal ministry has been clearly established, and this chapter will argue that this relational ministry should define the bishop's way of being. For that to happen, the bishop needs to be aware of competing demands. These demands are common to all those who hold positions of leadership. The assertion therefore is that the temptation to be defined by these other demands is real and has the potential to displace the primacy of the relationship established at ordination. The bishop and the institution therefore need to consciously affirm the primacy of their relational ministry.

Bishops 'are ordained and consecrated to the office of bishop in the Church of God' (*CW:OS* 56). Their ministry therefore transcends the limits of the hierarchy of the institutional Church. The nature of the ministry and ontology of the relationship established needs to be described, defined and formed on a theological basis, and not an institutional one. This is emphasized by the ordination of a bishop preceding their enthronement, which makes clear that the ordination establishes the relationship on which the enthronement depends. This is not to dismiss the needs of the institution, which are real, but rather to contextualize those needs by the ecclesial relationship, which cannot simply be assumed.

David Stancliffe articulates this importance of the ontology of bishops for the Church worldwide, not just in their local context: 'Ordination places a person within that catholic order and is not primarily concerned with the way in which that ministry will be exercised in the local context.'[1] The existence of bishops therefore says something significant about the nature of the Church as well as about the ministry of the person within the Church. The very existence of bishops, before considering their function or anything they might do, is significant for the nature of the Church. There is therefore a fundamental relationship between the bishop and the rest of the Church, which the ordinal affirms at *The Welcome* and *Sending Out*, when the newly ordained bishop's new relationship with the rest of the Church is made visible and celebrated.

This is the foundation for the bishop's ministry in a particular context within the institutional Church.

The bishop, especially a diocesan one, must therefore balance the needs of the Church as an institution and as the body of Christ. Significant for Anglican polity is the legitimacy of making such a distinction, in the ecclesiological affirmation that the Church is a legitimate but partial expression of the body of Christ. The tension between the institutional needs and the ecclesial needs is brought to light by James Jones, who notes: '[T]he centralizing of funding and decision-making about mission may well put at risk [the] universal presence [of the Church].'[2] The distinction is not necessarily between the needs of the diocese and the parish, as expressions of the local and wider Church, but between the needs of the Church as an expression of the body of Christ in the world and the institution that makes that presence a reality. As Jones notes, it is the institutional aspects of centralization, funding and deployment that endanger the Church. Although the institution is a necessity for the Church to be in the world, there is a danger that the institution and its needs become the controlling factor in the life of the Church.

The needs of the institution are significant, as Julian Hubbard affirms:

> No church can avoid having institutional elements in its life and its ministries. They are inevitable and necessary, but admittedly a risk in a body whose true citizenship (*politeia*) is in heaven (Phil. 3.20) and whose end lies in the kingdom rather than earthly power.[3]

Roger Standing places even greater importance on the institution for the way in which the bishop relates to the Church:

> Of course, there is also the shift from working with a local congregation that is by its very nature more relational and organic, to working within a denominational infrastructure or organizational network. The latter is far more institutional and, whether structured along charitable or entrepreneurial lines, far less relational and controlled by organizational policy and structural processes.[4]

However, this is not affirmed by the ordinal. The ontology of the bishop's relationship with the rest of the Church is not defined by function. If the bishop is to be a 'shepherd' in the way affirmed by the ordinal, the relationship cannot be defined by the needs of the institution. While the needs of the institution, and the authority that the institution gives the bishop, are necessary, the institutional need must be secondary to the ecclesial: the institution should not be an end in itself, but rather a tool for the furthering of the kingdom of God.

Within this context, the diocese, as the base unit of the Church, has both an ecclesial and an institutional element. Paul Avis defines the bishop within the diocese in terms of the Christian commonwealth:

> The diocese, like the parish, is a geographical area, not a gathered community. You can opt out of the bishop's care, but you do not need to opt in. Just as the good parish priest bears a pastoral concern for all within the parish and seeks as far as possible to offer Christian ministry to all who are willing to receive it, so the good bishop bears the care of the whole diocese on their heart.[5]

While not all bishops are diocesan bishops, all bishops minister within the diocese. Moreover, once again ecumenical differences between ministers with translocal oversight and diocesan bishops are highlighted; in Anglican polity there is a tension in which both the parish and the diocese are expressions of the local church. The diocese therefore is not a conglomeration of parishes, but the local area ministered to by the diocesan bishop.[6] The diocesan bishop, although often an infrequent visitor to the parish church, is not simply an external moderator but the principal, if not usual, minister in the parish, sharing the cure of souls with the parish priest and, when present, the president of the eucharistic assembly. It is often the institutional role of the diocesan bishop, which is more apparent to many laity, as the face of the diocese which, among other functions, administers faculties and collects parish share. While these elements are significant for the diocese as an institution, they only have moral legitimacy when built upon a carefully cultivated ecclesial relationship which the diocesan bishop shares not just with the suffragan or area bishops, but with all the bishops who minister within the diocese. As the ordinal puts it, 'With the Shepherd's love, they are to be merciful, but with firmness; to minister discipline, but with compassion' (CW:OS 61). It is engagement with the rest of the Church as a shepherd that defines and facilitates the institutional engagement: trust is more important than power.

Roger Standing affirms the importance of this relationship when he states that the nature of the representative role of the bishop 'is primarily relational, and the minister acts out of who they are as a disciple of Christ'.[7] But it seems that functional necessity drives his next sentiment that 'on undertaking translocal ministry there is a subtle change and the representative role shifts to being primarily institutional'. It is not clear why this should be the case. For the ordinal, such a shift is not an ontological necessity, and the inference is that the change is driven by practical necessity caused by current institutional arrangements. While the diocese is an essential unit of Church for the Church of England, the shape and size of the diocese are not, and have often changed in history. From the perspective of the ordinal, if the bishop is unable to relate to the diocese in ecclesial terms, and becomes reliant on the institutional relationship, then the diocese is too big. The institutional needs of economy of scale and the institutional desire to maintain the status quo are in contrast with the Church's need for an ecclesial relationship with the bishops of the diocese. It is a theological necessity that Standing's bold statement ('The reality is that the default position in engaging with someone exercising *episkope* is institutional rather than relational')[8] be challenged not only in principle but in praxis. The institutional structures of the Church need to facilitate ecclesial rather than institutional relationships.

The role of bishop, especially a diocesan bishop, is shaped therefore in vocational terms, and the successful fulfilling of the institutional role must be considered as such. Anyone could be the CEO of a charitable organization administering groups across a translocal area; only a bishop can be a diocesan bishop. As Stephen Cottrell defines the bishop, the institutional aspects of the role are subordinated to the ecclesial reality of the community of the followers of Jesus Christ:

> Therefore, the main task of the bishop is to oversee the Church in such a way that it remains focused on the apostolic work that is the transforming power of the gospel itself ... It is not an institution that needs managing, but the community of men and women who have been impacted by Christ and who are now his presence in and for the world.[9]

He continues: 'The bishop is therefore not the Managing Director of Church of England plc but storyteller, poet and theologian.'[10] And further: 'If we only look and sound like managers, the Church is in big trouble.'[11] As Paul Goodliff observes, this focus on ecclesial relationship and vocation leads to the 'quality of the man [sic] that is remembered, not the office he held' and further that, 'Those who are remembered with affection, or revered as examples to follow, are those who are wise counsellors, caring pastors and hard workers.'[12] Thus the ordinal's emphasis is affirmed as not only possible but of the essence of the role, to which the needs of the institution must be subordinated, and in which the true needs of the institution are best met.

However, the ordinal's emphasis should not be confused with individualism or even a cult of celebrity, in which the emphasis shifts completely on to the office holder rather than the office itself. As Paul Avis notes, 'Anglicans generally tend to have an ambivalent attitude to bishops, almost a love-hate relationship. They love the idea of episcopacy, but sometimes strongly deprecate particular examples of it!'[13] What underlies this truism is that Anglicans expect to have some sort of relationship with their bishop that is more than institutional, as an integral aspect of the life of the Church. While bishops are unlikely to be a regular part of almost all worshipping congregations, they are expected to have a relationship with the diocese and, as outlined by Avis earlier, the nature of the relationship is crucial.

Specifically, the ordinal does not conceive of the bishop in managerial terms. Indeed, Standing distinguishes between 'an organization that is formed to accomplish an objective and an institution that is more organic, formed as the response to prevailing needs and social pressures to promote and protect certain values'.[14] An integral aspect of this distinction is the prevalence of management and managerialism within an organization as a necessary aspect of the organization achieving its objectives. Paul Goodliff notes the 'trend in the Church today towards an ever-increasing managerial mode'[15] and there has been considerable criticism of the Church's adoption of managerial techniques, supremely in the Green report.[16] Martyn Percy expresses this criticism in the strongest terms:

> In the actual text of the Green report, there are a couple of serious issues to wrestle with. First, it has no point of origination in theological or spiritual wisdom. Instead, on offer is a dish of basic contemporary approaches to executive management, with a little theological garnish. A total absence of ecclesiology ... it is steeped in its own uncritical use of executive management-speak.[17]

The move towards managerialism is undoubtedly one of attempted control, likely in response to anxieties about the decline and future shape of the institution; it is also indicative of a failure to prioritize the ecclesial relationship. The theological foundation, which Percy emphasizes, is an integral aspect of prioritizing the ecclesial relationship of the bishop over the needs of the institution.

The Church as the body of Christ is of a different order, and leadership within the Church is therefore predicated differently, not on the authority of the bishop to command the rest of the Church, but upon the trust that the people have in the bishop. The managerial mode itself is indicative of a breakdown of trust within the community, and the sense among the rest of the Church of there being a managerial mode is itself corrosive of the trust within any community.[18] The Church as the body of Christ cannot be managed in these terms, and any need for management of the Church as an institution must be secondary, dependent upon the relationships affirmed between the bishop and the Church, as made manifest at *The Welcome* (*CW:OS* 68).[19] At this point in the ordinal, the Church expresses their welcoming of the bishop, affirming the new relationship, having affirmed their support for the candidate to be ordained. However, the significant question is whether this welcoming of the bishop is a once and for ever moment, giving the bishop authority to relate to the Church as they wish, or whether this is an indicative moment in which the people subtly demonstrate that the bishop's authority rests on their consent. The consent and trust of the people in the bishop are vital, and although withdrawal of consent by a diocese is rare, it does happen – for example, in the removal of the Channel Islands from the care of the Bishop of Winchester.[20] In the ecclesial dimension the relationship between the bishop and the rest of the Church is not a given, but instead a foundation that needs constant attention to flourish. The relationship is therefore analogous to that of a marriage, where the relationship is intended to be lifelong, but also must be life-giving, and this relationship must be nurtured rather than taken for granted.

This is not to say that the bishop does not have any responsibility for governance within the Church. Clearly, in institutional terms there are significant responsibilities, but there are ecclesial responsibilities too. As Roger Standing notes:

> Governance and management are impossible to avoid if anything is to be accomplished ... Many in positions of translocal oversight tend to gravitate to the leadership function, but without appropriate levels of governance and management their leadership can be quickly compromised or corrupted.[21]

However, in order to exercise this governance, the bishop must have a foundation for the authority to seek to shape the community. While the institution gives some authority to this, most notably in the Canons, the ordinal establishes the new relationship between the bishop and the Church community. This new relationship provides the more significant ontology, and the Canons, rather than being the primary point of reference, are better understood as safeguards to provide boundaries if things go wrong. Moreover, the ecclesial authority of the bishop is that which is given at ordination, through the invocation of the Holy Spirit and the welcoming consent of the people, and is distinct from the institutional authority given to diocesan bishops in particular.

Here again, the marriage analogy is helpful. While the expectation is that relationship within the marriage will be such that it will be lifelong, the lifelong endurance of the relationship is based on the quality of the relationship. The Church recognizes that marriages can break down and even end in divorce. The primary ontology of a marriage is therefore the nature of the relationship, which is significantly shaped by the expectation that it will be lifelong. However, the couple are not committed to a lifelong union of misery, should that relationship break down. The same tension is present in ordaining people to lifelong roles within the Church: the consent and welcome at ordination must be indicative of the kind of relationship that the bishop and the wider Church will enjoy throughout their life, rather than a preliminary to investing the bishop with a power that is no longer accountable to the people. As a 'shepherd', the bishop cannot take for granted that the sheep will follow; they will only follow while there is a trusting relationship.

Although within the institution the bishop is seen as being more 'senior',[22] such a view is inimical to the view of the ordinal which represents not a *cursus honorum*, whereby the bishop has reached the highest echelons of the ecclesiastical hierarchy, but a polity within which certain members of the Church are ordained to particular relationships with the world and the Church by the power of the Holy Spirit. Not only are bishops therefore not senior to deacons, for example, neither are they senior to any other member of the Church. Any authority given to the bishop by the Church is therefore within these terms and challenges the institutional and managerial move towards hierarchy and centralized authority. In particular, this tension is brought to light in the diocesan bishop as one who holds both a role as judge in any disciplinary proceedings and as pastor. The authority of the bishop as a pastor cannot be separated from, and is more significant than, the authority of the bishop as upholder of good discipline. For the ordinal, the role as pastor cannot be subsumed to that of governor; the bishop is always primarily pastor, and it is this that should determine the way in which they approach issues of discipline. Hubbard affirms: 'A Church includes both organizations and institutions. Translocal leaders need the skills that belong to each, and the fundamental relational skills to lead the Church in its primary category as a community.'[23] However, the organizational, institutional and ecclesial realities of the Church in which the bishop exists are not discrete entities but instead overlapping layers, and so identifying which layers are primary and which are secondary is therefore essential.

The significance of successive ordination, with bishops being baptized, confirmed, ordained deacon and priest, before their ordination is not hierarchical, but instead indicative of the nature of the relationship that the bishop has with the body of Christ. Rather than successive ordination giving a sense of superiority, the bishop is as much a deacon as any other deacon, and foundationally a member of the Church, sharing in the same baptism that is fundamental to the Church's and the person's life. The unity therefore that the bishop offers to the Church is not in their ability to manage the institution in such a way that it behaves like an organization, with all the members working together to achieve an agreed goal, but in their ontology as someone who inhabits all roles within the Church. Akin to naval chaplains assuming the rank of whoever they are speaking to,[24] the bishop is one whose authority is welcomed by the Church and who is able to speak to any person within the Church as an equal. Rather than successive ordination, a better term is cumulative ordination, speaking as it does of the layers of ordination rather than discrete episodes through history.

The authority of the bishop is therefore necessarily and importantly of a soft nature. As Standing states: 'While such authority may be acknowledged in theory, in practice it does not have much clout.'[25] While Standing relies on Max Weber's three levels of authority – traditional, legal-relational and charismatic[26] – the Church also has the ontological-relational level established in baptism, and shaped for the bishop at ordination. Any authority that the bishop enjoys is couched, in ecclesial terms, in the authority of Christ himself, who has ultimate authority of the Church and all the baptized. It is Christ's own ministry that the bishop shares, with its emphasis on pastoral care. As Standing affirms:

> Historically speaking, the priority given to the pastoral dimension of the role has been constant over the centuries and is illustrated by the

symbolism of the bishop's crozier shaped like a shepherd's crook in Western Christianity or the designation of a diocesan bishop as its 'chief pastor'.[27]

However, he goes on to note, 'The pastoral dimension of translocal oversight can easily be subverted too.'[28] The most significant issue for the bishop is being aware that the authority in pastoral matters is of a different order to that in governance: the pastoral relationship requires vulnerability to be offered by the one receiving the pastoral care, looking to the pastor to protect them. The authority in governance is one that requires vulnerability to be imposed on the one being held to account. As Standing states: 'It is about a much deeper awareness, especially for clergy and church-leaders, of where power lies in relationships and how easy it is to abuse that power.'[29]

In conclusion, the ecclesial relationship is predominantly pastoral, theological and spiritual. The bishop's primary ontology is as a child of God. Increasingly, organizations are emphasizing the importance of pastoral care of their workforce[30] for reasons of productivity, recognizing that workers who are content can offer more in the workplace than those who are stressed. The bishop in the Church has that affirmed at their ordination, not to increase productivity but simply because a truly pastoral relationship is at the heart of the way in which they relate to the Church. This is true of all bishops, and is particularly difficult for diocesan bishops, who more clearly inhabit the institutional as well as the ecclesial spheres. The ecclesial reality is not simply an ideal or ephemeral theological concept, but rather the foundation for the praxis of episcopal ministry, directing and defining the use of the authority invested in a bishop by the institution. The ecclesial relationship is therefore both the means and the telos of episcopal ministry, manifesting the kingdom of God through a way of being for the Church in general and the bishop in particular.

It requires practical measures to ensure that the primacy of the pastoral relationship is maintained. These measures are especially important in matters of clergy discipline when the jurisdiction of the bishop within the institution may confer powers that are in conflict with their role as pastor. The primacy of relationship for the bishop is therefore essential in both ontology and praxis. The use of practical tools of delegation of their institutional authority – for example, through independent investigations – are therefore essential to maintain the primacy of the pastoral relationship between the diocesan bishop and the rest of the Church, and with other clergy in particular. The quality of the relationship that the bishop has with the people is first and foremost as minister or servant of the community.

Notes

1 David Stancliffe, 2023, 'Ordination in the Church of England: Theology and Practice in the Common Worship Ordinal' in Thomas Pott, James Hawkey and Keith Pecklers (eds), *Malines: Continuing the Conversation*, London: SPCK, pp. 141–52, p. 143.
2 James Jones, 2020, 'Church of England Bishops as Religious and Civic Leaders' in Roger Standing and Paul Goodliff (eds), *Episkope: The Theory and Practice of Translocal Oversight*, London: SCM Press, pp. 81–92, p. 86.
3 Julian Hubbard, 'Translocal Ministries in the Church of England as Institutional Leadership in Personhood' in Standing and Goodliff (eds), *Episkope*, pp. 93–102, p. 93.
4 Roger Standing, 'Episkope, Identity and Personhood' in Standing and Goodliff (eds), *Episkope*, pp. 203–12, pp. 207–8.
5 Paul Avis, 2020, 'Anglican Episcopacy' in Standing and Goodliff (eds), *Episkopet*, pp. 61–70, p. 62.
6 Roger Standing, 2020, 'Theological Issues: Constants in Context' in Standing and Goodliff (eds), *Episkope*, pp. 14–43, p. 20. Cf. Church of England, GS Misc 733, 'Suffragan Bishops', <https://www.churchofengland.org/sites/default/files/2023-01/gs-misc-733-suffragan-bishops.pdf>, p. 88, accessed 23.03.2025.
7 Roger Standing, 2020, 'The Shape of Translocal Oversight', in Standing and Goodliff (eds), *Episkope*, pp. 213–24, p. 215.
8 Standing, 'The Shape of Translocal Oversight', p. 216.
9 Stephen Cottrell, 2020, 'Church of England Bishops as Pastor and Evangelist' in Standing and Goodliff (eds), *Episkope*, pp. 71–80, p. 71.
10 Cottrell, 'Church of England Bishops as Pastor and Evangelist', p. 74.
11 Cottrell, 'Church of England Bishops as Pastor and Evangelist', p. 77.
12 Paul Goodliff, 2020, 'Contemporary Models of Translocal Ministry: Ecumenical Landscapes' in Standing and Goodliff (eds), *Episkope*, pp. 44–60, p. 57.
13 Avis, 'Anglican Episcopacy', p. 68.
14 Standing, 'Theological Issues: Constants in Context', p. 26.
15 Paul Goodliff, 2020, 'Translocal Ministry and Scholarship', in Standing and Goodliff (eds), *Episkope*, pp. 225–31, p. 228.
16 The Green report defines itself as: 'At the request of the Archbishops and the Development and Appointments Group (DAG), Lord Green was asked to chair this project and also to review talent management and leadership development for senior clergy. The terms of reference required the review to meet the Archbishops' challenge of being sufficiently radical and imaginative in response to new contexts. His Steering Committee started work in January 2014, with the goal of presenting proposals to the Archbishops' Spending Task Group on 11th June 2014. The Steering Committee worked closely with the Archbishops in finalizing these proposals.' Green et al., 2014, 'Talent Management for Future Leaders and Leadership Development for

Bishops and Deans: A New Approach Report of the Lord Green Steering Group', <https://www.churchofengland.org/sites/default/files/2017-12/gs%201982%20-%20discerning%20and%20nurturing%20senior%20leaders.pdf>, accessed 25.03.2023, p. 3.

17 Martyn Percy, 2014, 'Are these the leaders that we really want?', *Church Times*, 12 December, <https://www.churchtimes.co.uk/articles/2014/12-december/comment/opinion/are-these-the-leaders-that-we-really-want>, accessed 12.07.2022.

18 See, for example, David Bell, 2007, 'Foreword' in Julia Middleton, *Beyond Authority*, Basingstoke: Palgrave Macmillan, pp. vii–ix, p. vii: 'It happens again and again. Bright, aggressive managers move quickly up an organization and then, quite suddenly, find themselves becalmed. The skills that seemed to be serving them so well are just not enough. We have all seen the heads shake. He, or she, is *'not very good with people'* or *'doesn't seem able to see the wood for the trees'* or *'is not very good at lateral thinking'*.

19 The congregation responds: 'We welcome you as a shepherd of Christ's flock.'

20 Hattie Williams, 2019, 'Channel Islands to leave the see of Winchester', *Church Times*, <https://www.churchtimes.co.uk/articles/2019/11-october/news/uk/channel-islands-to-leave-the-see-of-winchester>, accessed 11.09.2025.

21 Standing, 'The Shape of Translocal Oversight', p. 221.

22 Hubbard, 'Translocal Ministries in the Church of England as Institutional Leadership', p. 94.

23 Hubbard, 'Translocal Ministries in the Church of England as Institutional Leadership', p. 100.

24 'With no rank of your own, you share that of the person you're talking with, from Rear Admiral to the most junior rating.' Royal Navy, 'Chaplain', <https://www.royalnavy.mod.uk/careers/roles-and-specialisations/services/surface-fleet/chaplain>, accessed 11.09.2025. This understanding is distinctive for the Royal Navy among the armed forces.

25 Standing, 'The Shape of Translocal Oversight', p. 217.

26 Standing, 'The Shape of Translocal Oversight', p. 216. For sociologist Max Weber, there are three types of authority: Charismatic authority is held by individuals on their ability to personally win the trust of others, and can therefore spring up spontaneously, and often in response to specific need – for example, Nelson Mandela or Martin Luther King Jr in response to racial inequality. Traditional authority is most clearly seen in monarchical government, when subordinates accept a person's authority because it is an inherited part of the structure of society. The third form is rational-legal authority, as seen in bureaucracy or meritocracy, where people are able to gain power through the function they perform for the society. In this instance the authority is tied to a particular role, and when the person no longer holds that role they no longer have any authority. Cf. Max Weber, 1978 [1922], *Economy and Society*, edited by Guenther Roth and Claus Wittich, Berkeley, CA: University of California Press.

27 Standing, 'The Shape of Translocal Oversight', p. 218.

28 Standing, 'The Shape of Translocal Oversight', p. 219.

29 Standing, 'The Shape of Translocal Oversight', p. 219.

30 Cf. Susan K. Wintz and George F. Handzo, 2005, 'Pastoral Care Staffing and Productivity: More than Ratios', *Chaplaincy Today*, 21 (1), pp. 3–10.

7

The Church Needs Foot Washers

The previous chapters have affirmed and elaborated on the relational nature of episcopal ministry in both theory and praxis. In this chapter particular attention is paid to the innovation in CW:OS of the bishop washing the candidates' feet as part of the rite for the ordination of deacons. In light of the import of this ritual and its significance for episcopal ministry, consideration will be given to the discernment process for identifying candidates for episcopal ministry.

The introduction of foot washing by the bishop at the ordination of deacons[1] is a distinctive and unique aspect of the *Common Worship* ordinal. The introduction of the ritual has intended significance for the deacons being ordained. However, it is also significant for the congregation to witness, and for the bishop's self-understanding and expression of their episcopal ministry. In continuity with the ordinal's focus on ecclesial relationship, the ritual speaks loudly against a detached, hierarchical understanding of the relationship affirming that ordinations are cumulative, as it highlights the bishop's common status as a deacon with the newly ordained. The ritual is also sacramental and indicative of the nature of the relationship between bishops and other clergy, especially between the diocesan bishop and the clergy in their diocese, as a relationship of attentive care and service.

Although only appearing as an option, the foot washing is a significant innovation in the corpus of Anglican ordinals. This is therefore a significant moment in which the bishop, often vested as a deacon,[2] emphasizes their solidarity with the deacons in their new foot washing ministry. For Rosalind Brown, foot washing is as distinctive a diaconal expression of Christ's ministry as table presiding is for presbyters.[3] The inclusion of foot washing in the deacons' ordination rite speaks powerfully of the bishop's own diaconal ministry. It is not simply as a bishop that the bishop washes feet, but as a bishop who is also a deacon. In so doing, the bishop identifies themself with the ministry of the newly ordained deacons. The bishop therefore washes the deacons' feet as an experienced co-deacon, and as a fundamental act of solidarity.[4]

The theological focus of the foot washing is placed in the loving relationship between people that is symptomatic of the work of God in the world. It is therefore both a pastoral and eschatological act, which speaks of the establishment of the kingdom of God on earth. The suggested chant of *Ubi Caritas et amor, Deus ibi est*, 'where there is love and charity, there is God', draws out this emphasis. This is not an act of duty, humiliation or penance for the bishop, but rather an embodiment of the loving relationship between bishop and deacon. It speaks of both the support and care that the deacon will need to accept from the bishop, that they will not carry out this ministry in their own strength, and of the importance that the bishop should place on caring for the deacons, whose feet are going to need tending after they have been ministering at the margins of society.

The foot washing is also indicative of the nature and shape of diaconal ministry. Thus, for David Stancliffe, the ritual speaks both about the nature of the deacon-bishop relationship and the future shape of the deacon's own ministry: 'commend[ing] itself as a visible sign of the way in which the new deacon's ministry should be exercised and has made visible the relationship between the deacon and their bishop'.[5] However, as the bishop is also in deacons' orders, the importance of the ritual for the bishop is no less than that for the newly ordained deacons. Moreover, the foot washing is more than a temporary reclamation of the bishop's diaconal orders, for the bishop is still in diaconal orders themselves. Therefore, the foot washing speaks of the nature of the bishop's ministry, which must be diaconal in nature throughout. There is no way to be a bishop other than by being a deacon.

Cumulative orders are therefore highly significant for both ordained ministry and the whole Church. The question as to whether direct ordination is efficacious therefore misses the point.[6] The significance for each of the orders lies in the shaping and nature of the ministry being undertaken. As James Monroe Barnett notes: '[T]he shift from a Church whose ministry encompassed all its people, each with a special function for the good of the whole, like organs of the body, to a Church whose ministry was one of ascending grades characterized by rank, status and power is to be found wanting when tested by the revelation of Christ.'[7] Cumulative orders are therefore an important bulwark against the hierarchical tendency, which separates the bishop from not just the other orders but from the Church as a whole. Furthermore, cumulative orders are highly significant in the shaping of episcopal ministry in maintaining the bishops' commonality with all the other members of the body of Christ; that the bishop identifies with all people in the Church whether lay, deacon, priest or bishop. Therefore, any tendency towards a *cursus honorum* view, whereby the bishop is given greater rank, status or power, undermines not just the ministry of the bishop but the nature of the whole Church.

The ordinal stresses the equality of the orders from the outset of the deacons' rite, citing John 13.14, 'as [Christ] washed the feet of his disciples, so they must wash the feet of others' (*CW:OS* 10). The ministry of the deacon therefore cannot be relegated to only a transitional or training role for the subsequent orders. The diaconal ministry is the foundational ordination for the subsequent orders, which remains active and definitive of Christian ministry both for each ordained person and for the nature of the Church. The diaconal nature of all ordained ministry is based in the ministry of Christ himself, and therefore to abrogate the diaconal nature of episcopal ministry is to undermine the foundations for Christian ministry set by Christ himself. The deacon does not carry out their ministry in a vicarious manner but in a prophetic one, holding up a mirror to each person in which they can reflect on whether they, personally and corporately, are being true to the diaconal calling of the whole Church. The prophetic character of the bishops' ministry as deacons is therefore both highly significant for the Church as a whole and vital for each bishop in their inhabiting of the role. Cumulative orders, unless its significance is ignored, actively undermines any institutional tendency to treating those in leadership, especially bishops, with greater privilege and deference.

The integrity and distinctiveness of Christian ministry and leadership is also made clear in the reading of John 13.12–17. Here the emphasis is again placed on the common Christian calling to mutual service. Jesus does not suggest that specific people wash feet, but instead that his followers should wash one another's feet (John 13.14). Christ's form of leadership is countercultural not just in his own day but in any context. Repeatedly, Christ demonstrates a new way of being a leader, rooted and grounded in his own kenosis. Any Christian ministry must therefore itself be kenotic in nature. This is not the same as the personal sacrifice that many make to take up Christian ministry. This is clear in comments such as those of Marla Martin-Hanley: 'I joke, though not really, and say that in my first year as bishop I lost my prayer life, my family life, and my exercise life. It took me several more years to get those things back in line.'[8] However, the significance for the ordinal is clearly on the nature of the ministry: the isolation and loss described by Martin-Hanley reflect not so much the diaconal nature of episcopal ministry but rather a common experience of those who undertake hierarchical leadership in institutions.[9] Kenosis, and emphasis on active claiming of the baptism, which is common to all Christians, is therefore both ontologically significant and addresses the potential for bishops to become isolated leaders.

The foot washing is more than a reclamation of the bishop's previous ministry as a deacon. Integrated into the liturgy, it speaks as clearly as the laying on of hands of the nature of episcopal ministry. Therefore, Steven Croft's triangular model of the threefold ministry, in which diaconal, presbyteral and episcopal ministries are held in tension, fails to grasp the true foundational significance of diaconal orders for all Christian ministries. It is not enough to state that:

> The ministry of any person who is ordained is likely to contain different elements of each of these three focal areas of ministry ... The balance and movement between these three poles or dimensions of ministry will change and evolve over time.[10]

To narrate Christian ministry in these terms overly separates the three orders and fails to emphasize that the diaconal nature of ministry is more than an emphasis: it is of the essence of all orders. In the same way, the triangular model used in *Senior Church Leadership* overly separates the leader from the people of God.[11] To place the leader, people and God at the three apexes is to overly separate and distinguish them, as in the Shield of the Trinity,[12] where the apexes of the triangle are used to distinguish the persons of the Trinity rather than affirming their unity. Both these triangular models of ministry fail to emphasize the inter-connectedness and cumulative nature of orders: that the ordained are rooted in and remain very much a part of the community of the Church, and that diaconal ministry is an inherent part of episcopacy.

To draw on *Senior Church Leadership*'s conductor analogy, the shape of Christian ministry therefore is not as conductor in the way the report suggests.[13] The analogy is helpful, but the focus on the conductor as distinct from the leader of the orchestra is unhelpful. The advent of the non-playing conductor is a relatively modern invention.[14] More appropriate is the *konzertmeister*, one who leads the group from the harpsichord or violin, and whose role has been revived by early music ensembles in recent decades. In this arrangement, the leader is not removed from the orchestra but is an integral part of it contributing their own sounds to the music-making as well as having oversight of the whole. Interestingly, to lead the orchestra in this way limits the number of musicians in the group, as they rely on being able to hear the leader's playing and observe their subtle movements of the head or bow. Most importantly, the hierarchical significance of the conductor is greatly diminished, both for the orchestra and the audience, as they are no longer physically separated from the orchestra, but are an integrated part of the ensemble.

The definition of the conductor as 'itinerant, trans-local, visionary, charismatic',[15] reflects a specific form of conducting, which is not universally true and, importantly, is inappropriate for the ecclesial context. It is significant, although unintended but congruent with the triangular model of leadership, that the report focuses on a particular manifestation of conducting which places distance between the conductor and orchestra, and literally places the leader on a podium. Even the reference to the handshake between orchestra leader and conductor speaks not so much of the integration of the conductor with the orchestra, but of a distance bridged by the shaking of hands. Conversely, the *konzertmeister*, as an integral part of the ensemble, has to model the music-making personally, be ready to move between prominence and even silence in the piece of music, and also has significantly reduced ability to wield power over the players. It is this model that is a helpful analogy for the ordinal's vision of kenotic leadership, based on Jesus' own example and teaching, as exemplified by the bishop washing the newly ordained deacons' feet.

The foot washing in the deacons' rite is therefore a highly significant liturgical innovation, which speaks profoundly of the bishop's ministry more than it does of that of the newly ordained deacons. It places the bishop alongside the newly ordained in sharing their diaconal ministry and demonstrates the kind of care that the bishop has for those in their care. Furthermore, this ritual is not a moment in which the bishop steps back from being bishop, but one in which the bishop's diaconal ministry is brought into focus. Just as the bishop does not cease to be bishop to undertake this diaconal ministry in the liturgy, so the bishop never ceases to be a deacon in their wider ministry as bishop. The fullness of episcopal ministry rests on embodying diaconal ministry, which marks and shapes the nature of the bishop's relationship with the whole of the body of Christ, both lay and ordained. In contrast to models that distinguish the leader from the people, the ordinal promotes an understanding of the bishop as one who is deeply connected with the people, ready to listen and serve, rather than one who comes in from outside to offer their expertise. Based on Christ's own kenotic ministry, kenosis is the hallmark of Christian leadership. Stripped of power and privilege, the bishop leads as one who knows and is known by the people of the Church. They are trusted because the people have experienced the diaconal ministry of the bishop and recognize the authenticity of their moral authority in their modelling of Christian discipleship.

The process of discernment that identifies candidates for episcopal ministry must therefore be theologically predicated on, and rooted in, the ecclesial relationship that will be established at ordination. The process should be first and foremost an ecclesial outworking based in the ontology of being God's children, rather than an institutional recruitment process. The role of the Church as a whole is therefore highly significant and, in this ecclesial light, the contemporary process and reports of the Church will be evaluated.

The ecclesial, diaconal focus of the ordinal raises significant questions about the selection of candidates for the episcopate. Candidates cannot be discerned without first having a clear understanding of what is required of them and what character traits are best suited to the role. The focus must therefore be on the nature of the relationships that the bishop will need to have with the rest of the Church. The selection of the bishop is a prerequisite for ordination which is brought to completion and made visible in the rite at the presentation and the declarations (*CW:OS* 56, 63). The selection process is therefore both external to the rite, having taken place before the service begins, and an integral part of it. For the selection process to have integrity there must be congruency between the elements that happen before the service and that which happens within it. Thus, the descriptors in the ordinal must be the key determinants in the selection process. If the selection process is going to be successful, it must produce someone who is appropriate to be ordained according to the requirements and description of a bishop in the ordinal. Moreover, since the focus of the ordinal is ecclesial rather than institutional, this should also be reflected in the selection process, with a focus on ordination being as 'a bishop in the Church of God' as the primary role of any bishop, with a secondary concern for the needs of a given vacancy.

The variety of discernment processes is made clear in the ordinal at the presentation, with two routes depending on whether the candidate is going to be a diocesan or suffragan bishop. For diocesan bishops, the selection process is focused on the Crown Nomination Commission and, for suffragans, the appointment is in the gift of the diocesan bishop. There is therefore a distinction made in the rite over who is most appropriate to make the presentation (*CW:OS* 73). Since there are no unifying selection criteria for bishops, this reflects the potential for very different selection processes and criteria, in marked contrast to the process for the selection of candidates for ordination to the diaconate and priesthood.[16] It is also significant that the one aspect of the selection process that is uniform is the Royal Mandate, whose focus is not on the fundamental ecclesial relationships but on the needs of the institution as a feature of it being enmeshed in the state through establishment. This apparent diminishing of the ecclesial significance of the bishop is congruent with, and highlighted by, *Discerning in Obedience*, which considers the role of the Crown Nominations Commission. Although the report recognizes the place of the ordinal, it ranks its significance in third place for consideration, behind the 'profiles of the candidates and diocesan needs' and 'the way God's grace is served by a bishop as distinct from another minister'.[17]

An additional tension noted in *Discerning in Obedience* is the balance between the needs of the local, in terms of the diocese, and the needs of the Church of God. While these should not be mutually exclusive, the local often requires particular emphases from their bishop to address specific institutional needs. The primacy, however, must always remain on the character of the bishop within the Church of God, based on the relationship they will have with the body of Christ. Without this focus, there is the danger that the process will select a candidate who is nearer to being the CEO of the charity, who may be very adept at addressing the current issues, but who is not suited to the ontology of being a bishop. The report notes the significance of the ecclesial relationship when it states, 'without an understanding of what a bishop *essentially is*, no one is in a position to discern God's will for who the next bishop is'.[18] However, the report goes on to confuse the ontology of being a bishop with the function of the diocesan, mirroring the confusions noted earlier in other Church reports. It defines the essence of the bishop in purely diocesan terms: 'The bishop watches over the life of word and sacrament in the diocese as a whole, the local community of churches into which the Holy Spirit has breathed life.'[19] Aside from the ecclesiological question of whether the diocese is the base unit of Church, or a community of Churches, there is a significant omission in failing to recognize that the essence of being a bishop is not defined by the diocesan bishop.

The only legitimate success criterion for the selection process is whether the candidate is the person whom God is calling the Church to ordain in the power of the Holy Spirit. The significant test for the Church in selecting a candidate is whether the candidate is able to grow into the role as described by the ordinal. The report's criteria for a successful process are therefore lacking:

> If, at the end of the day, it can be said that the ministry of bishops **is a continuous ministry of word and sacrament,** faithful from generation to generation; **that the church as a whole recognises and accepts the episcopal ministry** sent to it; and that the selection of bishops is based on **a careful discernment informed by knowledge of the candidates and the situation,** then the process of selection has proved itself.[20]

Aside from questions about the recognition of episcopal ordination for women by the whole Church, there is an overly local and mechanical focus in the criteria. The litmus test, aim and essence of the success of the appointment process is the success of the bishop's ministry. In the light of Jesus' own ministry, the success of Christian ministry cannot be measured in simplistic external criteria. Rather, the ontology of being a successful bishop is in inhabiting the episcopal relationship with the rest of the Church, and, in common with all Christian disciples, the nature of their relationship with God. It is only on this foundation that they will be able to respond to the needs of the local context as a Christian minister, as opposed to responding as might any CEO of a charity.

Moreover, not only may the local context change over the term of the bishop holding that office, but also the person is ordained as a bishop in the Church of God and may minister in many contexts. The context of their first appointment is therefore necessarily secondary to the characteristics and qualities that are the ontology of being a bishop. This brings the selection process for bishops more in line with the process for selection to other orders, where, for example, the needs of a title parish are not even considered at the time of selection of a candidate for ordination to the priesthood. The report does recognize this, stating: 'The requirements of the office of bishop outlined in the Pastoral Epistles (Tit. 1:7–9; 1 Tim. 3:1–7) are not centred on gifts and skills but on moral character.'[21] However, this affirmation is contrary to earlier statements, and it is unclear as to whether this aphorism defines the selection process in the way that it should.

Martyn Percy clearly articulates the distinction between the character of being a bishop and how that character can be undermined by a focus on function. His use of the word 'job' is significant, in elucidating the way in which a clear understanding of the nature of the role defines the selection criteria. The specific needs of a diocese at any given time are much nearer to a 'job description' than the characteristics required to inhabit the ecclesial relationships that define the ontology of being a bishop:

> Bishops in their oversight should really function as public apologists, in the public square, when they defend the foolishness of the cross and the truth of the gospel, and so facilitate and enable lived corporate demonstrations of faith's endurance – and of the love, forgiveness and communion that is to be found in Christ. The primary calling for our bishops is to mediate the wisdom and compassion of God: to be truly good teachers and pastors, after the example of Christ himself, no less. Being a bishop is not an ecclesiastical 'job'. It is, rather, an 'occupation'. Bishops are to be occupied with God (for which they need theology and spirituality); and then to be occupied with what they think might preoccupy God's heart and mind – the cares and concerns Christ has for our broken world and its needy people (and so engage in pastoral care). Thus occupied, a bishop might then be said to be doing the 'job' the church believed and discerned that they were actually called to do.[22]

Percy not only clearly identifies some legitimate organizing principles in assessing a bishop's 'success', he also tacitly highlights how these qualities can be easily undermined by alternative criteria for success, often generated by the needs of the institution. It is not difficult to imagine how a bishop might be viewed as successful because of their ability, particularly in a diocesan role, to slow decline, oversee reorganization or stabilize the diocesan finances, without fulfilling any of the principles laid out here. Equally, and importantly in the light of Jesus' apparent failure to overthrow Roman oppression or avoid execution, it is possible to envisage a bishop whose worldly success is difficult to measure, but who has been successful in the way in which they have inhabited their relationship with the other members of the Church and Christ.

Percy goes on to suggest that not only is this a potential pitfall, but that the current leadership's unconscious anxieties mean that the essence of being a bishop is actually being lost. In place of the essential priorities of a bishop, he suggests priorities similar to those generated in any institution attempting to reverse decline are being given primary concern. For example, the gracious by-product of faithful living, which is Church growth, becomes the end goal to be managed, measured and achieved through the work of the bishop's leadership. To invert the priorities in this way is a theological crisis because it shifts the bishop from being the servant of God to being the leader of the institution. In so doing, the true divine telos – union with God – is not just marginalized, but is undermined. The ecclesial nature of the Church is subordinated to the institutional needs of the Church, and God's grace is replaced by carefully constructed programmes to develop specific skills. Thus, unconsciously, as Percy suggests, the Church morphs away from being God's Church and becomes primarily a human institution seeking to achieve specific ends. Simply by failing to ground the Church sufficiently in a strong theology of God's grace, and the mission of the Church as obedience to God's will, these essential aspects of the life of the Church are lost. The candidate selected in this context is therefore a radically different candidate to the one the ordinal has in mind. This is the point at which the selection process starts looking for a leader in the institution rather than a bishop in the Church of God.

The importance of the ecclesial relationship between the bishop and the Church is also lost when it is assumed. While Percy argues that the ecclesial relationship is subsumed by pressing institutional concerns, it is also easily lost when it is so obvious that it is not clearly articulated and investigated as part of the selection process. The danger of under-emphasizing the essential nature, and necessary qualities, of a bishop is that they then become assumed within the selection process, and overshadowed by those aspects of the selection process that should be secondary, including the needs of the context and the institution. The focus of the selection process is therefore skewed; no longer prioritizing the qualities that will enable the bishop to respond appropriately in any given context and grounded in their relationship with God and the body of Christ. More importantly, this shift moves the selection process away from being a discernment process. The report is clear that discernment is significant: '**Discernment involves a step of faith enabling us to conceive something that God will bring about, which is not yet visible**'.[23] Therefore, the process of selection, theologically, is to attend to God's will and discover whom God is calling to be a bishop.

This is radically different to selecting someone to undertake a specific job, where the needs of the particular role can be carefully measured against the experience and aptitudes of prospective candidates. In a job interview, the interviewer acts as judge and examiner in a process of examination in which the interviewee seeks to convince the interviewer that they are the person who will best meet the needs of the role as it has been articulated in the job description. It is clear how a selection process focused on filling a particular vacancy might tend towards that model, especially when power and ecclesiastical politics will also have a role to play on both the local and national levels. In contrast, discerning a candidate leaves God as the judge, with interviewer and interviewee both seeking God's will, which is a significant shift in dynamic. Moreover, discernment includes both clear boundaries about the character traits of the person, so that they are suited to fulfil the episcopal relationship with the Church, and also the expectation that this person selected will be in some way surprising. They will be beyond the immediately obvious, expedient or natural choice because they will be God's choice and they will be open to God's grace to grow into the role.

Whatever form the selection process takes, therefore, those making the discernment are primarily acting on behalf of God and the Church of God, into which the candidate will be ordained bishop. The report is aware of the need for God's grace in the process,[24] and for the process itself to be prayerful. Here the spiritual element of the process is significant: as a discernment process, it must be a prayerful seeking of God's will, rather than a decision made by the panel. Prayerfulness is of the essence of the process, and it is this dependency on the Holy Spirit that connects and integrates the selection process into the liturgy of ordination. The nomination of a candidate is therefore recognition, through the selection process, of a vocation by God, as is recognized by the report.

However, the report goes on to suggest that this vocation to be a bishop is of a different order to that of vocations to the priesthood:

> One can know oneself called to be a bishop only as one is invited to become one; vocation to be a bishop is unlike vocation to be a priest, in that the question cannot be raised initially by the candidate.[25]

If the selection process is to be rooted and grounded in the discernment of the will of God through the Holy Spirit, it is not clear why, when it is deemed appropriate for a prospective candidate to initiate the process for ordination to the priesthood, the same should not be true for prospective candidates for ordination to the episcopate. Equally, if it is inappropriate for candidates to initiate the process for discernment to be a bishop, it is not clear why the candidates for ordination to the priesthood should be able to respond to personal promptings of the Holy Spirit in offering themselves for consideration. Presumably it is only because of the relative scarcity of bishops in comparison with priests that makes this the case, as both processes are seeking to discern the will of God, with the agreement of panel and candidate being the basis for believing that the candidate is called by God. There is therefore no ontological need for different understandings of vocation for different orders. Moreover, the report is over-confident in the infallibility of any process when it states: 'The call of God is proved by a convergence of the judgement of the nominators with a personal conviction of vocation on the part of the nominee.'[26] Whatever the system, there remains an aspect of fallibility, whereby a vocation is discerned in error or missed, or where the prejudices of the nominators cloud their ability to discern the will of God. What can be said is that the Church's recognition of a vocation requires the convergence of judgement, and that everyone needs to have confidence in whatever discernment process is in place so that the whole Church is prepared to delegate the process of discernment to the panel, and ultimately accept the nomination at the point of ordination.

Here again there is an important, if subtle, articulation needed of the relationship between the Church as institution and the Church as spiritual community. It is essential to recognize both an understanding of, and trust in, the ability of the Church as an institution, to be able to discern God's will, and to recognize and accept the institution's limitations in acting as a conduit of the divine will. At its best, the Church is able to attend to, and be empowered by, the Holy Spirit to enact God's will. However, it is vital to understand that it is not infallible in discerning God's will, and that therefore there is epistemic distance between the will of the Church as identified by the panel and the will of God as expressed by the Holy Spirit. The will of God and the will of the Church are not synonymous; the will of the Church is its imperfect discernment of the will of God. This brings about an essential humility on the part of the Church as a whole, emphasizing its dependency on God's merciful forgiveness, with an explicit awareness and readiness to own its shortcomings.

A sound ecclesiology is therefore essential for a successful discernment of candidates for ordination in terms of the nature of the process, trust in the process, and the successful identification of the candidate nominated by the process. Inadequate understandings of ecclesiology and of the essential nature of episcopal ministry, as distinct from the nature of bishoprics, make the Church vulnerable through the potential for the erosion of trust in the process, an inability to recognize the potential for fallibility in the process of selection, and ultimately in the potential for the wrong person with the wrong characteristics being ordained bishop in the Church. The selection process is significant, therefore, not just because it shapes the collective qualities of the bishops of the Church as well as producing nominations for specific roles, whether that selection process be overseen by a diocesan bishop or the Crown Nominations Commission. Moreover, the selection process also plays a significant role in fostering or undermining the necessary trust of the whole Church in both the process of appointment and, through those appointed, the institution's ability to fulfil the ecclesial responsibilities of discerning God's will, which have been delegated to the process for the good of the Church and of the world.

This is not to say that specific contexts and the institution itself do not have specific needs; these are well represented in the current process, but what is significant, as Rowan Williams has identified above, is when these needs become dominant in the discernment. This could be with good intentions, such as to address a particular discrepancy within the diversity of representation among the existing bishops, to rely on the security of appointing diocesan bishops from among those who have already 'proved themselves' as suffragans – as would be appropriate for a job interview – or from a desire to find a candidate who will foster unity through being 'merely bland and inoffensive'.[27] However, the will of God is not confined to any of these categories. On the contrary, it is often challenging and surprising since the wisdom of God is not confined to human wisdom. Moreover, the bishop's essence is not to be found in their ability to bring a particular skill or fix a specific problem; the ordination of a bishop is about establishing a relationship, a way of being with God and with God's Church. This is about Christian virtues and characteristics, the embodiment of the gospel for the sake of the world, in a particular ministry of relating to the whole Church. At the heart of this is the bishop's ability to relate to the Church as a shepherd; to have the understanding and empathy with the flock that means that they trust the bishop as someone to follow. It is only when this ecclesiology, spirituality and understanding of episcopal ontology is at the forefront of the discernment process and the selection criteria that the Church can be confident in the process and trusting of the nomination process.

The ordinal's focus on ontology over institutional needs, or functionality, has been clearly established. Moreover, it has been demonstrated that this focus is not an instance of distanced or abstracted theology and spirituality. The theological foundations for ordination are of pragmatic and vital significance for the Church and the person inhabiting their place within the Church of God as a bishop. This foundation is liturgical, not in the sense of being reserved for the rite of ordination, but liturgical in the sense of being at the heart of the work of the people of God. The ecclesial relationship between the bishop and the Church is the primary description of the ontology of the role and is the foundation on which any institutional relationship is built. Therefore, rather than being assumed, and often subsumed, this foundational relationship must be the primary focus of the ministry of any bishop and the expectation of the Church as a whole. It must therefore also be the primary consideration of the selection process, above any other need that may have been identified in a given bishopric or role. It follows that it is vital that there is a conscious, explicit and careful articulation of the nature of the relationship between the bishop and the rest of the Church; for the institution in discerning ordinands; for those ordained bishop to understand their role; and for the body of Christ to be able to build up a trusting relationship with the bishops.

That this consciousness is still lacking in the Church has been evidenced through several reports. It would appear that the Archbishops of Canterbury and York and the Bishop of London want to address this in an unpublished paper: *A Consultation Document: Bishops and Their Ministry Fit for a New Context*. Given the secrecy surrounding the report, it is not possible to comment extensively on it. However, from what has been reported[28] it would appear that the foundations of the importance of ecclesial relationship as outlined here have not significantly shaped the proposals in the report. In particular, a reduction in the number of bishops has the potential to further distance bishops from the other members of the Church, and the proposal for specialist bishops would be congruent with a hierarchical understanding of bishop as spokesperson on specific issues. Both proposals seem to embody institutional understandings of the role of bishop. There is no suggestion of creating smaller dioceses in which the bishop would have greater connection with their diocese in exchange for a loss of hierarchical distance and power within the institution. Rather, the proposals once again seem to be placing the needs of the institution – to cut expenditure and maintain the kudos of bishops – above the ecclesial relationships that underpin their ministry. To establish this reconnection remains a significant challenge. The report apparently recognizes the difficulty in challenging the status quo; 'The structure and culture of the Church of England, and the proliferation of "vested interest" and diversified decision-making power structures make change difficult.'[29] However, the conclusions here suggest that the changes required are far more profound than the report apparently suggests.

The Church of England needs to reclaim and renew its ecclesial relationships, particularly between the bishops and the rest of the Church.

The bishop's divesting themself of the trappings of power is an essential aspect of their inhabiting their diaconal ministry, which is foundational to their episcopal ministry. At their ordination, a new relationship of mutual care is established, akin to the relationship established in a marriage, which is a lifelong way of being, no matter whether the bishop holds a diocesan, suffragan or other post within the Church. It is a relationship that is Christ-shaped, mirroring his own kenosis so that Christ's own faith can shape the bishop's life and relationships with others.

Notes

1 'Before the Welcome, the bishop may wash the feet of the newly ordained deacons' (*CW:OS* 29).

2 The ritual closely mirrors the washing of feet by the president of the rite on Maundy Thursday.

3 Rosalind Brown, 2008, *Being a Deacon Today*, Norwich: Canterbury Press, p. 9.

4 A similar connection is made when the bishop wears a pontifical dalmatic under the chasuble, which emphasizes the servant ministry that the bishop shares with all deacons. For a fuller discussion of pontifical dalmatics and their usage, see Shawn Tribe, 2018, 'The Pontifical Dalmatic and Tunicle: A Brief History and Consideration', *Liturgical Arts Journal*, <https://www.liturgicalartsjournal.com/2018/08/the-pontifical-dalmatic-and-tunicle.html>, accessed 11.09.2025.

5 David Stancliffe, 2018, 'Making Common Worship: Securing Some Underlying Theologies' in Aiden Platten (ed.), *Grasping the Heel of Heaven*, Norwich: Canterbury Press, p. 90.

6 See, for example, *Church Times*, 2015, 'Out of the question', <https://www.churchtimes.co.uk/articles/2015/9-january/regulars/out-of-the-question/out-of-the-question>, accessed 11.09.2025.

7 James Monroe Barnett, 1979, *The Diaconate: A Full and Equal Order*, Harrisburg, PA: Trinity Press International, p. 12.

8 Cited in Roger Standing, 2020, 'Episkope, Identity and Personhood' in Roger Standing and Paul Goodliff (eds), *Episkope: The Theory and Practice of Translocal Oversight*, London: SCM Press, pp. 203–12, p. 204.

9 See, for example, Helen Hall Jennings, 1950, *Leadership and Isolation: A Study of Inter-Personal Relationships*, second edition, London: Longmans, Green & Co.

10 Steven Croft, 2008, *Ministry in Three Dimensions*, second edition, London: Darton, Longman and Todd.

11 Archbishops' Council, 2015, *Senior Church Leadership: A Resource for Reflection*, <https://www.churchofengland.org/sites/default/files/2017-10/senior_church_leadership_faoc.pdf>, accessed 11.09.2025, p. 23.

12 Sharon Tam, 2015, *The Trinitarian Dance*, Eugene, OR: Wipf and Stock, p. 54, Figure 1.

13 Archbishops' Council, *Senior Church Leadership*, p. 26.

14 'Study of the History of Musical Criticism Reveals Reports about Orchestra Conductors to be Approximately 185 Years Old,' in Elliott W. Galkin, 1988, *A History of Orchestral Conducting in Theory and Practice*, New York: Pendragon Press, p. xxiv.

15 Archbishops' Council, *Senior Church Leadership*, p. 26.

16 Ministry Division, 2014, 'Criteria for Selection for the Ordained Ministry of the Church of England, <https://www.churchofengland.org/sites/default/files/2017-10/selection_criteria_for_ordained_ministry.pdf>, accessed 11.09.2025.

17 Church of England, 2017, 'Discerning in Obedience: A Theological Review of the Crown Nominations Commission', <https://www.churchofengland.org/sites/default/files/2018-01/gs-misc-1171-discerning-in-obedience-report-on-the-review-of-the-cnc.pdf>, accessed 11.09.2025, 2.6, p. 7.

18 Church of England, 'Discerning in Obedience', 2.6, p. 6.

19 Church of England, 'Discerning in Obedience', 3.2, p. 11.

20 Church of England, 'Discerning in Obedience', 2.8, p. 7. Emphasis in original.

21 Church of England, 'Discerning in Obedience', 3.9, p. 14.

22 Martyn Percy, 2021, 'Nuts and Bolts' (I): Reflecting on the Governance Review Group Report', *Modern Church*, <https://modernchurch.org.uk/martyn-percy-nuts-and-bolts-i-reflecting-on-the-governance-review-group-report>, accessed 11.09.2025.

23 Church of England, 'Discerning in Obedience', 2.4, p. 6. Emphasis in original.

24 Church of England, 'Discerning in Obedience', 2.7, p. 7.

25 Church of England, 'Discerning in Obedience', 2.11, p. 9.

26 Church of England, 'Discerning in Obedience', 2.11, p. 9.

27 Church of England, 'Discerning in Obedience', 1.3, p. 2.

28 Madeleine Davies, 2022, 'Fewer dioceses, specialist bishops: Archbishops' confidential paper revealed in detail', *Church Times*, <https://www.churchtimes.co.uk/articles/2022/11-february/news/uk/fewer-dioceses-specialist-bishops-archbishops-confidential-paper-revealed-in-detail>, accessed 11.09.2025.

29 Davies, 'Fewer dioceses, specialist bishops'.

8

The Use of Shepherd in the Anglican Ordinals of the British Isles

Thus far it has been clearly established that the bishop has a relational ontology with the rest of the Church, and the characteristic of that relationship has begun to be articulated with reference to the diaconal nature of episcopal ministry. In this chapter that articulation will be furthered through a consideration of the key words and phrases that *CW:OS* uses to describe bishops. The distinctive descriptors are 'shepherd', 'guardian of the faith of the apostles', and 'agent of unity' and the assertion of this chapter is that 'shepherd' is the primary descriptor, in the light of which the other two should be interpreted. Furthermore, it will be shown that 'shepherd' is a particular reference to the biblical understanding of the praxis of shepherding. The use of 'shepherd' in the ordinals of the Church of Ireland, Church in Wales and the Episcopal Church of Scotland will further elicit the use of the term in *CW:OS*.

The introduction to *CW:OS* sets out the three descriptors: the first named in the ordinal is as a 'shepherd of Christ's flock'. It is the term deserving most attention, and the defining characteristic for interpretation of the other descriptors and episcopal ministry in whatever form that may take. Second is in the continuation of the apostolic ministry, 'guardians of the faith of the apostles'. As has been discussed in Chapter 1, this concept is far broader than a mechanistic historical succession from the Apostles. These two aspects are linked with 'and', which connotes both distinction and connection between the two terms. While the link is implied in the sub-clause, 'proclaiming the gospel of God's kingdom and leading his people in mission', it is helpful here to distinguish the two elements to elucidate them more effectively. The third emphasizes the sacramental ministry of the bishop as a servant of God to 'gather God's people and celebrate with them the sacraments of the new covenant' and is therefore an agent of unity, forming the Church into a 'single communion' over time and space (*CW:OS* 55). All these descriptors have a theologically and ecclesial genesis, providing the basis and ontology for a bishop's relationship with the Church and the world.

'Shepherd' and 'shepherding' are significant biblical themes in both the Old and New Testaments, as a metaphor for God's relationship with his people. In the New Testament this metaphor becomes focused on Jesus Christ, as is clear from the Gospels and early mosaics[1] and, in a further development, in 1 Peter 5 when applied to the role of the *episkopos*. It is therefore not surprising that 'shepherd' is the key allegory, metaphor, basis and conceptualization of the role and ministry of a bishop in the ordinals of the Anglican churches of the British Isles. However, perhaps more than many metaphors, it is encumbered by a range of connotations and diverse interpretations that need to be identified and explored so that the helpful and authentic meanings can be separated from the chaff of unhelpful accretions. It is well known that ministry has pastoral, or shepherding, associations, but these are not necessarily well understood or sufficiently emphasized.

The most fundamental question concerns the relationship between a bishop as shepherd and Jesus himself as *the* shepherd. It is vital to identify which aspects of Jesus' shepherd-hood are being claimed for bishops and which should remain unique to Jesus himself. *CW:OS* contains both the potential for a transformative view of bishops, and at the same time would benefit from further development of the biblical background, which itself reflects issues within the Church's understanding of the role, status and place of bishops today. The assertion here is that the emphasis within *CW:OS* resonates with Pope Francis' words to priests on 28 March 2013, 'be shepherds with the smell of sheep'.[2] Central to the paradoxical nature of episcopal ministry is that bishops are both one of the sheep and those who distinctively share in Christ's own shepherding of the flock.

The significance of 'shepherd' in *CW:OS* lies both in its frequency of use and its placement within the text of the liturgy. The term is applied to both priests and bishops at their ordination, and it is in the bishops' rite that the use of the term and identification with the role is at its fullest. Given the cumulative nature of ordinations, all those who are ordained bishop are also priests and it is worth highlighting the usage in the priests' rite. At the ordination of priests, the 'Good Shepherd' is the example on whom the priests should model themselves. Although both John 10.11[3] and 1 Peter 5.1–4[4] are cited in the notes (*CW:OS* 32), there is no explanation of the way in which Jesus should be exemplary, other than the vague 'as their pattern and calling'. Later, in the ordination prayer, the concept is unpacked a little: they 'share as priests in the ministry of the gospel of Christ, the Apostle and High Priest of our faith, and the Shepherd of our souls' (CW:OS 42). The notes here reference 1 Peter 2.25,[5] but again associations are very vague and underdeveloped, not least in terms of whether as priests they actively share in the shepherding, or that their ministry is supportive of Christ's shepherding which he retains uniquely to himself: do the priests bring news of Christ who is the shepherd or actively participate in his shepherding themselves?

In the declarations, the priests are explicitly called 'servants and shepherds', with the notes referencing Ezekiel 34,[6] John 21.16,[7] Acts 20.28[8] and 1 Peter 5.2-4 (CW:OS 36). The terms are significant and given prominence at the beginning of the presiding bishop's address. Attributes are elucidated in the following sentences, but it is unclear whether this is an unpacking of the implication of being a 'servant and shepherd' or whether they are in addition to the initial terms. The prominence of the two terms is undermined by a lack of clarity around their juxtaposition. The text implies that neither is a controlling metaphor, and there may be an aspect here of priests standing between deacons as servants, and bishops as shepherds, and therefore inhabiting an overlapping ministry with elements of both the other orders. Moreover, it is unclear whether this 'and' is intended as a neutral conjunction; as a consolidation or emphasis, with 'shepherd' colouring the type of servanthood to which priests are called; or whether there is tension, paradox or even opposition between the terms, such that shepherds and servants are seen as distinct. It will be demonstrated in Chapter 9 that the biblical perspective naturally sees the terms as eliding, with shepherds being a form of servant, even though there is evidence of the latter in Church reports, as has been noted in previous chapters.

The bishops' rite builds on the analogy of priests as shepherds to make shepherd-hood the controlling metaphor for the ontology of the relationship that the bishop must embody with the other members of the Church. In the introduction of CW:OS, the presiding bishop explains that among the various ministries given by God: 'Bishops are ordained to be shepherds of Christ's flock and guardians of the faith of the apostles, proclaiming the gospel of God's kingdom and leading his people in mission' (CW:OS 55). The meaning of 'and' with regard to 'shepherd' and 'guardian' is unclear: is the guardian role distinct from the shepherd role or an expansion and explication of it? Rather than implying a tension between the servile shepherd and the authority of the guardian, the assertion here is that 'guardian' is a development of the definitive shepherd analogy, and that both require an emphasis on trust and good relationships rather than the power of the bishop over the Church. The paragraph ends with, 'Thus formed into a single communion of faith and love, the Church in each place and time is united with the Church in every place and time' (*CW:OS* 55). The notes highlight 1 Peter 2.9,[9] Exodus 19.6,[10] and Revelation 1.6[11] and 5.10[12] as a biblical basis, but once again there is no clear exegesis of these passages in the text. The metaphor of the shepherd, although controlling, needs greater exegesis[13] in the light of the biblical understanding of the role.

The implication of being a shepherd is returned to throughout the rite. During the declarations, the presiding bishop states: 'With the Shepherd's love, they are to be merciful, but with firmness; to minister discipline, but with compassion' (*CW:OS* 61). Christ is identified by the capital 'S' for 'shepherd' and the notes cite John 10.11–15.[14] However, it is unclear how John 10.11–15 relates to teaching about maintaining discipline and authority over the Church. As will be seen, the meaning of the passage is quite different. In the Ordination Prayer, a new term is introduced, a 'true shepherd', defined as one who 'govern[s] and feed[s] your flock, and leads them in proclaiming the gospel of your salvation in the world' (*CW:OS* 67). The false shepherds are implicit and it is unclear what their definitive characteristic would be. What is significant here is the direct association of the shepherd metaphor with the bishop's role in governance. As will be demonstrated below, governance as 'power over' is incompatible with the role of the shepherd. Rather than governance being an inherent aspect of shepherding, the association of governance and shepherd requires the nature of the governance to be determined by the shepherd metaphor, since a shepherd has no power over the flock; the shepherd's authority depends entirely upon the trust of the sheep.

Similarly, the way in which the shepherd feeds the flock is significant. It is not the case that the shepherd has huge personal stores from which to feed the passive sheep, as could be construed from some modern Western farming practices. To feed the sheep, the shepherd must lead them to the good pastures and through the times of danger. The shepherd has nothing to give except knowledge of the landscape, knowledge of the needs of the sheep, and the trust of the sheep that the shepherd can keep them safe and nourished. This is a significant aspect of the metaphor which, like governing, can be easily misread as implying the bishop's distance from, and power over, the Church. Instead, the hermeneutic of the biblical understanding of shepherding is the lens through which to understand these analogies and to understand the relationship between the bishop and wider Church, as envisaged by the ordinal.

While there is no explicit comment on any ontological change at ordination, there is a clear focus on the new relationship between the bishop and the Church that is established at ordination. At *The Welcome* the congregation states: 'We welcome you as a shepherd of Christ's flock. Build up the Church in unity and love, that the world may believe' (*CW:OS* 68). These few words are the most fruitful and biblically faithful evocation of the bishop as shepherd, drawing on Acts 20.28, 1 Peter 5.2, Ephesians 4.5[15] and John 17.21.[16] Here there is no mention of leadership in terms of power. Instead, the emphasis is on the Church as the flock to be cared for and drawn together by bishops who do so in the light of Jesus' own ministry and relationship with the flock as the Good, or archetypal, Shepherd.

The question of the identity of the flock is significant here: is the flock a synonym for the Church of God, Church of England, or a wider understanding of the people whom Christ has redeemed, including those for whom he died but who are yet to confess their faith in Christ? As will be seen, the bishop as missionary shepherd only makes sense if the flock is conceived of in much wider terms – or even in universal ones – redolent of the Church's historic vision of parochial ministry. The ordinal is not the rite by which someone is installed as bishop of a given diocese; the need of the diocese for a bishop prompts the ordination of a candidate as a bishop in the Church of God, who can then fulfil the role in that diocese. The flock that the ordinal envisages therefore cannot be a specific diocese, but rather refers to the fullness of the Church of God. The flock therefore should be understood in the widest possible terms: as those whom Christ has redeemed. The bishop's rescuing role is to help those who don't recognize that for themselves; those who somehow become detached from the flock and need to be enabled to re-join the flock to which they belong.

As in the priests' rite, in the declarations and the ordination prayer it is Christ who is identified as 'the Good Shepherd' (*CW:OS* 61) and 'Shepherd of our souls' (*CW:OS* 66). The nature of the relationship between Christ's identity as shepherd and the bishop as shepherd is not explained; it is assumed. However, there are many possible ways in which this might be understood, with various possible attributes of Christ's shepherd-hood and the ways in which the bishop's shepherd-hood might reflect that. This is brought into sharp focus when comparing *The Giving of the Pastoral Staff* and *The Welcome*. At *The Giving of the Pastoral*

Staff, the emphasis is on the bishop as shepherd, appointed by the Holy Spirit to be shepherd of the flock and who is exhorted to 'encourage the faithful, restore the lost, build up the Body of Christ' (*CW:OS* 71). However, earlier in the service at *The Welcome*, the emphasis is more clearly on the shepherd-hood of Christ, in which the bishop is one shepherd among many and in which Christ's ownership of the flock is affirmed: 'We welcome you as a shepherd of Christ's flock. Build up the Church in unity and love, that the world may believe' (*CW:OS* 68). There are clear echoes between the passages, voiced by the congregation, but also subtle and significant differences in emphasis as to whether the bishop is primarily among the people, under Christ, emphasizing commonality with the laity as part of the body of Christ; or whether the bishop is a shepherd over the flock in their care, emphasizing a distinction from the laity. It is only by defining the bishop's ontology in the essence of their relationship with the Church that the tension can be reconciled. It is only in understanding what it means for the bishop to be shepherd of the flock that a coherent articulation of the bishop as both one with the flock, yet distinctive within the flock, can be maintained.

The Scottish ordinal is much more careful and clearer that it is Christ who is the shepherd: 'There is one Shepherd, at whose call bishops seek to know his flock and be known by them.'[17] This emphasis is reinforced at the ordination prayer which asks for 'authority to shepherd your flock'. However, not only is Christ's ownership of the flock affirmed; the use of the verb 'to shepherd' is also significant, indicating the bishop's role in assisting Christ, who is the shepherd of the flock, as opposed to identifying the bishop themselves as the shepherd. The emphasis is very much on the relationship between Christ and his flock, and the bishop's personal relationship with the flock of which he or she is very much a part. Christ retains the direct shepherding of the flock.

The Welsh ordinal defines bishops as 'shepherds', and in the introduction identifies Jesus as the Good Shepherd. However, the connection is as obscure as it is in *CW:OS*. The presiding bishop instructs the bishop to be 'mindful of the Good Shepherd'.[18] At the Ordination Prayer the term 'true shepherd' is used, as in *CW:OS*, but it is defined differently as 'care for your people' and leadership 'in proclaiming the saving gospel of your love'.[19] Here the emphasis on pastoral care as opposed to governance is marked and significant. Furthermore, the bishop's relationship with Christ is articulated at the charge, which encourages daily renewal of vocation that 'you may follow the Good Shepherd wherever he leads'.[20] It is in Jesus, the Good Shepherd's name, that the bishop is sent out,[21] again affirming the bishop's identity with the flock, under Christ.

The term 'true shepherd' also introduces the possibility that not all shepherds will live up to their calling. The emphasis in *CW:OS* on governance directs the potential for failings in the shepherd in that direction. The emphasis in the Welsh ordinal is much more clearly pastoral: the false shepherd fails to care for the sheep appropriately. This is highlighted in comparison to The Church of Ireland Order Two which affirms, in the ordination prayer, that the 'true shepherd' is to 'feed and govern the flock'.[22] No exegesis of the shepherd metaphor is offered, although its connection to governance is again affirmed at the giving of the pastoral staff, where the bishop as shepherd is encouraged to look forward to receiving the 'unfading crown of glory' from Christ, the 'Chief Shepherd'.[23]

None of the contemporary language ordinals in the British Isles maintains the stark words of the *BCP 1662*: 'Be to the flock of Christ a shepherd, not a wolf; feed them, devour them not' (*BCP 1662* 108).[24] Although the bishop is 'a' shepherd, it is in the context of the shepherd-hood of Christ: this is Christ's flock, which the bishop is to help care for. The contrast with the wolf could not be sharper. The bishop might not just fail to live up to the high ideals of Christ's shepherding. He or she may well end up being the very source of danger from which Christ is protecting the sheep, echoing Jesus' warning about the hired hands in John's Gospel (John 10.12).

The term 'shepherd' is so loaded because of its ecclesiological and Christological significance. In a society in which shepherding is at best a marginal pursuit, outside of the experience of the vast majority of the population, its theological use becomes grounded in Christology, completely disconnected from any lived experience. Whereas first-century shepherds were understood in humble terms, the shepherd-hood of the bishop is defined solely in terms of Christ's own shepherd-hood, with attendant Christological associations. To describe a bishop as a shepherd therefore is to identify them as being 'Christ-like'. While Christology is varied and ultimately rooted in Christ's sacrificial self-giving, there is also an attendant connotation of Christ who is divine and other. Unmoored from its practical and historical roots, the term 'shepherd', unless carefully couched and explained, is readily misconstrued to connote authority over, and distinction from, rather than humble attraction to and identification with.

The term 'pastor' is less tied in that way: with pastoral care being widely understood as care for people. *CW:OS*, the Welsh and Scottish ordinals, and the Irish Order Two, all describe the bishop as chief pastor. In *CW:OS* this defines the bishop in terms of the relationship with the presbyterate: 'As chief pastors, it is their duty to share with their fellow presbyters the oversight of the Church, speaking in the name of God and expounding the gospel of salvation' (*CW:OS* 61). The reference is to Canon C 18.1, and demonstrates the shared responsibility of the bishop as *primus inter pares*. However, the emphasis on the bishop's primacy as chief pastor among other pastors is congruent with, and opens the possibility of, notions of hierarchy over the Church. For the Welsh and Scottish ordinals, the term applies to the bishop's care for the whole Church, with the Welsh ordinal[25] emphasizing unity, but it is in the Scottish ordinal that the pastoral care of the bishop is most clear: 'Will you, as chief priest and pastor, encourage and support all the baptized in their gifts and ministries, nourish them out of the riches of God's grace, pray for them and celebrate with them the sacraments of our redemption?'[26] Here, 'chief pastor' emphasizes the bishop's responsibility for care of the whole body of the Church, establishing a new relationship between the bishop and all of the Church.

The dichotomy of the shepherd as governor and pastor is made manifest in the pastoral staff, the ultimate symbol of the bishop as shepherd, and key symbol of the bishop's office. As will be shown in Chapter 10, the shepherd's crook is primarily an instrument of rescue, to bring the lost sheep back, and draw them out of danger. However, it can also have a ritualized form, acting as a symbol of authority, the equivalent of the monarch's sceptre. In both the Scottish and Welsh ordinals, the words accompanying the giving of the staff emphasize the care that the bishop must show: 'care for the flock of Christ'.[27] 'Keep watch over the flock of Christ which has been entrusted to your care.'[28] Unlike the Welsh and Scottish ordinals, pastoral care is not explicitly mentioned in *CW:OS*: 'Keep watch over the whole flock ... Restore the lost' (*CW:OS* 71). Taken in isolation, there is some ambiguity about the way in which the watch will be kept, whether it be based in the authority over or care for. Hence it is vital to ground this reference in the ontology of biblical understanding of shepherding to understand properly the pastoral paradigm.

'Shepherd', like all metaphors, is polyvalent and there is evidence of this in *CW:OS* and in other Anglican ordinals of the British Isles. *CW:OS* fails to make the analogy clear, and in particular the way in which a bishop's shepherd-hood relates to that of Christ is not explained. Therefore the text, more so than other ordinals, could be misunderstood as describing shepherd-hood as authority over, and distinction from, the rest of the flock. Not only would this be at variance with the biblical understanding of the shepherd but would also fundamentally undermine the nature of the relationship that is understood and established in the ordination rite. The relationship is based on pastoral care of the body of Christ by the bishop and trust in the bishop by the Church community.

The possibility of misinterpretation is realized in the Revision Committee, in January 2005, responding to comments on the proposed *Common Worship* ordinal made by members of General Synod. They note the request to delete references to governance:

> We have rejected a proposal to delete 'and govern' ... 'Governing' is part of the office of a bishop (the 1662 Ordinal says that those ordained bishop are admitted 'to Government in the Church of Christ'), and 'govern' (from *gubernare*, to steer) is an appropriate word to use of a shepherd shepherding his flock. The shepherd kings were to rule compassionately, but they were nonetheless to rule (and Psalm 2.10 speaks of a 'rod of iron').[29]

While the report notes the importance of the shepherd as 'teacher'[30] and 'missionary',[31] and pastor,[32] which may be congruent with an emphasis on pastoral care, it is the reference to the 'rod of iron' as an instrument of control over the flock and also the prominence given to the shepherd kings that indicate the presence of misunderstandings; these will be explored further in the next chapter. Although the reference to the rod of iron is not itself in the ordinal, its presence in the comments of the Revision Committee demonstrates the prevalence of this damaging misunderstanding. A careful reading of the biblical use of the analogy in both Old and New Testaments not only furnishes a clearer understanding of the intended meaning of the shepherd analogy, but also makes clear both that the authoritarian use of the rod of iron is a misunderstanding, and also that this misunderstanding actively undermines and erodes the relationship that the ordinal establishes between the bishop and the rest of the Church.

Notes

1 See, for example, Jill Caskey et al., 'Mausoleum of Galla Placidia' in *Art and Architecture of the Middle Ages: Exploring a Connected World*, Ithaca, NY: Cornell University Press, <https://artofthemiddleages.com/s/main/item/90>, accessed 05.08.2025.

2 Catholic Telegraph, 2013, 'Pope Francis: priests should be "shepherds living with the smell of the sheep"', <https://www.thecatholictelegraph.com/pope-francis-priests-should-be-shepherds-living-with-the-smell-of-the-sheep/13439>, accessed 11.09.2025.

3 'I am the good shepherd. The good shepherd lays down his life for the sheep' (John 10.11).

4 'Now as an elder myself and a witness of the sufferings of Christ, as well as one who shares in the glory to be revealed, I exhort the elders among you to tend the flock of God that is in your charge, exercising the oversight, not under compulsion but willingly, as God would have you do it – not for sordid gain but eagerly. Do not lord it over those in your charge, but be examples to the flock. And when the chief shepherd appears, you will win the crown of glory that never fades away' (1 Pet. 5.1–4).

5 'For you were going astray like sheep, but now you have returned to the shepherd and guardian of your souls' (1 Pet. 2.25).

6 For example, vv. 11–12, 'For thus says the Lord God: I myself will search for my sheep, and will seek them out. As shepherds seek out their flocks when they are among their scattered sheep, so I will seek out my sheep. I will rescue them from all the places to which they have been scattered on a day of clouds and thick darkness' (Ezek. 34.11–12).

7 'A second time [Jesus] said to him, "Simon son of John, do you love me?" He said to him, "Yes, Lord; you know that I love you." Jesus said to him, "Tend my sheep"' (John 21.16).

8 'Keep watch over yourselves and over all the flock, of which the Holy Spirit has made you overseers, to shepherd the church of God that he obtained with the blood of his own Son' (Acts 20.28).

9 'But you are a chosen race, a royal priesthood, a holy nation, God's own people, in order that you may proclaim the mighty acts of him who called you out of darkness into his marvellous light'(1 Pet. 2.9).

10 'but you shall be for me a priestly kingdom and a holy nation. These are the words that you shall speak to the Israelites' (Exod. 19.6).

11 'and made us to be a kingdom, priests serving his God and Father, to him be glory and dominion for ever and ever. Amen' (Rev. 1.6).

12 'you have made them to be a kingdom and priests serving our God, and they will reign on earth' (Rev. 5.10).

13 While it is unsurprising that the text does not offer significant commentary on the biblical passages, the point here is that the term 'shepherd' in particular has become separated from its generative context and therefore its meaning is unclear to the contemporary reader. Even those involved in modern agriculture wouldn't make the connections originally intended. It is therefore highly unlikely that the day-to-day ministry of a bishop will be determined, as it should be, by the ordinal's description of them as a shepherd.

14 'I am the good shepherd. The good shepherd lays down his life for the sheep. The hired hand, who is not the shepherd and does not own the sheep, sees the wolf coming and leaves the sheep and runs away – and the wolf snatches them and scatters them. The hired hand runs away because a hired hand does not care for the sheep. I am the good shepherd. I know my own and my own know me, just as the Father knows me and I know the Father. And I lay down my life for the sheep' (John 10.11–15).

15 'one Lord, one faith, one baptism' (Eph. 4.5).

16 'that they may all be one. As you, Father, are in me and I am in you, may they also be in us, so that the world may believe that you have sent me' (John 17.21).

17 The Scottish Episcopal Church, 'Scottish Ordinal 1984', <https://www.scotland.anglican.org/who-we-are/publications/liturgies/scottish-ordinal-1984/>, p. 5, accessed 11.09.2025.

18 The Church in Wales, 'Alternative Ordinal', <https://churchinwales.contentfiles.net/media/documents/Alternative_Ordinal_-_2004.pdf>, p. 37, accessed 11.09.2025.

19 The Church in Wales, 'Alternative Ordinal', p. 41.

20 The Church in Wales, 'Alternative Ordinal', p. 17.

21 The Church in Wales, 'Alternative Ordinal', p. 37.

22 The Church of Ireland, 'The Ordination or Consecration of a Bishop', <https://www.ireland.anglican.org/cmsfiles/files/worship/pdf/Ord2Bish.pdf>, p. 582, accessed 11.09.2025.

23 The Church of Ireland, 'The Ordination or Consecration of a Bishop', p. 584.

24 The Irish ordinal maintains the exhortation in the traditional language, Order One. However, it is with Order Two that the natural comparison with *CW:OS* is to be made. It is interesting that this is said at the handing over of the Bible rather than the pastoral staff, the *traditio instrumentorum* having been removed from the liturgy. The Church of Ireland, 'The Form of Ordaining or Consecrating an Archbishop or Bishop', https://www.ireland.anglican.org/cmsfiles/files/worship/pdf/Ord1Bish.pdf, p. 549, accessed 11.09.2025.

25 The Church in Wales, 'Alternative Ordinal', p. 39.

26 The Scottish Episcopal Church, 'Scottish Ordinal 1984', p. 6.

27 The Scottish Episcopal Church, 'Scottish Ordinal 1984', p. 9.

28 The Church in Wales, 'Alternative Ordinal', p. 43.

29 Revision Committee, Ordination Service Report January 2005, p. 33, #133. The citation here is incorrect; the reference to the rod of iron is in verse 9.

30 Revision Committee, Ordination Service Report January 2005, p. 25.

31 Revision Committee, Ordination Service Report January 2005, p. 23.

32 Revision Committee, Ordination Service Report January 2005, p. 22.

9

Shepherd in the Bible and Ancient Near Eastern Culture

In the previous chapter, the significance of the term 'shepherd' in *CW:OS* as a descriptor of episcopal ministry was clearly established. Here it will be argued that 'shepherd' should be understood in its biblical context. A key text for unlocking the biblical narrative around the term 'shepherd' is Kenneth E. Bailey's magisterial *The Good Shepherd: A Thousand-Year Journey from Psalm 23 to the New Testament*. As in the ordinal, for Bailey, the evolution of the use of the shepherd analogy through the Old and New Testaments[1] results in the deliberate choice of the analogy in 1 Peter 5 as the defining characteristic of a Christian leader. Bailey notes that the author:

> does not reflect on a centurion and his soldiers, a master builder and his stone masons, a sea captain and his sailors or a governor and his administrative staff. Instead he turns to the picture of a shepherd and his flock.[2]

The choice of shepherd is not a given. When chosen, it had a pragmatic application, so the way in which first-century shepherds shepherded matters.[3] Shepherd is chosen as opposed to any of the other potential models of leadership open to the author of 1 Peter: it is not the necessary or obvious choice and furthermore it is the biblical, pastoral model of the shepherd that is significant in Jesus' own self-identification – for example, in John 10.1–18. The shepherd analogy defines the Christology, and hence ecclesiology, rather than Christology defining the use of shepherd. The choice of the powerless, caregiving shepherd is distinctive both for Christology and the understanding of the relationship between the bishop and the Church. Thus Christopher J. H. Wright's assertions about the use of shepherd for Israelite kings are equally applicable to bishops as shepherds:

> At the human level, shepherds had very responsible and arduous jobs but a comparatively lowly social status. Applied to kings, the comparison was a powerful reminder of the duties, not the glories, of kingship. The king was to see that justice was done among his people – God's idea of justice ..., which operated especially on behalf of the poor and downtrodden.[4]

In order to explore this further, three significantly erroneous understandings of shepherding in *CW:OS* need to be addressed: the rod of iron, the glory of the shepherd, and the shepherd as monarch.

The rod of iron is also mentioned in the key biblical shepherd text: Psalm 23. Meshach Paul Krikorian explains:

> The [rod] is a club about three feet long, ending invariably with a knob about the size of a human fist. Sometimes metals and nails are driven in the end to make the instrument more menacing. One good blow from it will kill or cripple to utter disability almost any ferocious animal, including the bear or the lion, that may endanger the safety of the sheep ... So, the sheep have learned to fear no evil, for the shepherd is there with his staff to support and defend them tenderly and protect them against all harm.[5]

It is therefore not at all intended as a way to discipline the flock. The only use of it directly on the flock was to help with counting the sheep in at the end of the day, held horizontally across the door of the fold.[6] Thus the rod is all about protecting the flock from external threat and helping to identify any sheep who may be lost. Even this offensive weapon speaks of the pastoral care of the sheep. As Bailey notes:

> The good shepherd does not direct his sheep with a stick and a bag full of stones gathered to arm his sling and drive them in the desired direction. Rather he leads them from the front with a gentle call, inviting the sheep to follow him.[7]

Moreover, the pastoral staff is not an offensive weapon to be used against the sheep but as a tool of rescue. It is directed towards the flock 'to *gently assist the flock* in its daily grazing'.[8] The crook is to help release sheep that have been trapped in a crevice or thorn bush. The rod and staff therefore both speak of the shepherd's care and even love of the flock; neither is a tool of authority and control over the flock. In fact, the shepherd has no *ex officio* authority over the sheep, and no tool to insist on their conformity. The shepherd relies on the trust that the sheep have for him or her: the sheep know the shepherd's voice and follow of their own free will.

Second, one of the issues with Christological titles is that they have a tendency to bleed into one another: they describe the same Christ and so Christ the shepherd becomes overlaid with connotations of Christ in glory or Christ as pantocrator, for instance. Thus there is a danger that bishop, as shepherd, accrues to himself or herself aspects of other Christological titles which are wholly inappropriate. Key here are the concepts of honour and glory, both mentioned in 1 Peter 5.1–4. As Bailey notes, 'When we discuss "glory" in Scripture (Hebrew or Greek), we are discussing *weight* and *wisdom*, not *earthly power and wealth* … The true glory of God shines forth through the weakness and suffering of the cross.'[9] The 'crown of glory' in 1 Peter 5.4 is therefore not a magnification of the honour given bishops in this life, but an eschatological glory that, in Pauline terms, is 'not built on splendour and acclaim, but on "the wisdom of God" that will be revealed to believers at the end (1 Cor 2.7)'.[10] Here again, the glory of the shepherd is both a reflected glory from God, not intrinsic to themselves, and also a glory that stems from the way in which they inhabit the wisdom and gravitas of God. In short, the glory does not come from the office – shepherding has no intrinsic glory, but the good shepherd's glory comes from their ability as a shepherd. It is not therefore that the office of bishop should have glory and wisdom, but it is the sort of people who humbly exhibit these qualities that the Church should be encouraging and facilitating as its bishops; those who bring glory to the office of bishop.

These two errors come together in seeing the shepherd as a monarch. Monarch shepherds do form part of the biblical narrative, but it is their shepherd-hood that informs their rule as monarch, not an intrinsic link between shepherding and monarchy. Study of the biblical text reveals the extent of the perversion involved in the Church's implicit, and in places explicit, readiness to attribute monarchical associations to the bishops through use of the shepherd analogy. For the biblical narrative, the intuitive understanding is that the monarch is the antithesis of shepherding, and the association of the terms is intended to be inherently arresting. Thus, in Mark 6, Jesus the Good Shepherd is juxtaposed with Herod who relies on the authority of being a monarch and fails to care for those for whom he has responsibility. Bailey explains:

> The good shepherd takes over after the failures of the bad shepherd to care for his flock. Herod fed the rich and powerful while Jesus feeds the common folk. The first became the *banquet of death*; the second turns into a *banquet of life*.[11]

Jesus the Good Shepherd is not identified as a monarch. Instead, he demonstrates the authenticity and goodness of his shepherding in stark contrast to the monarch of his time. In being the Good Shepherd, Jesus 'deliberately set aside all violent options',[12] and so inherent in the shepherd paradigm is a determination not to use force or violence on the sheep.

Like the shepherd in Psalm 23, Jesus does not control the sheep, but draws them to himself because they trust him; he provides for their needs of food, water and safety, as Bailey affirms: 'There is no hint of any need for power or control.'[13] 'Without hesitation, the sheep confidently follow the shepherd, knowing that with him in the lead all will be well.'[14] The shepherd can no more make the sheep lie down in green pastures, than one can force a horse to drink from the trough. W. Phillip Keller explains:

> The strange thing about sheep is that because of their very makeup it is almost impossible for them to be made to lie down unless four requirements are met. Owing to their timidity they refuse to lie down unless they are free of all fear. Because of the social behaviour within a flock, sheep will not lie down unless they are free from friction with others of their kind. If tormented by flies or parasites, sheep will not lie down. Only when free of these pests can they relax. Lastly, sheep will not lie down as long as they feel in need of finding feed. They must be free from hunger.[15]

It is the trust of the sheep in the shepherd that keeps them safe, and it is only because they know and trust the shepherd so well that the shepherd is able to lead them and keep them safe from threat and from wandering off after strangers.[16] To identify a bishop as a shepherd is therefore not to emphasize their sole leadership of the flock as monarch, but rather to demonstrate the form of humble, powerless leadership that the shepherd has over the sheep: the only influence the shepherd has is through the sheep's trust and the shepherd's ability to build on that trust by meeting the needs of the sheep.

However, the most perilous association of the shepherd is the description of God himself as Shepherd of Israel. This is the foundational understanding of Psalm 23.1, 'The Lord is my shepherd'. It is not so much that shepherds inherently reflect God's way of being, or that there is a useful analogy in the way shepherds shepherd that helps elucidate the way in which God is with his people; this is about God's direct relationship with his people. The ontological difference cannot be overplayed: as much as the humanity of shepherd is distinct from the animal nature of the sheep, so God is by nature a divine leader of his people. Thus Ezekiel, in Chapter 34, 'is confident that a human shepherd cannot accomplish these tasks; only a divine shepherd can manage'.[17] When Psalm 23 affirms 'the Lord is my shepherd', the tacit implication is that God is the shepherd who succeeds where other human shepherds have failed. Theologically, spiritually and practically, therefore, the significance of God in Christ as the archetypal shepherd is key for the relationship between the bishop and the Church. Christ's active shepherding over the whole body, the fullness of the Church, including the bishops, is what prevents the bishop from becoming distanced from the other members of the Church and undermines the potential for a *cursus honorum* in the orders of the Church. Under Christ, the bishop must have a close pastoral relationship with the rest of the Church if they are to inhabit the relationship established at ordination.

This is not to say that there is no place for the bishop to have influence. The bishop as shepherd is one who leads the people through adversity, as Bailey explains: 'When in trouble, this person will be able to help you solve your problems. Their thoughts are deep and balanced. When all hell breaks loose he or she will know what to do.'[18] The shepherd therefore has no authority beyond the trust that he or she engenders in the flock. To call bishops 'shepherds' is to undermine the desire to rest on the authority of the role. It is the trust in the person who inhabits the role that gives the bishop authority. The bishop is the one who enters the danger first, and who through experience, faith, and care of the flock is trusted to bring them through.

Just as the flock is led through the valley of the shadow of death in Psalm 23, Christ's distinctive shepherd-hood sees him leading his flock through death itself on the cross. Just as a shepherd builds trust with the flock by leading them through lesser danger, before they will trust the shepherd in greater danger, so too Christ's sacrificial leadership is not in isolation on the cross, but as a fulfilment of a self-sacrificial ministry. Enlarging on Peter's self-description, Bailey explains:

> In short, Peter saw Jesus suffer painful rejection, and also saw how Jesus *responded* to that rejection. As a member of the apostolic band, Peter was united with Christ in that suffering. He watched how Jesus dealt with 'the agony of rejected love' and that agony became Peter's agony.[19]

Rather than being trusted as one who manages to avoid controversy and keep their 'hands clean', the bishop as shepherd is one who leads into danger as part of the body of Christ, confident that it is Christ who truly leads the way and will bring the flock safely through. The bishop as shepherd is an incarnational minister, who in Henry Scott Holland's famous sentiment has a care for drains.[20] This is the essence, although implicit in the bishops' rite of CW:OS, of the sequential ordination. To be a bishop is not to have moved beyond being a deacon, but rather diaconal ministry is an essential aspect of the bishop's ministry: the bishop cannot be a bishop without first being a deacon. It is one of the more significant shortcomings of the bishops' rite in CW:OS that this is not made explicit.

The bishop as shepherd is one who has a strong connection with the other members of the Church, and it is in their inhabiting of their identity as one of the baptized that their ministry is rooted: 'Through baptism and faith they were united with him and his life produced in them the power to reprocess their suffering into glory/gravitas.'[21] The first task of the shepherd is to understand the needs and fears of sheep, so that, in thinking like the sheep do, the shepherd can build the relationship of trust with the sheep that is needed to shepherd effectively. The bishop has the advantage of already being a member of the baptized, deacon and priest, and their effective ministry as a bishop is not in forsaking these aspects of their Christian life but in being able to reconnect with them and identify with the variety of people within the life of the Church.

Moreover, within the diversity of the Church there will be many different life experiences of which the bishop will have no personal experience, and essential to the bishop's good relationship with the flock is their ability to be humble, like the shepherd before the sheep, and learn from them and understand the world from a variety of perspectives. The bishop as shepherd is therefore far from the pomp of the mitred, or even a qualified leader. He or she is much closer to the example of Nelson Mandela whose prison sufferings were described by Desmond Tutu. Thus, Bailey explains:

> In the crucible of his soul, Mandela transformed his suffering into gravitas (*kabod*). He managed to reprocess his anger into grace, and that grace flowed from his life into the life of his nation and out into the wider world.[22]

The bishop is one who is able to identify with the other members of the Church, and build a relationship of trust in which they recognize the bishop's care for them and offer the bishop their trust and willingness to follow where the bishop leads: inherent in this is not the bishop's ability to distinguish him or herself from others, but to identify with and emphasize the closeness of the relationship they have with the whole Church, and in particular their readiness to share in the sufferings of the shepherd. In this way, Bailey describes the shepherd as a 'weighty' person:

> In Middle Eastern culture, a 'weighty' person (*rajul thaqil*) has to do with wisdom, balance, stability, reliability, sound judgement, patience, impartiality, nobility and the like ... Every family, community and church desperately wants and needs such a person to guide them, comfort them and help them solve their problems.[23]

The extent of the shepherd's love for the flock means that they are prepared to endure sufferings and hardships for the sake of the sheep. The nature of the relationship means that suffering is not an additional aspect of being a shepherd that may need to be endured from time to time, but rather that it is an integral part of what it means to be a shepherd. Thus, Psalm 23 couches the suffering of the shepherd in terms of their own integrity, 'which he will not violate'.[24] The external sufferings that the shepherd endures are therefore manifestations of the intrinsic readiness of the shepherd to suffer for the sheep because of their love for them. The shepherd is therefore different to the hired hand, whose primary interest is his or her own preferment and wealth, as Jesus explains in John 10.12. The dangers to the sheep come from thieves who steal, strangers who lead astray, wolves who devour, and hired hands who lack integrity and lack in care for the sheep.[25] The bishop as shepherd is realistic about the dangers and is prepared to lead the sheep through them in hope of resurrection. Bailey movingly quotes Matta al-Miskin, 'They loved because they felt his love for them.'[26] Once again it is pastoral care that is emphasized as the key attribute of the shepherd: the people trust and follow the bishop because they experience him or her as trustworthy and they know that the bishop loves them, being motivated by what is in the flock's best interests.

The care of the shepherd is for the flock. Bailey opens the question about whether the flock are limited to the baptized, quoting a pastor's view of non-Christians: 'Oh they are all my people, it is just that some of them don't know it yet.'[27] Here there is an important dissonance between the missionary bishop as shepherd and as fisherman. Both terms are authentic to the New Testament, but it is noticeable that while used of the Disciples – for example, in Matthew 4.19 – the epistles do not refer to the early church leaders as fishermen. There are two key differences between the shepherding of the flock and catching fish. First, fishing is not in the fishes' best interests, because they are literally food for others, whereas shepherding is in the best interests of the sheep: it is how they are cared for and nourished. Second, the fish are 'out there' and have to be brought in forcibly, against their will, whereas the shepherd has care over the sheep who are already in the flock and respond willingly and trustingly to the shepherd's leadership. In a time of heightened awareness of mission in the Church, it is important to note that describing a bishop's missionary activity in terms of the shepherd has significant, if unrealized, connotations. The sheep are already part of the flock: this is not about proselytizing, but relates to personal care for the sheep who has wandered off or got stuck and so has become separated from the flock. The shepherd doesn't have a net to throw over the sheep, but only their trusted call and, if necessary, the staff to help the sheep who wants to be rescued but is stuck. The question therefore is not so much 'catching' people as caring for people in such a way that they re-join the flock of which they are already a part: theologically the bishop as shepherd is going out to the lost sheep of the house of Israel,[28] making visible the redemption that Christ the true shepherd has already achieved.

The shepherd's care for the flock is therefore characterized by the personal care that the shepherd has for each and every sheep, rather than over the flock as a whole. This is the emphasis of both Psalm 23 and the Gospels. Psalm 23 is a personal account by the Psalmist in the first-person singular. In the Gospels, the shepherd's care of the individual is demonstrated by the shepherd's willingness to risk the flock by going in search of the one lost sheep. Bailey, drawing on the explanation of Andrew Roy, elucidates this for the individual as care for the flock: the good shepherd does not care for the flock *per se*; he or she cares for each sheep. Thus 'By going after the *one* Jesus gave the *herd* boundless security in that each of them knew "If I get lost he will come after me".'[29]

The bishop as shepherd cares not for the Church's reputation or the survival of the institution, but for each member of the Church in his or her care: 'The parable of Jesus is a bold and daring statement affirming the worth of the one, *even when lost*, and the willingness of the good shepherd to expose the flock to danger in order to seek that flawed "little one".'[30] The relationship has marital overtones, and the bishop is called to show a love towards the sheep that is close and personal, reflecting the close personal love between the Father and the Son, which Jesus demonstrates on the cross.[31] The bishop-as-shepherd's leadership is not to be seen in overarching visions, strategies and programmes for the diocese, but rather in attentive care for the flock when they're in trouble. There is a strong mutual trust: by the bishop that the people are capable of getting on with being Church, and by the people that the bishop will care for them and lead them through difficulty. Here it is important to note Valentine Muller's affirmation of the prehistory of the Good Shepherd as one who has pastoral care, rather than one who bears a sacrificial lamb:

> It seems likely that some oriental deities dating from imperial times must be interpreted as caretakers and not sacrificers ... It is obvious that the Christian Good Shepherd follows the oriental branch in regard to meaning, but with modification. The caretaking is intensified to redemption.[32]

This is in sharp contrast to the bad shepherds, who bring death and destruction: 'starting with Jeremiah 23, the bad shepherd destroys everything'.[33] The destruction, as already seen, comes through self-interest, typified by the monarch and the hired hand, which prevents them from offering the costly love required of the good shepherd. But the failures of the shepherd can go further, and 1 Peter 5.2 speaks of *aischrokerdos*, which Bailey renders 'money acquired in shameful ways'.[34] The false shepherd not only neglects their duty, but they also actively seek their own betterment at the expense of the sheep they were meant to be caring for. The false shepherd's lack of care for the sheep manifests itself in a lack of pastoral care and the embodiment of a lack of love: they develop a 'domineering style';[35] 'These shepherds are "in it for the money" and bully the sheep rather than lead them by example.'[36] This is the moment at which the primary function of the shepherd moves from care to governance: the shepherd should not primarily be interested in building and maintaining their authority over the sheep, but in the relationship with the sheep as a trusted leader. The bishop as shepherd connotes one who, following Christ's example, lays down the tools of coercion and relies completely on building a strength of relationship with each of the sheep that they not only trust but love him or her sufficiently to follow of their own volition.

The shepherd's relationship with the sheep therefore needs to be particularly close; the sheep need to know the shepherd and the shepherd needs to know the sheep. Bailey explains:

> The shepherd must lead the flock, but needs to do so willingly, spontaneously, and not because of external pressure. It is not an easy life, but when there is a deep love for the sheep it is a joyful calling. 'As God would have you do it' rings with the references to God as good shepherd that appear all throughout the tradition.[37]

The theological and therefore primary motivation for bishops daring to adopt this leadership style is because it is the way of God: 'The movement from "the good shepherd is God" to "the good shepherd is Jesus" and finally "the good shepherd is a model for church elders" is clear and unmistakeable.'[38] Thus the bishop as shepherd both emulates and communicates the love of God in their leadership of each of the people entrusted to their care. It is a relationship in which both bishop and people grow in love, for one another and in their capacity to love. It is also therefore a relationship in which the bishop is ready to suffer for the body of Christ because of their love for them, and in which others in the Church are ready to follow the bishop's lead through hardship, trusting that the bishop will lead them to where their needs can be met. This is the way in which the shepherd is the hallmark of Christian leadership, based in the costly personal love that is the hallmark of the Good Shepherd.

In identifying bishops as shepherds, CW:OS draws on a firm biblical and historical basis for Christian leadership, which has a distinctive Christian character. Although CW:OS fails to make the richness of that heritage sufficiently explicit, it is this biblical basis that must be the hermeneutic for reading the text. That there is an opportunity for misconception about the shepherd analogy is evident in the discussions at the preparation of the ordinal, where it is equated with power and authority over the Church. Theologically, it is Jesus as the Good Shepherd who provides not just the example for bishops, but the context in which they establish their pastoral relationship with the other members of the Church, emphasizing the importance of the bishop's identification with the whole Church, under the active shepherding of Christ. Walter Brueggemann affirms the direct shepherd-hood of Yahweh:

> The image evokes a wise, caring, attentive agent who watches over, guards, feeds, and protects a flock that is vulnerable, exposed, dependent, and in need of such help ... The work of the shepherd Yahweh is to gather the sheep in safety, often when they are exposed to serious danger.[39]

In these terms, shepherding is the antithesis of the power and authority of the monarchical bishop. As shepherd, the bishop guides (governs) with love and personal knowledge of the people, who follow where he or she leads not because they are under any compulsion to do so, but because they want to in response to what the bishop has done for them and most significantly, the bishop does so in the context of God's own primacy as shepherd of his people.

Notes

1 For an overview of the shepherd motif in the Ancient Near East, see Jack W. Vancil, 1992, 'Sheep, Shepherd' in Noel Freedman (ed.), *Anchor Bible Dictionary*, vol. 5, New York: Doubleday, pp. 1187–90.

2 Kenneth E. Bailey, 2015, *The Good Shepherd: A Thousand-Year Journey from Psalm 23 to the New Testament*, London: SPCK, p. 250.

3 Also significant and importantly congruent with Bailey's emphases is the prehistory of the shepherd analogy. For a discussion of this, see Valentine Muller, 1944, 'The Prehistory of the "Good Shepherd"', *Journal of Near Eastern Studies*, 3 (2), pp. 87–90.

4 Christopher J. H. Wright, 2004, *Old Testament Ethics for the People of God*, Leicester: Inter-Varsity Press, p. 233.

5 Meshach Paul Krikorian, 1999, 'The Spirit of the Shepherd: An Interpretation of the Psalm Immortal' in Miriam Taylor Wert, *Meshach Paul Krikorian*, Nappanee, IN: Evangel Press, p. 179. It's important to note that Krikorian identifies the 'rod' as the pastoral staff and the 'staff' as the offensive weapon, so in the above quotation 'staff' has been changed to 'rod' to avoid confusion.

6 Bailey, *The Good Shepherd*, p. 51.

7 Bailey, *The Good Shepherd*, p. 265.

8 Bailey, *The Good Shepherd*, p. 53.

9 Bailey, *The Good Shepherd*, p. 257.

10 Bailey, *The Good Shepherd*, p. 265. Cf. Edward G. Selwyn: 'The Reward of the Faithful and Humble Minister is that He Will be Given a Share in the Glory and

Joy of his Lord' in Edward G. Selwyn, 1947, *The First Epistle of St Peter*, London: Macmillan, p. 233.

11 Bailey, *The Good Shepherd*, p. 171.
12 Bailey, *The Good Shepherd*, p. 176.
13 Bailey, *The Good Shepherd*, p. 39.
14 Bailey, *The Good Shepherd*, p. 38.
15 W. Peter Keller, 1970, *A Shepherd Looks at Psalm 23*, Grands Rapids, MI: Zondervan, pp. 41–2.
16 Bailey, *The Good Shepherd*, p. 219.
17 Bailey, *The Good Shepherd*, p. 89.
18 Bailey, *The Good Shepherd*, p. 259.
19 Bailey, *The Good Shepherd*, p. 258.
20 Michael Wheeler, 2018, 'Much more than nothing at all – Henry Scott Holland', *Church Times*, <https://www.churchtimes.co.uk/articles/2018/8-june/faith/faith-features/much-more-than-nothing-at-all-henry-scott-holland>, accessed 11.09.2025.
21 Bailey, *The Good Shepherd*, p. 262.
22 Bailey, *The Good Shepherd*, p. 260.
23 Kenneth E. Bailey, 2011, *Paul Through Mediterranean Eyes*, London: SPCK, pp. 110–11.
24 Bailey, *The Good Shepherd*, p. 46.
25 Cf. the introduction of care in the shepherd theme in Zechariah 10.2–12. Bailey, *The Good Shepherd*, p. 99.
26 Bailey, *The Good Shepherd*, p. 115, quoting Matta al-Miskin, 1998, *The Gospel According to Saint Luke* (Arabic), Cairo: Dayr al-Qiddis Anba Maqar, p. 568.
27 Bailey, *The Good Shepherd*, p. 237.
28 Cf. Matthew 15.24 '[Jesus] answered, "I was sent only to the lost sheep of the house of Israel."'
29 Bailey, *The Good Shepherd*, p. 200.
30 Bailey, *The Good Shepherd*, p. 201.
31 Bailey, *The Good Shepherd*, p. 230.
32 Muller, 1944, 'The Prehistory of the "Good Shepherd"', *Journal of Near Eastern Studies*, 3 (2), pp. 87–90, p. 90.
33 Bailey, *The Good Shepherd*, p. 228.
34 Bailey, *The Good Shepherd*, p. 264.
35 Bailey, *The Good Shepherd*, p. 266.
36 Bailey, *The Good Shepherd*, p. 367.
37 Bailey, *The Good Shepherd*, p. 263.
38 Bailey, *The Good Shepherd*, p. 171.
39 Walter Brueggemann, 1997, *Theology of the Old Testament*, Minneapolis, MN: Fortress Press, pp. 259–60.

10

The Pastoral Staff

In the preceding chapters the significance and distinctive connotation of 'shepherd' have been demonstrated. In this chapter, these arguments will be drawn together in a consideration of the place of the pastoral staff in the bishops' rite in *CW:OS*, to demonstrate further the pastoral and relational nature of the relationship that should exist between the bishop and the Church.

The pastoral staff, or crozier, is the key element of the *traditio instrumentorum* for those ordained to episcopal ministry, being the only piece of liturgical vesture given at ordination (*CW:OS* 71). Other items associated with the ministry of a bishop in Anglicanism are the episcopal ring, mitre and pectoral cross. But it is the pastoral staff that is clearly associated with the pastoral ministry of the bishop as a shepherd of Christ's flock. Moreover, the use of the pastoral staff during the liturgy is a significant area of study to elucidate the pastoral role of the bishop when presiding over the eucharistic assembly.

Although it is widely suggested that the familiar Western form of the crozier resembling a shepherd's crook is due to 'later symbolism',[1] the connection between the crozier and the shepherd's crook is key for *CW:OS*. First, the shepherd's crook is expected to be recognizable in the pastoral staff; it would be very unusual, possibly unacceptable, for the newly ordained to be presented with a *bekteria* (*dikanikion*), a crozier based on the *Tau* or double serpent, which is expected in the Syriac and Eastern Orthodox traditions.[2] Second, there is the nomenclature itself: the giving of anything other than a Bible is absent from the 1662 and the *ASB* rites, so the inclusion of the giving of the pastoral staff is a significant reintroduction for *CW:OS*, and the choice of 'pastoral staff' over 'crozier' is therefore a significant statement of the intended pastoral, shepherd-like significance. Third, the words of the rite at the giving of the pastoral staff define the significance in pastoral and shepherding analogy:

> *Archbishop*: Keep watch over the whole flock in which the Holy Spirit has appointed you shepherd.
> *All*: Encourage the faithful, restore the lost, build up the Body of Christ. (*CW:OS* 71)

Therefore, while the origins of the pastoral staff as 'a rod used by Roman augurs in divination' or 'the ordinary walking stick'[3] may be true, the significance for *CW:OS* is explicitly and significantly in the realm of the shepherd's crook and its pastoral connotations; as such, it is congruent with the emphases being advanced here as definitive of the relationship the bishop will have with the rest of the Church.

Paul Avis dismisses the significance of the pastoral staff: 'It would not be appropriate to go into any detail about what the bishop should wear and other protocols of episcopal ministry in parish church and cathedral.'[4] While Anglicanism rejoices in its diversity of liturgical expression, and regards such matters as *adiaphora* – literally, indifferent – this does not mean that they are of no significance. For the ordinal, the pastoral staff is significant, and the bishop's use of the staff is also significant liturgically both for the way in which it speaks of the bishop's ministry outside of the liturgy and for the way in which during the liturgy it speaks of the way in which the bishop inhabits their relationship with the rest of the Church. Just as it would be inappropriate to dictate the style of the pastoral staff, for instance, so it would be an oversight if no attention and thought were given to the way in which the use of the pastoral staff speaks of the bishop's role and relationships. Furthermore, failure consciously to consider the liturgical use of the pastoral staff will often lead to unconscious inferences for both the bishop and the rest of the Church. Rather than being dismissive of its significance, the use of the pastoral staff is therefore highly significant in its symbolism, whether it be intended and unintended.

David Stancliffe explains the symbolism of the pastoral staff in his practical notes for the newly consecrated:

> The staff is a walking stick, and you hold it with the crook facing the assembly and walk with it in your left hand. You may hold it as you confirm and walk with it in your left hand. You always hold it as the gospel is read – it is a sign of readiness for action. Its connotations are

with shepherding – the crook end hauls the flock together away from danger: the pointed end prods them to go out and find fresh pasture. The staff is a reminder of the bishop's pastoral office, not a sign of jurisdiction. Never let anyone lay it on the altar.[5]

The foundational question here is about the authority connoted by the pastoral staff. While Stancliffe wishes to affirm that the pastoral staff is not a sign of jurisdiction, there is a tension with the use of the pastoral staff to prod the sheep. In the light of the understanding of the shepherd's crook as being exclusively a tool of rescue, as established in Chapter 9, the implication that the staff is to be used for prodding is unhelpful. If the pastoral staff were to be a tool to prod people with, it would necessarily suggest an aspect of jurisdiction or authority for the bishop to discipline other members of the Church in this way. When solely a tool of rescue, the pastoral staff both emphasizes the bishop's responsibility for ensuring the safety of the sheep and, at the same time, speaks of their lack of ability to exert their authority over the Church. The pastoral staff therefore becomes symbolic of the nature of the relationship that the bishop has with the Church, which mirrors the relationship between the shepherd and the sheep and ultimately between Christ and the Church.

Thus, the pastoral staff speaks of the trust between the bishop and the rest of the Church, with the bishop leading from the front and the sheep willingly listening to and following the voice of the shepherd. Any sense of the pastoral staff as a tool for prodding shifts the emphasis to one where the shepherd is using some form of force to move the sheep against their will. It moves the pastoral staff from being a reassuring tool of rescue, reminding the flock that none will be forsaken, into a tool for control. Only when the pastoral staff is devoid of any aspect of coercion can the exhortation to 'watch over the flock' connote simple reassurance. Any aspect of coercion opens the possibility of something more menacing, whereby the bishop's watch is not to protect the flock from external threat but subtly moves it to watching-over so as to keep in line, like an officer watching over prisoners.

In using the term pastoral staff rather than crozier, *CW:OS* diminishes and even disavows the connotations of authority and jurisdiction that the crozier is given and assumed. However, in other contexts these are the primary foci of the crozier; James Noonan defines the crozier 'as a symbol of jurisdiction and authority'.[6] In the Roman Catholic tradition, the crozier is also explicitly defined as symbolic of jurisdiction in the *Caeremoniale Episcoporum*, which states that a bishop uses the crozier within his territory, or with the diocesan's consent, and that only one bishop may use the crozier in liturgical celebrations.[7] The assertion by Stancliffe, supported by careful reading of *CW:OS*, that the pastoral staff is not a symbol of authority and jurisdiction, is therefore made in a context in which the authority and jurisdiction embodied by the crozier are often affirmed and assumed, both outside of the Anglican Communion and within through the liturgical use of the pastoral staff, their design, and the understanding of those who carry them.

To suggest that the pastoral staff gives the bishop the authority to 'prod you', emphasizing the sharp end of the staff as opposed to the hook of rescue, immediately shifts the emphasis away from pastoral care to enforced compliance, in the same way that a police officer has the authority to carry a truncheon to legitimately enforce the law. This aspect of jurisdiction is also seen when a diocese has a specific pastoral staff, often ornate, for use by the diocesan bishop at diocesan events. Here again the pastoral staff carries a connotation that is far removed from the simple pastoral staff which emphasizes the pastoral office. Moreover, with many Church dioceses having more than one bishop, it is interesting to note that often it is only the diocesan bishop who processes with their pastoral staff, presumably based on the Roman Catholic praxis. Therefore, while the concept might be clear that the pastoral staff is a symbol of the pastoral office of the bishop – as much a reminder for the bishop as the congregation – the praxis of having a special pastoral staff for the diocesan bishop, and no pastoral staffs for assisting bishops, communicates a diametrically opposed emphasis on the jurisdiction and authority of the diocesan bishop. Moreover, the absence of the pastoral staffs of the assisting bishops shifts the emphasis on to the mitres as the distinctive vesture of bishops in the liturgy, an emphasis not supported by *CW:OS*; this further undermines the clearly intended pastoral focus for bishops, as made visible in their pastoral staffs.

Stancliffe's preference for the giving of the pastoral staff at *The Sending Out* addresses the practical aspect of what to do with the pastoral staff for the rest of the liturgy. It also relies on an expectation that the newly ordained bishop will be a diocesan bishop, referring to separation of ordination from enthronement in 'their cathedrals'.[8] Here again is an implication that the pastoral staff is indicative of the bishop's jurisdiction. The question therefore arises as to what is meant by the words of the rite at the giving of the staff: 'Keep watch over the whole flock in which the Holy Spirit has appointed you shepherd.' The case for giving the pastoral staff at *The Sending Out* would be strengthened if the reference here was to a specific flock within the body of Christ, giving the pastoral staff as a mandate to go and take up the authority of the diocesan bishop in a given place, as embodied by the bishop elect striking the west doors of the cathedral with their staff before their enthronement.[9] However, the rite does not have a specific flock in focus but rather the 'whole flock' 'in which' and not 'over which' the bishop will keep watch. Moreover, the congregational response speaks of the general building up of the 'body of Christ'.

Congruent with the pastoral staff being a symbol of the pastoral responsibility of the bishop, the text of the rite at this point reflects the new relationship between the bishop and the rest of the Church. This would be better reflected liturgically by the giving of the pastoral staff to the newly ordained before *The Welcome*. While Stancliffe is aware of the dangers of confusion, whereby the *porrectio instrumentorum* becomes associated with 'effecting ordination',[10] such confusion is no more inevitable than in the giving of the Bible after the ordination prayer. While the giving of the pastoral staff at *The Sending Out* has a practical and missional emphasis, the giving of the pastoral staff after the ordination prayer is a clearer demonstration of its primary function, speaking of the relationship between the bishop and the rest of the Church, and should be in the hand of the newly ordained at the celebration of that new relationship at *The Welcome*.

The implication of Simon Jones' directions on the use of the pastoral staff by bishops at initiation is that the pastoral staff is a constant part of the bishop's vesture. Although, like Stancliffe's walking stick description, Jones emphasizes the importance of the pastoral staff for movement, there is a sense in his description that it isn't just, or even primarily, for movement. There seem to be just two reasons for the bishop to 'give up the crozier'.[11] The first is practical; the bishop only has two hands and at various points in the service needs them both. The second is at points of prayer. While this too could have a practical aspect, to enable the bishop to adopt a symmetrical orans position for prayer, there is also a theological significance here. Laying aside mitre and pastoral staff for prayer can provide a powerful symbol of the bishop's unity with the rest of the Church in prayer, and help to reaffirm in praxis the bishop as leading the congregation in prayer, rather than praying on behalf of the people.[12] The practical question is what to do with the pastoral staff when it is not being held by the bishop. Neither propping it against a pillar, as in many parish churches, nor a cathedral's purpose-built stand, seem sufficient. The first often leads to the pastoral staff being largely left out of the liturgy, to be brought on stage for specific moments, as implied by Ormonde Plater's identification of the procession, absolution and blessing, and gospel as moments for the bishop to hold the pastoral staff.[13] The second seems to emphasize the jurisdictional role of the pastoral staff, akin to the mace in Parliament. If the pastoral staff is to be with the bishop as a matter of course, as a reminder to the bishop and the Church of the primacy of their pastoral role, then asking someone nearby to hold it briefly for the bishop is surely the most eloquent and practical solution.

As the key element of the *traditio instrumentorum*, the pastoral staff speaks of the primacy of the pastoral role of the bishop, which is expressed as the faith placed in them and their accountability. The faith placed in a bishop is twofold. First, from the Church, who place their faith in the bishop at the declarations.[14] An essential prerequisite for ordination as a bishop is the election and endorsement of the candidate by the laity, and the clergy's endorsement, on behalf of the Church, then made visible at the imposition of hands by the other bishops (CW:OS 67). This is not simply a preliminary for ordination but instead speaks of the faith placed in the bishop, which will then lead to the bishop's role whereby 'the church as a whole recognises and accepts the episcopal ministry sent to it'.[15] To place acceptance of the bishop's ministry outside of the bishop's election shifts the basis of bishop's authority from being relational, based in their relationship with the rest of the Church, to being based in the bishop's own personal authority as bishop; to put it another way, the bishop moves from being authoritative to being authoritarian, and consequently relies more on their authority than on their relationship with the Church. In giving the pastoral staff, the presiding bishop is placing in the hands of the bishop a symbol of the trust the Church is placing in the newly ordained bishop, a trust that must be respected and nourished.

Second, the pastoral staff also represents the faith that God places in the bishop. Vocation is a key aspect of the discernment of the candidate for ordination: those making a nomination 'are looking for the direction where God is leading – leading the candidates, the diocese and themselves, and through them the wider church – a path on which they are being invited to set foot together'.[16] As a sharer in Christ's own shepherd-hood, the bishop is being trusted to inhabit and exhibit the ministry of which Christ himself is the archetype. Hence, the bishop is primarily accountable to God, not in the sense that they are not accountable to any human authority, but that they will have to give account for the flock at the last judgement, as is implied in the ordination prayer's intercession that the bishop 'be presented blameless' and 'enter your eternal joy' (*CW:OS* 67). It is in synod that the bishop is held to account by the laity, and this raises significant questions about the monarchical overtones and the suggestion above by Colin Podmore that diocesan synods do not have that kind of authority over their bishop. Although it might not be possible or acceptable for a diocesan synod in the Church of England to mandate the bishop, as they might in the Episcopal Church of the United States, the synod can withhold support for the bishops, as seen when General Synod rejected the House of Bishops' report on human sexuality in February 2012.[17] More directly, a diocesan synod can refuse to support the diocesan bishop's vision and mission by voting down the budget or even by tabling a vote of no-confidence in the bishop, as was reportedly planned against a former Bishop of Winchester.[18]

To deny that the pastoral staff has any connotation of authority is counter-intuitive; it clearly symbolizes the office and therefore authority of the bishop. However, it is essential to clearly articulate that the authority of the bishop is based on a trusting relationship to which the Church willingly assents, and for which the bishop will be held responsible at the last judgement. This authority is very much one that is offered to the bishop, rather than extending from the bishop, and it must be so to remain an authority that has no reliance on coercion. Just as the shepherd's authority relies on the trust placed in them by the sheep and is accountable to the sheep's owner for their well-being, so the bishop's authority within the Church cannot be expected or demanded, but rather is earned and a fruit of the relationship that bishop has with the Church.

The pastoral staff symbolizes not the bishop's authority to constrain or force others, but rather their authority to authorize and liberate in the name of the Church and of God. As Rowan Williams states: 'the bishop is very much a giver of permission'.[19] This is also an ontological aspect of the distinctive ministry of the bishop, distinguishing them from other orders. This distinction is most clear at an ordination, where the bishop presides over the prayers of the Church and is also present in the licensing and commissioning for ministry. Thus, the pastoral staff speaks of Malcolm Grundy's 'enslaved liberator';[20] it is both a symbol of their authority to liberate and a symbol of their lack of independent authority: their servanthood. As Roger Standing affirms, the diocesan bishop's role is to 'encourage and facilitate missional momentum in their jurisdiction'.[21] The relational, rather than legal, emphasis in this is most clearly seen in the words at an institution to a living, to 'receive this cure, which is both yours and mine',[22] emphasizing the ongoing relationship between bishop, priest and laity. It is not simply that the newly instituted priest is given authority by the bishop, but that the bishop and priest enter a new relationship, as the priest enters a new relationship with the Church in that place.

The pastoral staff therefore emphasizes the bishop as shepherd: one who enables and encourages mission and ministry, with the positive connotations of leading through mutual trust, in the discernment of gifts and vocation. Here the bishop as overseer is a sentinel, as highlighted by Cottrell, drawing on Gregory the Great.[23] However, given the scale of most Church dioceses, the relationships that the bishop, particularly the diocesan bishop, is able to foster are necessarily thin, with the bishop having little relational ministry with the people of the Church particularly in the parishes, other than at confirmations, ordinations, pastoral reorganization or a serious pastoral breakdown. The pastoral staff therefore is a significant symbol of the relationship to which the bishop is called but runs the risk of losing its power to remind, and becoming instead a proxy for an assumed relationship that is not evident in praxis,[24] whereby the bishop exercises their pastoral relationship with the rest of the Church through the bearing of the pastoral staff, rather than in the character of their relationships.

There are therefore significant resonances between the giving of the pastoral staff and the giving of a wedding ring. The intention of the ring is made explicit in the blessing of the ring: it is 'a symbol of unending love and faithfulness, to remind them of the vow and covenant which they have made this day'.[25] While there is no reciprocal gift for the pastoral staff and the intensity of the relationship is of a different order, nevertheless the function of the ring and pastoral staff is very helpful as a reminder of the nature of the relationship. The wearing of a wedding ring speaks of the nature of the marriage vows; that they are about love and that the relationship is intended to be unending. The pastoral staff too speaks of a relationship of love between the bishop and the rest of the Church, defined by the love of the Good Shepherd himself, and of a relationship that is unending, given the lifelong nature of Anglican orders.

It is important to note that the wedding ring too has the potential shadow of implying ownership, of one person in the relationship being owned by another, rather than the intended sacramental sign of the loving marriage relationship. The pastoral staff too has a shadow side, whereby it is assumed to speak of authority and power, particularly in relation to the diocesan bishop or presiding bishop at a service, and when the pastoral staff is particularly ornate and given to a diocesan bishop at their enthronement. Neither of these shadow meanings are intended, and there must be awareness that, just as when the marriage ring is reduced to a symbol of ownership or obligation, it fundamentally undermines its intended purpose; so too when the pastoral staff becomes a symbol of authority and power, it also fundamentally undermines the intended nature of the relationship between bishop and the Church, which is characterized by the shepherd's sacrificial and loving relationship with the flock.

The pastoral staff has the potential to be a hugely powerful and helpful symbol of the nature of the relationship between the bishop and the rest of the Church, firmly rooting the relationship in the analogy with the shepherd who has no authority over the flock other than the flock's willingness to follow based on their trust in them as a faithful leader. Moreover, the pastoral staff speaks of the bishop's role in keeping the flock safe, gathering together, rescuing those who have become lost, all of which is lost if the pastoral staff is confused with an instrument for doing violence to the flock to ensure conformity. Ultimately, therefore, the pastoral staff is not so much a symbol of authority, but of accountability. The nature of the bishop's relationship with the Church is one in which they will be held accountable for the flock, but that accountability does not confer authority over the Church. Instead, the bishop must earn the trust of the Church so that people will follow the bishop's lead, as the whole flock discern the will of the Good Shepherd, Jesus Christ, whom they collectively seek to follow. Jesus self-defined his leadership as one who 'came not to be served but to serve, and give his life a ransom for many' (Matthew 20.28; Mark 10.45) and is epitomized by the washing of feet (John 13.1–17), which bishops are encouraged to embody liturgically at the ordination of deacons (CW:OS 29).

Notes

1 F. L. Cross and E. A. Livingstone, 2005, *The Oxford Dictionary of the Christian Church*, third edition, Oxford: Oxford University Press, p. 437.

2 Wendy Doniger (ed.), 1999, 'Crosier', in *Merriam-Webster's Encyclopaedia of World Religions*, Springfield, MA: Merriam-Webster, p. 269.

3 Cross and Livingstone, *The Oxford Dictionary of the Christian Church*, p. 437.

4 Paul Avis, 2015, *Becoming a Bishop: A Theological Handbook of Episcopal Ministry*, London: Bloomsbury/T&T Clark, p. 149.

5 David Stancliffe, 2019, 'Episcopal Dress and Kit', An unpublished guidance document for new bishops in the Church of England, p. 2.

6 James Noonan, 1996, *The Church Visible*, New York: Viking, p. 197. See also Jack W. Vancil, 1992, 'Sheep, Shepherd', *Anchor Bible Dictionary*, edited by Noel Freedman, 5, New York: Doubleday, p. 1118, for a discussion of the usage of crozier symbolism in the Ancient Near East, in particular in Egypt: 'Evidence for the symbolic nature of the shepherd figure is found in the widespread use of the simple shepherd's crook as an insignia of kings, princes, and chieftains. The instrument symbolized the ruler's power and eminence, and especially the nature of his rule, the king's obligation to maintain order and justice (*maat*) in the land.'

7 *Caeremoniale Episcoporum*, 1985, Vatican: Polyglot Press, p. 59.

8 David Stancliffe, 2023, 'Ordination in the Church of England: Theology and Practice in the Common Worship Ordinal' in Thomas Pott, James Hawkey and Keith Pecklers (eds), *Malines: Continuing the Conversations*, London: SPCK, pp. 141–52, p. 150.

9 See, for example, The Guardian, 2013, 'Archbishop of Canterbury enthronement – in pictures', *The Guardian*, 21 March, <https://www.theguardian.com/uk/gallery/2013/mar/21/archbishop-of-canterbury-enthronement-pictures>, accessed 11.09.2025.

10 The Guardian, 'Archbishop of Canterbury enthronement – in pictures'.

11 Simon Jones, 2016, *Celebrating Christian Initiation: Baptism, Confirmation and Rite for the Christian Journey*, London: SPCK, p. 11.

12 A similar principle is expressed about musicians in the liturgy in Aidan Kavanagh, 1990, *Elements of Rite*, Collegeville, PA: Liturgical Press, pp. 32–3.

13 Ormonde Plater, 2009, *Deacons in the Liturgy*, second edition, London: Church House Publishing, p. 125.

14 The presiding bishop asks the congregation, 'Is it now your will that *he* should be ordained?' (*CW:OS* 62).

15 Church of England, 2017, GS Misc 1171, 'Discerning in Obedience: A Theological Review of the Crown Nominations Commission', <https://www.churchofengland.org/sites/default/files/2018-01/gs-misc-1171-discerning-in-obedience-report-on-the-review-of-the-cnc.pdf>, 2.8, p. 7, accessed 11.09.2025.

16 Church of England, 'Discerning in Obedience', 2.3, pp. 5–6.

17 Tim Wyatt, 2017, 'Archbishops propose new way forward on sexuality after Synod reject Bishops' report', *Church Times*, <https://www.churchtimes.co.uk/articles/2017/17-february/news/uk/synod-rebuff-for-bishops-report-on-sexuality>, accessed 11.09.2025.

18 Staff Reporter, 2021, 'Bishop of Winchester steps back after diocesan rebellion', *Church Times*, <https://www.churchtimes.co.uk/articles/2021/21-may/news/uk/bishop-of-winchester-steps-back-after-diocesan-rebellion>, accessed 11.09.2025.

19 Rowan Williams, 2020, 'Foreword' in Roger Standing and Paul Goodliff (eds), *Episkope: The Theory and Practice of Translocal Oversight*, London: SCM Press, pp. xxi–xxii, p. xxi.

20 Malcolm Grundy, 2011, *Leadership and Oversight: New Models for Episcopal Ministry*, London: Mowbray, pp. 58–69.

21 Roger Standing, 2020, 'The Shape of Translocal Oversight' in Standing and Goodliff (eds), *Episkope*, pp. 213–24, p. 220.

22 Steven Croft, 2022, 'The Cure of Souls', *Diocese of Oxford: Bishop Steven's Blog*, <https://blogs.oxford.anglican.org/the-cure-of-souls/>, accessed 11.09.2025.

23 Stephen Cottrell, 2020, 'Church of England Bishops as Pastor and Evangelist' in Standing and Goodliff (eds), *Episkope*, pp. 71–80, p. 75.

24 Cf. the analysis of War Memorials in Alan Bennett, 2014, *The History Boys*, London: Faber, p. 25. Bennett's suggestion is that the public remembrance is a way of sublimating the truth: '[A]ll this mourning has veiled the truth. It's not so much lest we forget, as lest we remember. Because you should realise the Cenotaph and the Last Post and all that stuff is concerned, there's no better way of forgetting something than by commemorating it.' In like manner, the suggestion here is the pastoral staff becomes a ritualized way of claiming the pastoral care of the bishop, investing the object with a meaning and significance that, rather than inspiring or enabling pastoral care, therefore becomes the primary locus of the pastoral identity and undermines the emphasis that should be placed on pastoral relationships with the Church. To put it another way, the pastoral staff has the potential to become a totem for the bishop's pastoral care, rather than the relationships themselves.

25 Archbishops' Council, 2000, *Common Worship: Pastoral Offices*, London: Church House Publishing, p. 109.

11

Shepherd is the Defining Metaphor

Having extensively articulated the significance and meaning of 'shepherd' in *CW:OS*, this chapter will demonstrate the way in which 'shepherd' acts as a hermeneutic for the descriptor of the bishop as 'guardian of the faith of the apostles' and as an 'agent of unity'. As has been noted above, bishops in historic succession are an important indicator and manifestation of continuation of apostolic ministry in the Church. However, *CW:OS* modifies the bold claims of the 1662 ordinal. This modification is a significant reflection not only of developing Anglican polity, as has been noted in Chapter 1, but also of the role of the bishop and the nature of their relationship with the rest of the Church, in continuity with the bishop as shepherd of Christ's flock.

The theme of apostolicity becomes increasingly significant in the sequence of ordination rights, reaching the strongest associations in the bishops' rite. The deacons' rite makes no reference to 'apostle' at all, and in the priests' rite there are two references, one referring to Jesus as the 'Apostle and High Priest of our faith' in the ordination prayer (*CW:OS* 42) and Jesus' own apostles in the Prayer after Communion (*CW:OS* 46). In the bishops' rite there is both the fullest reference to apostolic ministry, and a connection made between the ministry of the Apostles and the bishop. In addition to the references in common with the priests' rite, reference is made to the 'teaching of the apostles' (*CW:OS* 61) as an example for bishops to follow. However, building on the shepherd analogy, 'guardian of the faith of the apostles' (*CW:OS* 55) is the second descriptor of the bishop and the most significant reference to the Apostles. This is an important change from the 1662 ordinal, which makes a more direct correlation between the ministry of the Apostles and the bishop in the opening collect:

> Almighty God, who by thy Son Jesus Christ didst give to thy holy Apostles many excellent gifts, and didst charge them to feed thy flock; Give grace, we beseech thee, to all Bishops, the Pastors of

thy Church, that they may diligently preach thy word, and duly administer the godly discipline thereof; and grant to the people, that they may obediently follow the same, that all may receive the crown of everlasting glory through Jesus Christ our Lord. Amen. (*BCP 1662* 101)

The shift in emphasis is subtle but significant, and correlates well with Paul Avis' affirmation that apostolicity should not be seen as residing with the bishops alone, but with the whole Church: 'The apostolicity of the Church does not pivot on episcopacy or "apostolic succession" in a narrow sense: it is conceived to rest on a broader basis.'[1]

Within the shared apostolicity of the Church, for bishops to be 'guardians' may imply some form of defensiveness, protecting the faith of the Apostles from becoming damaged or polluted. Thus for Stephen Cottrell:

The bishop is the one who ensures the unity and continuation of God's mission through the Church. The bishop ensures that the life and ministry of the Church in each and every place and time is the same as in every place and time. The bishop embodies and carries this apostolic vocation.[2]

There are therefore three significant functions to the bishops' guardianship. The first is ontological: by their very existence, they evidence the legitimacy of the continuity with the Church of the Apostles; second, in their teaching bishops have a key role in maintaining sound doctrine; and third, there is an element of governance, in ensuring that the life of the Church continues to reflect the true teaching about it.

However, in the context of the bishop being primarily a shepherd and the attendant relationship with the other members of the Church, there is an underlying foundation for all these aspects, which is the primary role that the bishop has in guarding or preserving the trust that Christ places in the Apostles. The nature of this faith or trust is explored in *Discerning in Obedience*:

In the New Testament 'trust' and 'faith' are one and the same concept, pistis, which refers to a relation of trust and trustworthiness, faithfulness and good faith. The trusting relation in which Christians stand to one another is an expression of the faith each has in Christ. Oriented to Christ in pistis, members of the community are bound together in pistis. Pistis not only characterises the community, but constitutes it as a community, allowing it to act together coherently.[3]

While there might be specific functions of the bishops as guardians of the faith of the Apostles, the underlying hermeneutic, rationale and purpose of these functions is to maintain and pass on the relationship of trust in Christ, made manifest in the trust within the body of Christ. It is this grounding that determines the way in which the bishop should carry out the functions of their office and inhabit their ministry: to do otherwise is not only to make an erroneous split between the bishop as shepherd and as guardian; it also undermines the relationship between the bishop and the rest of the Church, not just the clergy, which is the very essence of their *episcope*.

The bishop's role in governance is particularly emphasized by Roger Standing, who sees the bishops as 'the pre-eminent guardians of the application of doctrine in the life of the Church'.[4] The nature of this governance is significant for the Church, where bishops may not have any institutional authority over others to discipline them. The bishop's role as guardian of the faith is not therefore to be inquisitorial, seeking to preserve the doctrinal purity of the Church by removing or punishing those considered heretical; to be a guardian of the faith cannot be identified with a bishop's ability to penalize other members of the Church, especially other clergy. The emphasis for the bishop must therefore be on their ability to positively promote and assert the faith of the Apostles, rather than in being able to suppress or restrain anything that may undermine the faith of them. The notes in *CW:OS* affirm this by citing 1 Timothy 6.20: 'Timothy, guard what has been entrusted to you. Avoid profane chatter and contradictions of what is falsely called knowledge.' The emphasis here is not on controlling others, but maintaining personal purity and leading by example.

Therefore, instead of the bishop as one who drums out heresy, the emphasis here is far better seen as the bishop being one who embodies and encourages trust in the life and resurrection of Jesus. This is congruent with Acts 1.22,[5] where the qualification for potential replacements for Judas Iscariot is someone who trusted Jesus sufficiently to follow him in his earthly ministry and who subsequently trusts sufficiently in Jesus' resurrection that they can witness to it to others. Here the role of the bishop as guardian of the faith of the Apostles mirrors the role of the shepherd who does not keep the flock locked up in the sheepfold, but leads them out to find nourishment. To nourish the flock, the shepherd must know both the needs of the sheep and where those needs can be met. To be a guardian of the faith of the Apostles is to be engaged in mission, as distinct from proselytizing. The missional imperative of the bishop is pastoral, in seeking to find nourishment for the relationship between Christ and his people and between the people. Thus the introduction to the ordination rite explains that bishops are to be 'proclaiming the gospel of God's kingdom and leading his people in mission' (*CW:OS* 55). When viewed through the prism of relationship, leading the people in mission and proclaiming the kingdom of God are two aspects of the way in which the bishop fosters the relationships established by and in Christ.

Paul Goodliff notes the importance in history of missionary bishops,[6] and James Jones, in a very different context, emphasizes the importance of morality as a missional aspect of the life of a prominent diocesan bishop: 'It seems to me that the calling of the Church is to help people trace back from their moral intuition to the divine source and especially the figure of Jesus Christ, who personified [the] values of justice and mercy.'[7] To be a guardian of the faith is therefore to be prominent in society, while maintaining trust in Jesus' teaching and resurrection; a guardian of the faith is a kind of modern-day stylite, one who is not set apart from the wider society but acts as a kind of lighthouse to those passing by or, as Cottrell prefers, a sentinel.[8] The faith of the Apostles is guarded, therefore, not by being kept safe but by being shared with others, so that relationships, which cannot exist in isolation, can grow.

Relationship is also the primary rationale for the distinctive liturgical functions of the bishop – namely, confirmation, ordination and licensing for ministry. Rather than being seen as the preserve of those who have achieved this 'rank' within the Church, or as an outworking of the authority placed in the bishop by the Church, this is a ministry of enabling and establishing new relationship which is at the heart of the bishop's ministry. Instead of being the climax of the *cursus honorum*, these ministries flow from the bishop's relationship with the rest of the Church, and are in continuity with the ministry that the bishop has as a result of being baptized, confirmed, and ordained deacon and priest. So too the bishop's natural place as the president at the celebration of the Eucharist is an outworking of the relationship the bishop has with the Church, which the bishop is seeking to foster within the body of Christ and, most significantly, between the Church and Christ. Thus the introduction affirms that the bishop will be the one whose responsibility it is to 'gather God's people and celebrate with them the sacraments of God's love' (*CW:OS* 55).

The bishop as guardian of the faith of the Apostles is responsible for the oversight of the relationships that constitute the body of Christ. Fostering this trust and faith within the Church is the primary ministry of the bishop, which they inhabit by developing and maintaining a good relationship with themselves, with other members of the Church, and with God in Christ. Bishops seek to nourish these relationships in teaching and sacramental worship and in drawing people into a deeper relationship with Christ and one another. As guardian, like the guardian of cultural heritage or language, the guardianship requires the bishop to be missional, and to encourage the faith in others to be explored and deepened. This is because the faith of the Apostles is a living relationship requiring people to be in relationship to exist. The bishop as guardian of this faith is therefore one who both oversees the sharing of this relationship with those outside the Church and the encouraging of the relationship among those already within the Church.

Previous themes of the tension between the institutional and ecclesial, and the temptations to clericalism, demonstrate the significance and distinctive nature of the unity engendered by the bishop as 'shepherd'. The introduction to the ordination rite for bishops concludes: 'Thus formed into a single communion of fellowship and love, the Church in each place and time is united with the Church in every place and time' (*CW:OS* 55). As is consistently the case in the ordinal, the focus here is on the ecclesial unity of the Church, made manifest at the celebration of the Eucharist, at which the bishop presides. This is distinct from the institutional unity that is the particular responsibility of the diocesan bishops and the House of Bishops in General Synod.

For the ordinal, the Eucharist is the natural and necessary context for ordinations, where the body of Christ is gathered together and meet with Christ in word and sacrament. The Eucharist is therefore the foundational unitive act. Impaired communion within the Church, whereby the Eucharist is not shared because of concerns over the ordination of women, for example, is an ecclesial crisis. Once there is a break in eucharistic communion, the ecclesial unity of the Church has been broken. In this context the bishop can maintain unity by ministering alongside other bishops to meet the needs of various groups within the diocese, most notably in the case of 'provincial episcopal visitors', but unless the bishops themselves are in communion the unity ceases to be an ecclesial unity, and is reduced to an institutional unity.

It is in presiding at the Eucharist that the bishop is shepherd and host, as an embodiment of Jesus' gathering and feeding his people. The connection between shepherd and host is clearly made in Psalm 23, where in verse five the shepherd becomes the host of the banquet.[9] Presiding at the Eucharist therefore is symbolic, or more accurately sacramental, of the relationships within the Church both within and beyond the liturgical celebration. The ministry of the bishop fosters unity in the Church in an ontologically distinctive way, defined by the bishop's role as pastor and enabler of relationship, defined by the shepherd metaphor and as guardian of the faith of the Apostles. This is significant for the way in which unity in the Church is engendered, with an emphasis on mutual acceptance rather than imposed uniformity or authoritarianism. It is as an agent of unity that the bishop offers a ministry of oversight, and the governance of the diocesan bishop is to be inhabited in such a way that the Church is kept together and kept safe, in the same way that the shepherd leads and cares for the needs of the sheep. It is this ecclesial relationship that defines the nature and style of institutional leadership required of a diocesan bishop.

The praxis and understanding of institutional unity within the Church must therefore be built upon the ecclesial unity. The nature of institutional unity is brought into clearest focus when considering the relationship between the monarch and the episcopate in the Church. Ordained ministers are required to give both allegiance to the monarch and obedience to the diocesan bishop, as a prerequisite for ordination and being licensed to minister.[10] Both bishop and monarch are the sole authority in certain matters within their respective institutions, and have looked for support from each other at various points in history. However, neither are absolute rulers: the British monarch's authority is largely moral and ritualized in nature, with little expectation that they will exert anything other than 'soft' power, and certainly not use their authority to do anything other than the will of the elected government. The nature of the bishops' authority within the Church is highly complex and evolving in the contemporary Church, particularly with regard to their relationship with their diocesan synods. Just as monarchs cannot assume the goodwill of the people, so the willing submission of the Church to the will of the bishop should not be taken for granted, but instead is the fruit of a trusting relationship between bishop and the rest of the Church.

The relationship between monarch and bishops is significant for the

Church. For James I, as exemplified by his statement at the Hampton Court Conference of 1604, 'no bishop, no king',[11] the bishops were a necessary tool for ruling not just the established Church, but through the Church for the nation. With the decline in the relevance of the Church for the nation, the dependency is set in much the other direction: the Church now depends on its established status for attempting to exert an influence beyond what it could reasonably expect based on its committed membership.

Although all orders in the Church must take the oath of allegiance,[12] the dependency on the monarch is most clearly seen in the bishops' rite where the Royal Mandate is required to authorize the ordination (*CW:OS* 56). While the Church ordains the bishop, it can only do so with the monarch's authority. This is in marked contrast with the Church in Wales, where the mandate is also significant in the liturgical text,[13] but where the mandate comes from the election by the Bishop's Electoral College, as set out in Chapter 5 of the constitution.[14] The involvement of the monarch in the Church's rite brings to the fore questions about the established nature of the Church, including that the Prime Minister's role in appointments on the monarch's behalf had to be passed to the Lord Chancellor when the Prime Minister identified as Roman Catholic.[15] However, the primary question here relates not to establishment *per se*, but to the influence and appropriateness of monarchical metaphors for the episcopate.

The diocesan bishops are those who are most identifiable with monarchical leadership, but the only reference to this in the ordinal is the assumption that the diocesan bishop will preside at the ordination of priests and deacons, and the archbishop will preside at the ordination of bishops. In terms of unity, the role is therefore not so much one of honour but facilitation and service, as a focus for unity. To facilitate this unity, it is both ecclesially and institutionally essential that the archbishop presides, and recent ordinations of bishops in which the archbishop does not clearly preside over the rite, while an accommodation in institutional terms, make clear the lack of unity in ecclesial terms.[16] Where the monarchical analogy is more hazardous is where the bishop becomes the sole authority or leader, in a move towards managerialism, as seen in initiatives such as the remodelling of the Church.[17] In a time of significant change for parish priests, where the monarchical model has been significantly revised, either through multi-parish benefices or through recognizing the importance of lay leadership, there are significant questions about how the institutional role of bishops can be remodelled to better facilitate the ecclesial reality of the Church with the current resources.

Among possible avenues for exploration is the relationship between diocesan bishops and diocesan secretaries, with the latter possibly taking on greater strategic leadership and the bishop offering a sacramental and teaching ministry devoid of their current institutional authority and responsibilities. If the ecclesial unity, grounded in relationship, is of primary importance over the institutional unity, then such questions, while almost unthinkable in institutional terms, become not only more credible but essential for the relationships that lie at the heart of the nature of the Church. To elucidate more clearly, the Episcopal Church of South Sudan has 61 dioceses[18] serving a population of 12.5 million,[19] compared to the Church of England's 42 dioceses[20] serving a population of 56.5 million.[21] Smaller and more numerous dioceses, possibly with a greater role for more regional provinces, would dilute the institutional authority and prestige of bishops, but would create far better relationships within the Church, and a greater ministry of presence in the locality.

Aspects of leadership in the Church, as human institution, are no different than leadership in any other group of people. The institution offers authority to the leader that they can choose to rely on, but the assertion here is that this is a temptation, or false leadership. Rather, the bishop must lead by seeking to engender authority through the trust of other members of the Church. The shepherd metaphor is key in reminding bishops that their authority is not based on the institutional relationship; their effectiveness is not based in their role, but in the trust they can engender in those they seek to lead. Julia Middleton explains: 'The point is that they don't *need* authority to be able to [lead].'[22] This leadership mode is closely aligned with the bishop's ability to engender unity in the Church as there is a further correlation between distance from those being led and the need for authority: the less connected the bishop is with the wider Church, the greater the need to rely on institutional authority. As Vaughan S. Roberts and David Simms note:

> In most organisations, it is hard for those at the top to be well in touch with what is happening on the ground. The more uncertain we are, the more we may be prone to feeling that all would be well if only everyone else did what we would do if we were in their situation, or, in other words, if they were under our control.[23]

Within the shepherd metaphor the significant difference is between driving the sheep with fear and drawing the sheep with trust. The comparison is brought out clearly by travel writer Chris Stewart, reflecting on the love of his *gandano*, flock of sheep, which he cared for in Alpujarras, Spain. He thought he loved his flock, but to the local shepherds he didn't; they believed he had distanced himself from the flock:

> [N]either I nor the sheep had quite mastered the easy technique of the Alpujarran shepherd who strides at the head of a flock, whistling for the sheep to follow. Instead I would be left bringing up the rear, shouting and pitching stones.[24]

Although his sheep were healthy, he hadn't been able to nurture the kind of bond that would mean that they wanted to follow him: he had to rely on his authority through imposition, rather than gaining authority by being a shepherd. Although both driving and drawing the flock result in a semblance of unity, the character of that unity is significantly different. Good relationships with the rest of the Church therefore cannot be taken for granted by the bishop but must be a focus for continued effort as the way in which unity is engendered in the community.

The unity that the bishop embodies is not just within the local church, as Stancliffe affirms: 'the newly ordained minister has a responsibility to and in the whole church, not just to the local community'.[25] However, there is a danger that ecclesial unity fostered by good relationships between bishops is undermined by a hierarchical culture, in which the bishop is seen to have climbed the *cursus honorum* of having passed from laity, to deacon to priest, finally to become a bishop. Although Hanson[26] and others have highlighted the need for distinct, non-hierarchical roles, deference to the bishop remains a distinctive aspect of the culture of contemporary Church, as recognized by senior clergy in the Diocese of Blackburn: 'The report has a great deal to say about "clericalism" and about an inappropriate culture of deference to clergy, especially senior clergy, which has resulted in cover-up and in the voices of the vulnerable being silenced.'[27] The potential for conflict between ecclesial unity and institutional unity is seen most clearly in the diocesan bishop's central judicial role in the Clergy Discipline Measure.[28] The role places the bishop in a complex and compromising place of being both the pastor and the judge, and as has been evidenced by the Sheldon Community,[29] these are roles that often do not sit happily together, with the pastoral role being subsumed into the judicial.

An additional aspect of clericalism is that fellowship between the bishops can resemble more networking with people of a similar status within an exclusive club rather than facilitation of unity on behalf of the whole Church. This is reflected by Giles Fraser when he speaks of the 'boss class and the workers',[30] referencing the numbers of parochial clergy who are joining unions to protect themselves. The concerns he raises are redolent of the potential for the bishop to be different in the same way that the human shepherd is not a sheep, for the pastoral staff to be misconstrued as symbolic of power and authority and for the guardian of the faith to be seen in exclusivist terms, as the one who knows better than the rest of the Church. This is the enforced unity from outside, provided by the diocesan bishop who is distanced from the rest of the Church and must find solidarity and kinship with those of similar class – that is, other bishops. It is only by rooting the unifying role of the bishop in relationship with the life of the Church that any institutional roles undertaken by a bishop can be authentically inhabited.

Since they are funded by the Church Commissioners, there is a danger that the bishops are disconnected from concerns at the parish level about numbers of parish clergy and the demands of the parish share. This distance is fuelling a growing disgruntlement among laity in particular who are being asked to give more for less as the cost of ministry is borne by fewer people and local clergy are being stretched further. In this context centralized initiatives such as the Archbishops' Council's *Setting God's People Free*,[31] rather than creating unity through a uniform solution, reflect the distance within the Church between the bishops and the parishes. In its most extreme form, the decrying of the Archbishop of York's plans for radical solutions,[32] including the founding of the Save the Parish network,[33] is further evidence of the gulf that is emerging between the episcopate and the laity, with a deficit in shared vision and mutual trust. The importance of the ecclesial foundation of the primary importance of trust, particularly between lay and ordained, is made evident by the nature of – and response to – centralized institutional initiatives.

Notes

1 Paul Avis, 2020, 'Anglican Episcopacy' in Roger Standing and Paul Goodliff (eds), *Episkope: The Theory and Practice of Translocal Oversight*, London: SCM Press, pp. 61–70, p. 66.

2 Stephen Cottrell, 2020, 'Church of England Bishops as Pastor and Evangelist' in Standing and Goodliff (eds), *Episkope*, pp. 71–80, p. 72.

3 Church of England, 2017, GS Misc 1171, 'Discerning in Obedience: A Theo-

logical Review of the Crown Nominations Commission', <https://www.churchofengland.org/sites/default/files/2018-01/gs-misc-1171-discerning-in-obedience-report-on-the-review-of-the-cnc.pdf>, p. 10, accessed 11.09.2025.

4 Roger Standing, 2020, 'Theological Issues: Constants in Context' in Standing and Goodliff (eds), *Episkope:*, pp. 14–43, p. 26.

5 'beginning from the baptism of John until the day when he was taken up from us – one of these must become a witness with us to his resurrection' (Acts 1.22).

6 Paul Goodliffe, 2020, 'Contemporary Models of Translocal Ministry: Ecumenical Landscapes' in Standing and Goodliff (eds), *Episkope*, pp. 44–60, p. 57.

7 James Jones, 2020, 'Church of England Bishops as Religious and Civic Leaders' in Standing and Goodliff (eds), *Episkope*, pp. 81–92, p. 85.

8 Cottrell, 'Church of England Bishops as Pastor and Evangelist', p. 75.

9 'You prepare a table before me in the presence of my enemies' (Ps. 23.5).

10 See 'The Oaths and the Declaration of Assent' (*CW:OS* 6).

11 David Harris Wilson, 1956, *King James VI & I*, London: Jonathan Cape, p. 207.

12 Church of England, 'Canon C13', <https://www.churchofengland.org/about/leadership-and-governance/legal-services/canons-church-england/section-c>, accessed 11.09.2025.

13 The Church in Wales, 'Alternative Ordinal', <https://churchinwales.contentfiles.net/media/documents/Alternative_Ordinal_-_2004.pdf>, p. 38, accessed 11.09.2025.

14 Chapter V; part iii; 10. The Church in Wales, 'Chapter V: The Archbishop and the Diocesan Bishops', <https://www.churchinwales.org.uk/en/clergy-and-members/constitution/chapter-v-archbishop-and-diocesan-bishops/>, accessed 11.09.2025.

15 Madeleine Davies, 2021, 'Lord Chancellor "likely" to pass names of new C of E bishops to Queen', *Church Times*, <https://www.churchtimes.co.uk/articles/2021/11-june/news/uk/lord-chancellor-likely-to-pass-names-of-new-c-of-e-bishops-to-queen>, accessed 11.09.2025.

16 Cf. earlier discussion around the lockdown ordinations in Lambeth Chapel on 15 July 2020. See also the then Archbishop of York's explanation of arrangements for the consecration of Philip North as Bishop of Burnley, at which the archbishop delegated the ordination to a traditionalist bishop. John Sentamu, 2015, 'Statement by York on the Consecration of a Traditionalist Bishop for Burnley', *Anglican Ink*, <https://anglican.ink/2015/01/23/statement-by-york-on-the-consecration-of-a-traditionalist-bishop-for-burnley/>, accessed 11.09.2025.

17 Madeleine Davies, 2021, 'Synod to discuss target of 10,000 new lay-led churches in the next ten years', *Church Times*, <https://www.churchtimes.co.uk/articles/2021/2-july/news/uk/synod-to-discuss-target-of-10-000-new-lay-led-churches-in-the-next-ten-years/>, accessed 11.09.2025.

18 The Episcopal Church of South Sudan, 'About', <https://southsudan.anglican.org/about/>, accessed 11.09.2025.

19 Country Meters, 'South Sudan Population', <https://countrymeters.info/en/South_Sudan>, accessed 11.09.2025.

20 Church of England, 'Diocese: Our Regional Presence', <https://www.churchofengland.org/about/diocese-our-regional-presence>, accessed 11.09.2025.

21 UK Population Data, 'Population of England 2022', <https://populationdata.org.uk/population-of-england/>, accessed 11.09.2025

22 Julia Middleton, 2007, *Beyond Authority*, Basingstoke: Palgrave Macmillan, p. 12.

23 Vaughan Roberts and David Simms, 2017, *Leading by Story: Rethinking Church Leadership*, London: SCM Press, p. 15.

24 Chris Stewart, 1999, *Driving Over Lemons, An Optimist in Andalucia*, London: Sort of Books, p. 215.

25 David Stancliffe, 2023, 'Ordination in the Church of England: Theology and Practice in the Common Worship Ordinal' in Thomas Pott, James Hawkey and Keith Pecklers (eds), *Malines: Continuing the Conversation*, London: SPCK, pp. 141–52, p. 152.

26 R. P. C. Hanson, 1969, 'The Nature of the Anglican Episcopate' in Michael Ramsey (ed.), *Lambeth Essays on Ministry*, London: SPCK, pp. 79–86.

27 Julian Henderson et al., 2019, 'Letter from Senior Clergy Reflecting on IICSA Reports on Chichester Diocese and Peter Ball', *Blackburn Diocese*, <https://www.blackburn.anglican.org/news/274/letter-from-senior-clergy-reflecting-on/>, accessed 11.09.2025.

28 Church of England, 'Clergy Discipline', <https://www.churchofengland.org/about/leadership-and-governance/legal-services/clergy-discipline/>, accessed 11.09.2025.

29 Cf. Sarah Horsman et al., 2011, '"I Was Handed Over to the Dogs": Lived Experience, Clerical Trauma and the Handling of Complaints against Clergy in the Church of England', <https://www.sheldonhub.org/usercontent/sitecontentuploads/3/1A10E25DCB7DB5E02AB69C0188CF7975/handed%20over%20to%20the%20dogs%20final.pdf>, accessed 11.09.2025.

30 Giles Fraser, 2022, 'The Church's War on the Clergy', *UnHerd*, <https://unherd.com/2022/02/justin-welbys-war-on-the-parish/>, accessed 11.09.2025.

31 Archbishops' Council, *Setting God's People Free*, <https://www.churchofengland.org/sites/default/files/2017-11/gs-2056-setting-gods-people-free.pdf>, accessed 11.09.2025.

32 Catherine Pepinster, 2021, 'Looking for Radical Solutions to Decline, Church of England Debates Lay-led House Churches', *Religion News Service*, <https://religionnews.com/2021/07/09/looking-for-radical-solutions-to-decline-church-of-england-debates-lay-led-house-churches/>, accessed 11.09.2025.

33 Save the Parish, <https://savetheparish.com/>, accessed 11.09.2025.

12

Conclusions for Contemporary Episcopal Ministry

It has been clearly shown that the institution of the Church is a manifestation of the body of Christ and that *CW:OS* gives a distinctive interpretation to the inheritance of the institution to emphasize the significance of the active ecclesiological role of both lay and ordained. Just as candidates 'affirm [their] loyalty to this inheritance of faith as [their] inspiration and guidance under God' (*CW:OS* 6), so *CW:OS* is loyal to, but not bound by, previous interpretations of the inheritance. In particular, the influence of baptismal ecclesiology on *CW:OS* has been established and the role of the bishop in the ordination rite, as one of the baptized, has articulated the integrated and active nature of the community of the Church. This relational ontology has been articulated as an expression of sacramental ecclesiology, in which the body of Christ is manifested through the gathering of the Church in *leitourgia*.

Christian ministry is therefore an aspect of the full life of the Church in which the ordained, through the instruments of the institution that make manifest the body of Christ, inhabit a new relationship with the rest of the Church. The nature of that relationship emphasizes the importance of the bishop as an integrated member of the Church community with a close pastoral relationship being at the heart of the bishop's ministry.

In this concluding chapter, the argument established thus far will be applied to the contemporary Church. At a time when the Church is producing reports on how to change to meet current challenges, this section will assert that the ontology of the nature of the Church, with whom the bishop is called to a relational ministry, should be the key factor in any reform of the Church.

While a detailed analysis of the current state of the Church is beyond the scope of this thesis, the relational nature of the shepherd paradigm means that the discussion cannot be held in a vacuum. The need to reclaim the shepherd-hood of the bishop is evidenced from contemporary studies of the Church experience of episcopal ministry. Salisbury Diocese has benefited from a serious and wide-ranging study, which will be shown to be congruent with the national experience evidenced by research from the Sheldon community, and with the work of Fiona Gardner. The case will then be made for institutional reforms to better facilitate the ecclesial relationship between bishop and the rest of the Church – namely, increasing the number of bishops and decreasing the size of the dioceses.

Veronica Hope Hailey's report *The Trustworthy Leader: A Report for the Diocese of Salisbury*[1] identifies criticisms of 'the diocese'[2] by the clergy. In her initial thoughts, Hope Hailey notes: 'It is indeed ironic that the keepers of a faith which is comfortable with the idea of an immortal and invisible God and Holy Spirit seem to be in such need for the support of a physical visible presence from the diocese.'[3] Such a need is not at all ironic, but rather to be expected: the care of the diocese mediates the care of the God whose care is experienced through the practical and mundane, as reflected in the foundational nature of diaconate for all ordained ministry. That the Church experiences the diocese, and bishops, as distant is again noted but within the apparent paradoxical criticism of the interfering nature of the diocese:

> And yet, so many clergy accused them of not being sufficiently visible, accessible, local, approachable, while many equally criticised them for interfering in the local parishes. In short, I was confused by what clergy actually wanted from a diocesan structure. It felt a little like whack a diocese at times.[4]

Although apparently irreconcilable, these two criticisms point towards a lack of relationship between the centralized institutions of the diocese and the people of the diocese; and in particular for the case being made here: between the bishop and the rest of the baptized. It is eminently possible for leadership to be experienced as both distanced and interfering when the underlying issue is a lack of trust and belief in the goodwill of the leader. As the report notes, it is largely in 'one-to-one' or personal interactions that trust is built up.[5]

The indications of the report are therefore that there is a need in Salisbury Diocese for a renewal of episcopal ministry as connection with the wider Church. It is noted in the report that the clergy are under significant stress and feel vulnerable. However, to call a bishop a shepherd requires their engagement with the challenges faced by the clergy, as an integral part of the Church. This is the significance of the parable of the lost sheep: that the bishop will feel called to reach out to help the clergy in their care, so that the trust engendered within the diocese, as a manifestation of the body of Christ, grows with a sense of both personal encounter with the pastoral care of the diocese, and an awareness that as and when such care is needed, it will be forthcoming – as it has been for others. This is not to suggest that bishops don't have wide-ranging commitments, but rather that there is a question here about priorities and the way in which the actions, or inaction, of the bishop has a profound effect on the culture and morale of the Church as a whole. Furthermore, the import is theological; it is the sense of distance from the diocese or isolation by the clergy that has a significant impact on the clergy's experience of God in Christ.

That the issues raised in Salisbury Diocese are in common with experience across the Church is affirmed in the report produced by the Sheldon Hub that looks at clergy experience of the Clergy Discipline Measure. It notes that many of the participants in the study did not experience their bishop as the shepherd of CW:OS, but rather as leader of the institution. As one participant explained:

> I didn't know when I went to this meeting that the bishop concerned was going to use it as a disciplinary meeting. I thought I was going for a pastoral chat. The bishop concerned ... just read these complaints to me as if they were gospel truth, tackling them one by one, like twisting a knife into an open wound. I collapsed into floods of tears and was then ordered to leave my post (effectively sacked).[6]

While another states: 'I was never granted a one to one with my Bishop and ultimately shepherd of the flock. My current bishop ... could not be more different and a refreshing cathartic change.'[7] The suggestion here is that the difficulty bishops experience in inhabiting their institutional and ecclesial relationships is not isolated, but to some extent endemic within an institution that creates processes that undermine the ecclesial relationship between bishop and the rest of the Church – in this instance, members of the clergy.

The abuse of power within the Church is also explored by Fiona Gardner, who notes both the active abuse by Christian 'leaders' within the Church and a passive permissiveness: 'Here is what one might call wilful blindness or a denial of awareness towards the victims and, indeed, the perpetrator ... The Church had no interest in them, only in turning away and blocking action that might cause difficulties.'[8] Further, Gardner explains: 'The issues of clericalism, deference to the institutional church and its reputation, and taboos around discussing the issues realistically and with appropriately qualified people, all contributed to the neglect, humiliation and further abuse of victims.'[9]

It is clear from internal and external reports that change is needed, but Gardner notes again that the Church repeatedly seeks institutional responses rather than the cultural change articulated here:

> There is no shortage of ideas around for significant changes but, as noted before, the Church appears stuck in a self-destructive and self-defeating pattern. This pattern, or modus operandi, is following bad publicity eventually to admit to past mistakes, issue apologies, then point to procedural and administrative changes and claim all is improved.[10]

There is a clear need for radical change if the Church is to live out its call to follow Christ and thereby engage seriously in mission in the world,[11] and enable a shepherd-like episcopal ministry. The institutional structures of the Church need reform to better facilitate the ecclesial relationships to which the children of God are called.

Institutional change has been a feature of episcopal ministry within the Church. R. P. C. Hanson notes, 'Episcopacy has in Anglican hands shown itself remarkably flexible and has manifested a surprising power of survival.'[12] In developing the role of the bishop, Hanson notes the influence of *quinquesecularism*, and in particular the appeal to Ignatius of Antioch and Cyprian of Carthage. He explains:

> The Ignatian traits are visible in the very strong moral, rather than legal, appeal which the Anglican bishop has always made to the loyalty of his flock, and in the emphasis upon the personal relationship which exists between the bishop and his clergy. The Cyprianic features are the concept that all bishops hold a common responsibility (*in solidum* is Cyprian's phrase) for the whole Church, manifested in the tendency of the bishops of an Anglican province to meet for common counsel, and in the Lambeth Conference.[13]

However, the ordinal suggests that this relationship is not restricted to the ordained; the relational and consultative approach should characterize the relationship that a bishop has with all those in their care. Thus Hanson surmises: 'If we next ask what is the nature of the authority of the Anglican bishop, we shall have to say that ultimately his authority is a moral authority.'[14] Recourse to legal authority and excommunication, for example, have therefore come to be regarded as 'only a last resort in extreme cases; the constant use of ecclesiastical coercion, whether exercised through the bishops or not, is not an Anglican characteristic'.[15]

Hanson also affirms the need for bishops to be integrated within the Church: 'Bishops do not constitute the Church, and they do not form a caste independent of the rest of the Church to which inferior clergy and laity are subordinated.'[16] Given the ordinal's emphasis on the shepherd analogy for bishops, the closeness of relationship often associated between presbyters and their congregations is also required of bishops, including between diocesan bishops and their diocese. What is immediately clear therefore is that the current diocesan structures in the Church are hampering the bishops' ability to create these sorts of relationships. The experience of clergy and laity has been shown to be far from the closeness envisaged. Given the geographical size of the current dioceses, this is unsurprising. Only with smaller dioceses, reflective of the polity in other Churches in the Anglican Communion,[17] is there the potential for this order of relationship.

The model of more dioceses within smaller provinces is suggested in Anthony Hodgson's reflection on Geoffrey Fisher's time as Bishop of London: 'With so many suffragans to manage, Fisher's role at London had something of the dimensions of a metropolitan overseeing a province.'[18] So the suggestion is not a novel one. It has many resonances with the Tiller Report,[19] but where the Tiller Report suggests a differentiation within the presbyterate,[20] the suggestion here is that the differentiation could be between the episcopate and presbyterate, preserving the identity and integrity of each order. The bishops in this vision would be integrated into the life of the local church, as suggested by David Prior; it would be good for bishops, in Tiller's terms, 'to be woven into the leadership and life (especially a home-cell) of a resource-parish'.[21] With bishops actively involved in ministry in the parishes, they could inhabit their primary pastoral and liturgical role. The question of funding, although not completely removed, would be recontextualized, administration could be dealt with at a provincial level, rather than a diocesan one, enabling the fiscal rationalization that has favoured suggestions to reduce the number of dioceses.

It is clear that the current diocesan structures of the Church are not fit for purpose. There is even a question as to whether they have *ever* really worked effectively. As C. A. H. Green notes, auxiliary or assistant bishops have been part of the Church's life since at least the fourth century when they are noted in the Canons of Ancyra (AD 314). The issue was not so much the existence of these 'Chorepiscopi' or 'country bishops' but their relationship with the diocesan bishop, and so bishops before the Reformation were regularly ordained *in partibus infidelium* to assist the diocesan bishops of the English Church.[22] The need for bishops to have a smaller cohort of people to care for is clear theologically, historically and ontologically.

The complexity of the suffragan system, as noted above, is highlighted in the Cameron Report, which wrestles with the relationship between monepiscopacy and the existence of suffragans who are fully bishops within the diocese. The distinction made is between 'personal' and 'general' episcopacy: '[The suffragan bishop] exercises an episcopal and personal *episcope*, not the general *episcope* which the diocesan bishop shares with all his presbyters.'[23] That this and other definitions of the distinction of ecclesial function between suffragans and diocesan bishops has been unsuccessful is clear from issues that continue to beset both suffragan bishops and the Church more widely. As has long been reported:

> There is evidence that some ... of the parish clergy and very many of the laity regard a suffragan bishop as an ... inferior substitute for their 'real' bishop, the diocesan, even in matters which have been agreed with him and the diocesan to be his sole responsibility.[24]

This monarchical experience of episcopacy was questioned in the 1920s:

> The institution of Episcopacy – that is, of oversight exercised under a continuously given commission – has taken a variety of forms, and it cannot be maintained that any one form of it is necessary. So, for example, the monarchical diocesan episcopate might conceivably be changed to a collegiate episcopate if this seemed likely to render better service.[25]

The criteria for assessing what would render 'better service' is the ability of the bishop to relate to the diversity of the body of Christ that facilitates their shepherd ministry.[26] Reducing the number of people to whom the bishop needs to relate is the principal argument that John Henry Newman employs to argue for increased numbers of suffragan bishops in 1835: 'The obvious reason for increasing our number of Bishops is the increase in the population.'[27] Further, Newman affirms the incarnational importance of the ability of members of the Church to relate to their bishop: 'Men do not like to attach themselves to an impalpable system, to a quality, but rather to an embodied form of religion.'[28] This personal relationship is also affirmed in the Cameron Report:

> Nor can the bishop's ministry be separated from the ministry of the whole people of God in the diocese: bishop, presbyter and people belong together. Amongst his people the bishop is the personal focus for their unity, and principal agent in maintaining and strengthening that unity.[29]

Therefore, the ordination rite is not an isolated ritual that must be passed through before the bishop can get on with the real work of 'leadership' within the institution. The rite defines the new relationship the bishop has with the rest of the Church, and that this relationship should be as a shepherd. As Stancliffe affirms, 'Yet it is in *how* the rites are celebrated that the underlying theology can be made explicit.'[30] The *leitourgia* of the rite is directly linked to the praxis of the bishops outside of the liturgical setting. They are to engender unity within the Church both sacramentally and pastorally, being – in Farrer's terms – a 'walking sacrament'.[31] The ecclesial relationship is established at ordination and it is through the praxis of inhabiting this shepherd relationship that the bishop should live out every aspect of their ministry. The relationship between the bishop and the Church is therefore a particularly close one; it requires the bishop to have a personal relationship with those in their care, knowing the people so as to be able to guide them towards having their needs met.

The bishop as shepherd, agent of unity, and guardian of the faith of the Apostles, resonates with the diaconal basis for episcopal ministry. Inhabiting this way of being requires the bishop and the other members of the Church to eschew the temptation to seek the trappings of power for their leaders. Their role is as a community facilitator, shaping the community through their own modelling of Christian discipleship, so that the community itself, albeit dispersed over disparate parishes in the case of a diocese, shapes the lives of the people within it, with the community as a whole taking responsibility for discerning the culture and direction that is God's will for it.

The temptation of worldly models of leadership is evident in the *ASB*, which offers a 'primary emphasis' on 'leadership'. The areas of episcopal leadership are stated as pastoral care, mission (baptizing new believers), proclamation of the gospel, and overseeing the people in their care.[32] *CW:OS* shares some of these references, but not all. The introduction, following *The Greeting*, speaks of 'leading [God's] people in mission' (*CW:OS* 55); the declarations speak of leading 'your people in proclaiming the glorious gospel of Christ' (*CW:OS* 62); and leading 'out to proclaim the good news of the kingdom' (*CW:OS* 63). The charge following the laying on of hands mirrors this: the bishop is to 'lead them in proclaiming the gospel of your salvation in the world' (*CW:OS* 67); there is also reference to liturgical leadership at the declarations: 'lead the offering of prayer and praise' (*CW:OS* 61). However, significantly, *CW:OS* also notes the importance of personal leadership by the bishop in their own discipleship: the bishop is to lead 'in the way of holiness' (*CW:OS* 61).

As with any ministry within the Church, that of a bishop is primarily relational, grounded in the relationship between Christ and the Church. As Stephen Cottrell affirms, 'I love being a bishop, but it is not what defines me. That is my baptism.'[33] The fundamental and primary ecclesial context for a bishop is their being part of the body of Christ, and it is this context that defines how they relate to others and how others should relate to them; it is this context that affirms that bishops are shepherds of the flock in which they are first and foremost sheep, and in which the chief shepherd is Christ himself. As the Office hymn for bishops in the *New English Hymnal* puts it:

> The Shepherd bled to save the sheep,
> And gave his own strict watch to keep,
> That souls bought at so great a cost
> Might never from the fold be lost.[34]

For the bishops of the Church to be shepherds of Christ's flock they must inhabit a difficult role of sharing in both Christ's own shepherding of his people but also being one of the sheep themselves: to be a shepherd bishop is not to be taken out of the flock that is the Church, but to be an integrated part of the flock, identified within the community as one who engenders unity within it and is able to inspire discipleship and protect the community from external threat. The real-life shepherd must bridge the ontological gap as a human leading sheep, learning to think like sheep do: the bishop has the advantage of already being part of the flock as lay person, deacon and priest. The new relationship that the bishop has with the Church is therefore built upon, and is dependent upon, that person maintaining an active connection with these ways of being within the Church. It is out of these ways that the bishop can establish meaningful and trusting relationships with the flock, nurturing the unity of the body and its head – Christ himself.

Shepherding is the defining feature of being a bishop and speaks of the closeness of relationship between the bishop and the Church. The willingness of the Church to follow the bishop depends on their trustworthiness; this trust must be earned and cannot simply be assumed as an aspect of their office. Like the shepherd in the twenty-third psalm embodied by Christ himself, the bishop as shepherd leads the people through danger by journeying through it with them and drawing people along with them through their demonstrable ability to care for the flock and lead them to safety. The future of the institution of the Church depends on its bishops embracing and embodying the true meaning of their shepherding, rendering it a practical reality rather than a notional ideal. This is nothing new; it was described 30 years ago by David Prior:

> If we want to de-centralize the power-structures of the church, the only effective (and biblical) way is to take the person at the top and put him at the bottom in a servant capacity. Fortunately, our bishops are rarely, if ever, prelatical today; but it would release much (and proclaim even more) if bishops and archdeacons were truly part of the fellowship-ministry of a resource-parish.[35]

However, this model is just one possible response, and mirrors the teaching-head model in many smaller primary schools where the head teacher has classroom teaching commitments alongside their oversight responsibilities. The essence is active engagement in the fullness of all levels of the life of the Church, rather than centralized, distanced, focused on oversight as management. Being a shepherd bishop requires embodying the cumulative nature of orders, identifying with the laity, deacons and priests as much as with other bishops, and an active participation in the cure of souls which is shared with the clergy. In short, a shepherd bishop is one who radically undermines the hierarchical and managerial tendencies within the Church, in favour of being a wise and humble pastor who journeys alongside the people, trusting them and being trusted by them.

This new relationship between bishop and the rest of the Church, established at ordination, is identified by the tool of rescue – that is, the pastoral staff – which symbolizes the bishop's care for the people and their determination to eschew the temptation to drive rather than draw the flock. In this way, the bishop cultivates trust within the community and between the community and Christ, who is the Good Shepherd.

The bishop offers a personal example to the Church community of their care and their Christ-inspired willingness to seek the glory that comes through suffering. Thus, the bishop presides at the Eucharist not as the distanced leader, but as the one who has shared in the trials of the community and whom the community trusts as their guide in seeking God. The bishop is therefore embedded in the community, with an active care for each person, the pastoral staff being a symbol of this new relationship in a manner akin to the sacramental purpose of a wedding ring.

Final concluding remarks can now be made with reference to the three questions articulated at the outset of this exploration into ecclesiology and Christian ministry through the lens of the ordinal. The first question set out in the Introduction was: What is the nature of the Church in which the bishop ministers? The primacy of the Church's ontology as a manifestation of the body of Christ has been affirmed. Within the Anglican inheritance, *CW:OS*, significantly influenced by baptismal ecclesiology, affirms the significance of the full active participation of the Church in *leitourgia*. This places the bishop, as the focal Christian minister, firmly within the Church community, sharing with them a common baptism and inhabiting the new relationship with them that is established at ordination. The nature of the relationships within the Church are sacramental of the relationship offered to all by God in Christ, and the term 'sacramental ecclesiology' has been used to best describe the way in which the Church both partakes in that divine relationship and points beyond itself to the fullness of that relationship in the body of Christ. Christian ministry is therefore both rooted in, and speaks of, the foundational sacramental ecclesiology in which relational ontology is of primary importance.

The second question was: How does ecclesiology inform episcopal ministry? Within the fullness of the life of the Church, paradigmatically manifested by the eucharistic assembly with the bishop presiding *in loco Christi*, the bishop has been shown to be a sign of Christ's presence in the community by being his ambassador. The bishop's ministry depends on the trust of the Church, which is corporately engaged in the mutual pursuit of the deepening relationship with God in Christ. This relationship is characterized by the bishop being a shepherd of the Church, with whom the bishop identifies and associates closely. Trust and eschewing of personal power have been shown to be key attributes of the relationship, which is modelled on the kenosis of Christ's own ministry. In so doing, the bishop seeks God's glory through being prepared to suffer for the sake of the people in their care. Thus the bishop's ministry is integrated into their own discipleship, and their modelling of the Christian life reflects the nature of the Church which nurtures the faith of the children of God and, through lives transfigured, proclaims the gospel in the world. The bishop is therefore radically countercultural and must be aware of the temptations of the worldly trappings of power: both their own desire for themselves and the desires of others projected onto them.

The third question was: How do 'shepherd' and other key terms define and elucidate the bishop's ontology? The bishop is one who leads by example, whom the Church follow because they trust that the bishop has a close relationship with God and a close relationship with them. The way in which the Church community knows this is threefold, relating to Weber's threefold forms of authority.[36] First, the Church has a trust in its tradition as an institution to successfully discern the person whom God is calling to be a bishop; second, the members of the Church have personal experience of the depth of pastoral care and spiritual wisdom that the bishop inhabits; third, the Church community experiences the ordered nature of the Church, that the bishop is able to 'govern' the Church well, creating a culture in which the body of Christ is nurtured, and facilitate one another in nurturing their personal and common discipleship. None of this can be taken for granted, and each aspect is readily undermined by errors, or over-confidence in discernment, distance and disinterest on the part of some bishops, and disorder or fear within the Church about its future.

The Church needs to restore trust that it can facilitate and support the ecclesial relationships articulated here, trust that has been significantly eroded in recent years. To minister in the way articulated here will require bishops to recognize and actively eschew the temptations of power, to close the distance between themselves and the rest of the Church, such that they are known by – and know – the people whom they care for on behalf of Christ. Only in this way will trust be restored, with the bishops modelling themselves and their ministries on the kenosis of Christ. The understanding of episcopal ministry advanced here is therefore closely aligned to presbyteral ministry.[37] For *CW:OS*, the Church of England bishop is not simply an overseer, or moderator, as they may be in other denominations or in secular management structures; there is a distinctive emphasis on the bishop being the local minister and on their closeness to the other members of the Church.

The potential implications for the institutional life of the Church can be seen in four key areas. First, there is an opportunity to revise the role of synods in the life of the Church. At deanery, diocesan and provincial levels, synods provide an opportunity for the full expression of the Church to gather and discern the will of God. The leadership of the diocesan bishop is akin to their role in presiding at the Eucharist, facilitating the unity of the Church, listening to the needs of the people, and articulating a way forward that the people will willingly follow. The place of authority is therefore between either the imposition of their will on the one hand, or a need for there to be unanimity on the other. There is something here about honouring the role of the whole Church in discerning the will of God, and in enabling that important creative tension between leader and led, which holds both to account and prevents either the autocracy of the bishop or the separatist tendencies that may exist within particular congregations or perspectives. This would also help develop a way of finding an institutional form of being that transcends the apparent dichotomy between those who wish to affirm a polity of 'bishop in council' and those who affirm 'episcopally led and synodically governed'.

Second, the discernment and training of candidates for episcopal ordination needs to emphasize the centrality of the relationships articulated here. This requires a shift away from a preference for those who have held other 'senior roles' or the specific needs of any given diocese. There is something here about the character and spirituality of the bishop being at the heart of their ministry. Recognizing that and fostering it must be at the heart of the discernment and preparation process to help a new generation of bishops inhabit the virtues and praxis envisaged by the ordinal.[38] Moreover, any model of leadership that identifies the bishop as leader, without the leadership of Christ being explicit, is always going to be fatally flawed. The bishop has a sacramental ontology in that their ministry is defined by their pointing beyond themselves to Christ, and thus the praxis of their ministry becomes a locus for the revelation of Christ in the world.

Third, the priorities established for the bishop's relationship with the rest of the Church at ordination need to be fostered by the way in which they are deployed by the institution. If they are to know and be known by the Church, the diocese must be a unit that is sufficiently small to facilitate this. The suggestions of larger dioceses, while possibly making financial savings and maintaining the kudos of the bishop, is diametrically opposed to the ontology and praxis established at ordination. It is a relationship that requires localism, and this defines the translocal ministry of the diocesan bishop.

Fourth, there is the question of discipline within the Church. As has been demonstrated, discipline is often equated in church reports with the ability to exert power over its members.[39] This has been codified by the diocesan bishop's role in the Clergy Discipline Measure. It is important to note that the pastoral metaphor, as used by Jesus in the Gospels, does not make provision for the misbehaving sheep. However, what can be affirmed is that the bishop's relationship with the members of the Church should be characterized by a desire for the good of each person. This is not the same as permissiveness. It considers the needs of each person, and the ultimate goal of facilitating right relationships within the body of Christ. In this way, discipline is returned to its root meaning – that is, a relationship that enables learning.[40]

It would take another book to explore further how this ideal is to be inhabited in the world, and whether there is an appropriate use of power when the diocesan bishop no longer enjoys authority for one of their flock. A fundamental question that is raised here is whether the right relationship, which the ordinal affirms as being at the heart of the bishop's ministry, and which Rohr suggests is at the heart of Jesus' teaching, is an ideal or a way of life. The suggestion here is that Jesus' articulation of the kingdom of God is nearer to a way of life than an ideal. Invitational authority characterizes this right relationship and should inform the daily praxis of bishops and all Christian leaders. The use of coercion is always symptomatic of failure and using power over someone when that is not in their best interests is never acceptable.[41] An essential aspect of bearing witness to the kingdom of God is in maintaining the kingdom of God way of life even when that is costly and counter to the worldly expectations. This is the goal to which the Church should seek to move; however, getting there may require an evolution that takes many years.

The right relationship advocated here is, while not absent from the life of the Church, something that needs to at least be nourished and prioritized within the life of the Church. Moreover, these relationships require a significant amount of self-awareness and a movement towards a parental relationship as enjoyed between adults, rather than envisaging the baptized as either naïve children or difficult teenagers. There is value here in the father title for bishops, if seen in the relationship that one might hope to have in adulthood with one's parent. Over time, in the familial context, a spectrum of healthy and appropriate relationship can be observed, depending on the context and as a child matures. Right relationship in the kingdom of God is closer to the adult-to-adult dynamic. This is based on the equal relationship as children of God offered by Christ and accepted in baptism, and it may be helpful to envisage the bishop as an elder sibling within the family of the Church. This elder sibling metaphor provides a way in which the equality of persons within the ecclesiology of the Church might interface with the hierarchy of roles within the institution of the Church, rooting the institutional roles in the values of the kingdom of God.

The establishing of right relationship is fundamental to the kingdom of God that the Church seeks to inhabit. The ministry of the bishop is as much defined by that as is every aspect of the life of the Church. Models of management and leadership from other contexts need not be eschewed, but they do need to be assessed in this light if they are to be employed for the furtherance of the kingdom of God. The eucharistic assembly, the focal *leitourgia* of the Church and the context for ordination, is a paradigm that shapes the whole of the bishop's ministry. The bishop gathers the Church together as their shepherd, so that both might be open and vulnerable with God. The bishop stands alongside them and *in loco Christi*, making Christ visible in their ministry, and leading the Church to find Christ in word and sacrament. As their trusted shepherd, the bishop is able to lead the Church through the valley of the shadow of death, the facing of their own mortality, and the letting go of their false self or ego so that they can find not their own glory but the gracious gift of the glory of God. For Kenneth Bailey, the links between the Eucharist and Christ's shepherd-hood are readily identifiable in the prominence of Psalm 23 for St Paul's recounting of the institution of the Eucharist.[42] In standing *in loco Christi*, the bishop inhabits their role as under-shepherd for Christ, drawing the community to Christ through their own faith in Christ.

The bishop's relationship with the Church is sacramental of the relationship between God and his people. God provides a bishop for the Church to act as Christ's ambassador, to nourish the trust that all are called to have in God. It is the personal and communal trust that the body of Christ have for God, which is at the heart of Christian ministry. It is a ministry based on trust, inherently vulnerable and costly, and is thereby an outworking of Christ's own ministry, rooted and grounded in the Church's common discipleship of Christ, in which people and communities grow as disciples of Christ in the world. This way of life, integrated into the celebration of the Eucharist, is the vocation, ministry and witness of the Church in the world for the bishop and all the baptized.

CONCLUSIONS FOR CONTEMPORARY EPISCOPAL MINISTRY

Notes

1 Copies can be obtained from the Bishop of Salisbury's office, South Canonry, Salisbury.

2 This is a complex concept, as the 'diocese' could connote the community of parishes; however, here it is understood to stand for the centralized structures, including – significantly for this study – the diocesan and suffragan bishops.

3 Veronica Hope Hailey, 2019, *The Trustworthy Leader: A Report for the Diocese of Salisbury*, p. 4.

4 Hope Hailey, *The Trustworthy Leader*, p. 6.

5 Hope Hailey, *The Trustworthy Leader*, p. 50.

6 Sarah Horsman et al., 2021, '"I Was Handed Over to the Dogs": Lived Experience, Clerical Trauma and the Handling of Complaints against Clergy in the Church of England', <https://www.sheldonhub.org/usercontent/sitecontentuploads/3/1A10E25DCB7DB5E02AB69C0188CF7975/handed%20over%20to%20the%20dogs%20final.pdf>, p. 16, accessed 11.09.2025.

7 Horsman et al., 'I Was Handed Over to the Dogs'.

8 Fiona Gardner, 2021, *Sex, Power, Control: Responding to Abuse in the Institutional Church*, Cambridge: Lutterworth Press, p. 52.

9 Gardner, *Sex, Power, Control*, p. 165.

10 Gardner, *Sex, Power, Control*, p. 162.

11 Here mission is conceived of as nurturing the relationships that lead to salvation, rather than proselytizing or marketing initiatives.

12 R. P. C. Hanson, 1969, 'The Nature of the Anglican Episcopate' in Michael Ramsey, *Lambeth Essays on Ministry*, London: SPCK, p. 80.

13 Hanson, 'The Nature of the Anglican Episcopate', pp. 81–2.

14 Hanson, 'The Nature of the Anglican Episcopate', p. 84.

15 Hanson, 'The Nature of the Anglican Episcopate', p. 85.

16 Hanson, 'The Nature of the Anglican Episcopate', p. 85.

17 For example, Hanson himself was Bishop of Clogher in the Church of Ireland from 1970 to 1973. He had about 40 clergy in his diocese.

18 Anthony Hodgson, 2018, 'The Origins and Evolution of Suffragan Bishops in the Church of England', Lambeth PhD Thesis, Chapter 6, p. 20.

19 John Tiller, 1983, *A Strategy for the Church's Ministry* (commonly called the Tiller Report after its author), London: CIO Publishing.

20 Tiller, *A Strategy for the Church's Ministry*, pp. 169–79.

21 David Prior, 1983, 'Resource Parishes – An Alternative Way Forward' in Graham Dow et al., *Whose Hand on the Tiller? The Future of the Church's Ministry as a Response to the Tiller Report*, Bramcote: Grove Books, pp. 20–4, p. 20.

22 'The rule has now been established that where an Assistant or Auxiliary Bishop is needed, and cannot be found among Bishops who have resigned their Sees, he may be Consecrated to a fictitious See or Diocese, in which there is no possibility of his exercising power of Order, or the power of Jurisdiction; so consecrated he is free to assist a Diocesan Bishop. In England this rule, which was confirmed by Acts of Parliament in the sixteenth century, is in constant operation.' C. A. H. Green, 1937, *The Setting of the Constitution of the Church in Wales*, London: Sweet and Maxwell, p. 20.

23 The Central Board of Finance of the Church of England, 1990, *Episcopal*

Ministry: The Report of the Archbishops' Group on the Episcopate 1990 (commonly called the Cameron Report after its author), London: Church House Publishing, p. 199.

24 Dioceses Commission, 1985, *Episcopacy and the Role of the Suffragan Bishop: A Second Report by the Dioceses Commission*, London: General Synod, paragraph 20.

25 Church of England, 1938, *Doctrine in the Church of England: The Report of the Commission on Christian Doctrine Appointed by the Archbishops of Canterbury and York in 1922*, London: SPCK, pp. 121–2.

26 In a similar vein, beyond a certain size, a sheep flock can no longer be shepherded by voice alone, dogs etc. are then needed to enforce control rather than win trust.

27 John Henry Newman, 1877, 'The Restoration of Suffragan Bishops' in *The Via Media of The Anglican Church*, Vol. II, London: Basil Montagu and Pickering, pp. 41–83, p. 50.

28 Newman, 'The Restoration of Suffragan Bishops', p. 80.

29 The Central Board of Finance of the Church of England, 1990, *Episcopal Ministry: The Report of the Archbishops' Group on the Episcopate 1990*, p. 94. Note the confusion between diocesan and suffragan bishops here, in the assumption that there is only one bishop in the diocese.

30 David Stancliffe, 2023, 'Ordination in the Church of England: Theology and Practice in the Common Worship Ordinal' in Thomas Pott, James Hawkey and Keith Pecklers (eds), *Malines: Continuing the Conversation*, London: SPCK, pp. 141–52, p. 152.

31 'And that's not all; the man who bears the Sacrament is sacramental himself; he is, one might almost say, himself a walking sacrament.' Austin Farrer, 1991, 'Walking Sacraments' in Lesie Houlden (ed.), *Austin Farrer: The Essential Sermons*, London: SPCK, Chapter 26.

32 The Central Board of Finance of the Church of England, 1990, *Episcopal Ministry: The Report of the Archbishops' Group on the Episcopate 1990*, pp. 83–4. Paragraph 182 notes the leadership claims in:

- the opening words of the Declarations remind the congregation that, 'a bishop is called to lead in serving and caring for the people of God and to work with them in the oversight of the Church'.
- the final question that is asked of the bishop-elect concerns his willingness to 'lead your people to obey our Saviour's command to make disciples of all nations'.
- the prayer that follows immediately upon the laying on of hands asks for grace and power that the bishop 'may lead those committed to his charge in proclaiming the gospel of salvation'.
- the post-communion Collect has at its heart the petition that the bishop 'may lead the people committed to his charge'.

33 Stephen Cottrell, 2020, 'Church of England Bishops as Pastor and Evangelist' in Roger Standing and Paul Goodliff (eds), *Episkope: The Theory and Practice of Translocal Oversight*, London: SCM Press, pp. 71–80, p. 79.

34 George Tims et al., 1986, *New English Hymnal: Full Music Edition*, Norwich: Canterbury Press, p. 506.

35 David Prior, 1983, 'Resource Parishes – An Alternative Way Forward', pp. 20–4, p. 20.

36 See the discussion in Chapter 6.

37 For instance, Lesslie Newbigin's *The Good Shepherd* is addressed mainly to the presbyterate. Cf. Lesslie Newbigin, 1977, *The Good Shepherd: Meditations on Christian Ministry in Today's World*, Leighton Buzzard: The Faith Press.

38 For a view of the current process and an alternative set of priorities, see Gerry Lynch, 2024, 'The Failure of Anglican Managerialism', *The Critic*, 11 January, <https://thecritic.co.uk/the-failure-of-anglican-managerialism/>, accessed 11.09.2025.

39 Cf. the misunderstanding about the shepherd's use of the rod to discipline the sheep in Chapter 9.

40 This way of being also offers hope for a new understanding of clergy discipline within the life of the Church of England, where the Clergy Discipline Measure needs significant revision. As the one who invites ministry within the diocese, the diocesan bishop is one who holds the boundaries of that invitation and, if necessary, as a last resort, rescind that invitation. The investigative role is best placed outside of this relationship, so that the diocesan bishop can retain the pastoral role until such time as the facts have been established and can be presented. Moreover, the bishop's place as pastor is to lament alongside all those impacted by failings, rather than to stand in the place of condemnation. As James Timpson notes, it is even possible to end someone's role on good terms and while being 'kind and compassionate'. Cf. James Timpson, 2024, *The Happy Index*, Manchester: Harper North, pp. 38–41.

41 It is worth noting here that to exert power over someone who is harming another to stop that harm is both in the interests of the person's victim and the perpetrator themselves.

42 Paul has apparently reflected deeply on Psalm 23 in the light of the life and sacrificial ministry of Jesus, the Good Shepherd (Luke 15.4–7). The result is that when discussing the Eucharist, Paul easily and naturally speaks of 'the cup' and the 'table'. Kenneth E. Bailey, 2011, *Paul through Mediterranean Eyes: Cultural Studies in 1 Corinthians*, London: SPCK, p. 277.

Bibliography

Liturgies

Archbishops' Council, 2000, *Common Worship: Pastoral Services*, London: Church House Publishing.
Archbishops' Council, 2000, *Common Worship: Services and Prayers for the Church of England*, London: Church House Publishing.
Archbishops' Council, 2006, *Common Worship: Initiation Services*, London: Church House Publishing.
Archbishops' Council, 2007, *Common Worship: Ordination Services*, London: Church House Publishing.
Church of England, 2004 [1662], *The Book of Common Prayer and Administration of the Sacraments and other Rites and Ceremonies of the Church according to the Use of the Church of England, 1662*, Cambridge: Cambridge University Press.
Church of England, 1938, *Doctrine in the Church of England: The Report of the Commission on Christian Doctrine Appointed by the Archbishops of Canterbury and York in 1922*, London: SPCK.
Church of Ireland, 'The Form of Ordaining or Consecrating an Archbishop or Bishop', <https://www.ireland.anglican.org/cmsfiles/files/worship/pdf/Ord1Bish.pdf>, accessed 11.09.2025.
Church of Ireland, 'The Ordination or Consecration of a Bishop', https://www.ireland.anglican.org/cmsfiles/files/worship/pdf/Ord2Bish.pdf, accessed 11.09.2025.
The Central Board of the Church of England, 1980, *The Alternative Service Book 1980*, London: SPCK.
The Church in Wales, 'Alternative Ordinal', <https://churchinwales.contentfiles.net/media/documents/Alternative_Ordinal_-_2004.pdf>, accessed 11.09.2025.
The Episcopal Church of the United States of America, 1979, *The Book of Common Prayer and Administration of the Sacraments and Other Rites and Ceremonies of the Church*, New York: The Seabury Press.
The Scottish Episcopal Church, 'Scottish Ordinal 1984', <https://www.scotland.anglican.org/who-we-are/publications/liturgies/scottish-ordinal-1984/>, accessed 11.09.2025.

Church publications, reports and canons

Anglican Communion, 1948, 'Committee Report on the Anglican Communion' in *The Lambeth Conference 1948 – The Encyclical Letter from the Bishops: Together with Resolutions and Reports*, London: SPCK, pp. 84–5.

Anglican-Orthodox Dialogue Joint Doctrinal Commission, 1984, *The Dublin Agreed Statement 1984*, <https://www.anglicancommunion.org/media/103812/the_dublin_statement.pdf>, accessed 11.09.2025.

Archbishops' Council, 1999, *General Synod Report of Proceedings July 1999*, 30 (1).

Archbishops' Council, 2015, *Senior Church Leadership: A Resource for Reflection*, <https://www.churchofengland.org/sites/default/files/2017-10/senior_church_leadership_faoc.pdf>, accessed 11.09.2025.

Archbishops' Council, 2017, *Setting God's People Free*, <https://www.churchofengland.org/sites/default/files/2017-11/gs-2056-setting-gods-people-free.pdf>, accessed 11.09.2025.

Catholic Church, 1985, *Caeremoniale Episcoporum*, Vatican: Polyglot Press.

Chartres, Richard, 2015, 'Islington 2015', https://www.thinkinganglicans.org.uk/wp-content/uploads/2015/03/20150101-London-Bishops-Council-item-9-Revival-of-The-See-of-Islington-2015.pdf>, accessed 11.09.2025.

Church of England, 'Clergy Discipline', *Church of England*, <https://www.churchofengland.org/about/leadership-and-governance/legal-services/clergy-discipline>, accessed 11.09.2025.

Church of England, 'Reviews and Reports', *Church of England*, <https://www.churchofengland.org/safeguarding/reviews-and-reports>, accessed 11.09.2025.

Church of England, 1990, 'Suffragan Bishops', GS Misc 733, <https://www.churchofengland.org/sites/default/files/2023-01/gs-misc-733-suffragan-bishops.pdf>, accessed 11.09.2025.

Church of England, 2005, GS 1535Y, *Report of the Revision Committee*.

Church of England, 2005, GS 1535Z, *Second Report of the Revision Committee*.

Church of England, 2017, 'Discerning in Obedience: A Theological Review of the Crown Nominations Commission', <https://www.churchofengland.org/sites/default/files/2018-01/gs-misc-1171-discerning-in-obedience-report-on-the-review-of-the-cnc.pdf>, accessed 11.09.2025.

Church of England, 'Canon B2', <https://www.churchofengland.org/about/governance/legal-resources/canons-church-england/section-b>, accessed 11.09.2025.

Church of England, 'Canon C1.1', <https://www.churchofengland.org/about/governance/legal-resources/canons-church-england/section-c#b59>, accessed 11.09.2025.

Church of England, 'Canon C13', *Church of England*, <https://www.churchofengland.org/about/governance/legal-resources/canons-church-england/section-c>, accessed 11.09.2025.

Church of England, Cf. Canon C15.1(1). Cited in *CW:OS*, p. 57.

Church of England, 'Canon C18.1', *Church of England*, <https://www.churchofengland.org/about/governance/legal-resources/canons-church-england/section-c>, accessed 11.09.2025.

Church of England, 'Canon C18.4', <https://www.churchofengland.org/about/leadership-and-governance/legal-services/canons-church-england/section-c>, accessed 11.09.2025.

Church of England, 'Canon C2.3', *Church of England*, <https://www.churchofengland.org/about/governance/legal-resources/canons-church-england/sec-

tion-c>, accessed 15.07.2022.

Church of England, *From Anecdote to Evidence: Findings for the Church Growth Research Programme 2011–2013*, Church of England, <https://www.churchofengland.org/sites/default/files/2019-06/from_anecdote_to_evidence_-_the_report.pdf>, accessed 12.11.2021.

Dioceses Commission, 1985, *Episcopacy and the Role of the Suffragan Bishop: A Second Report by the Dioceses Commission*, London: General Synod.

Green, S. et al., 2014, 'Talent Management for Future Leaders and Leadership Development for Bishops and Deans: A New Approach Report of the Lord Green Steering Group', <https://www.thinkinganglicans.org.uk/uploads/TalentManagement.pdf>, accessed 11.09.2025.

Henderson, Julian, et al., 2019, 'Letter from Senior Clergy Reflecting on IICSA Reports on Chichester Diocese and Peter Ball', *Blackburn Diocese*, <https://www.blackburn.anglican.org/news/274/letter-from-senior-clergy-reflecting-on->, accessed 11.09.2025.

Hope Hailey, Veronica, 2019, The Trustworthy Leader: A Report for the Diocese of Salisbury, p. 4.

International Anglican Liturgy Consultation, 2006, *The Berkeley Statement: To Equip the Saints Ordination in Anglicanism Today*, edited by Ronald L. Dowling and David R. Holeton, Blackrock: Columba Press.

Matta al-Miskin, 1998, *The Gospel According to Saint Luke (Arabic)*, Cairo: Dayr al-Qiddis Anba Maqar, p. 568.

Revision Committee, Ordination Service Report January 2005, p. 33, #133.

Sentamu, John, 2015, 'Statement by York on the Consecration of a Traditionalist Bishop for Burnley', *Anglican*, <https://anglican.ink/2015/01/23/statement-by-york-on-the-consecration-of-a-traditionalist-bishop-for-burnley/>, accessed 11.09.2025.

Stancliffe, David, 2019, 'Episcopal Dress and Kit', an unpublished guidance document for new bishops in the Church of England.

Stancliffe, David, 1998, 'Extended Authorisation for the Ordinal in the Alternative Service book 1980', GS 1319, London: General Synod, Church of England.

The Central Board of Finance of the Church of England, 1990, *Episcopal Ministry: The Report of the Archbishops' Group on the Episcopate 1990*, London: Church House Publishing.

The Church in Wales, 'Chapter V: The Archbishop and the Diocesan Bishops', <https://www.churchinwales.org.uk/en/clergy-and-members/constitution/chapter-v-archbishop-and-diocesan-bishops/>, accessed 11.09.2025.

The Liturgical Commission, 2007, 'Celebrating Ordinations: A Practical Guide' in Archbishops' Council, *Common Worship: Ordination Services*, London: Church House Publishing.

The Liturgical Commission, 2007, 'Commentary' in The Archbishops' Council, *Common Worship: Ordination Services*, London: Church House Publishing.

The World Council of Churches, 1982, *Baptism, Eucharist and Ministry*, Faith and Order paper no. 111, Geneva: World Council of Churches.

Secondary literature

Abbott-Smith, G., 1992, *A Manual Greek Lexicon of the New Testament*, London: T&T Clark.

Aldred, Joe, 2020, 'Foreword' in Roger Standing and Paul Goodliff (eds), *Episkope: The Theory and Practice of Translocal Oversight*, London: SCM Press, pp. xix–xx.

Avis, Paul, 1990, *Christians in Communion*, London: Geoffrey Chapman Mowbray.

Avis, Paul, 2008, *The Identity of Anglicanism*, London: T&T Clark.

Avis, Paul, 2015, *Becoming a Bishop: A Theological Handbook of Episcopal Ministry*, London: Bloomsbury/T&T Clark.

Avis, Paul, 2018, *The Anglican Understanding of the Church*, London: SPCK.

Avis, Paul, 2020, 'Anglican Episcopacy' in Roger Standing and Paul Goodliff (eds), *Episkope: The Theory and Practice of Translocal Oversight*, London: SCM Press, pp. 61–70.

Baier, Karl, 2010, 'Spiritual Authority: A Christian Perspective', *Buddhist–Christian Studies*, 30, pp. 107–99.

Bailey, Kenneth E., 2008, *Jesus through Middle Eastern Eyes*, London: SPCK.

Bailey, Kenneth E., 2011, *Paul through Mediterranean Eyes: Cultural Studies in 1 Corinthians*, London: SPCK.

Bailey, Kenneth E., 2015, *The Good Shepherd: A Thousand-Year Journey from Psalm 23 to the New Testament*, London: SPCK.

Ballard, Paul H. and Pritchard, John, 2006, *Practical Theology in Action*, London: SPCK.

Barton, John, 1988, *People of the Book*, London: SPCK.

Barton, John, 2022, *The Word, on the Translation of the Bible*, London: Allen Lane.

Bell, David, 2007, 'Foreword' in Julia Middleton, *Beyond Authority*, Basingstoke: Palgrave Macmillan.

Bennet, Alan, 2014, *The History Boys*, London: Faber.

Bradshaw, Paul, 1971, *The Anglican Ordinal*, London: SPCK.

Bradshaw, Paul, 2006, *A Companion to Common Worship*, vol. 2, London: SPCK.

Bradshaw, Paul, 2006, 'The Church of England' in Ronald L. Dowling and David R. Holeton (eds), *Equipping the Saints: Ordination in Anglicanism Today*, Blackrock: Columba Press, pp. 146–9.

Bradshaw, Paul and Jones, Simon, 2006, 'Daily Prayer' in Paul Bradshaw (ed.), *A Companion to Common Worship*, vol. 2, London: SPCK.

Brown, Andrew, 2020, 'Analysis: Church Commissioners Spend £24m to "Create 50,000 Disciples"', *Religion Media Centre*, <https://religionmediacentre.org.uk/news/analysis-church-commissioner-disciples/>, accessed 11.09.2025.

Brown, Rosalind, 2008, *Being a Deacon Today*, Norwich: Canterbury Press.

Brueggemann, Walter, 1997, *Theology of the Old Testament*, Minneapolis, MN: Fortress Press.

Burgess, Kaya, 2022, 'Behold the Bishop of Brexit as church models itself on politics', *The Times*, <https://www.thetimes.com/uk/politics/article/bishop-of-brexit-church-models-itself-politics-vd8mv2fgg>, accessed 11.09.2025.

Caeremoniale Episcoporum, 1985, Vatican: Polyglot Press, p. 59.

Chapman, Mark, 2013,'Does the Church of England have a Theology of General Synod?', *Journal of Anglican Studies*, 11 (1), pp. 15–31.

Charry, Ellen T., 2005, 'Sacramental Ecclesiology' in Mark Husbands and Daniel T. Treier (eds), *The Community of the Word Towards an Evangelical Ecclesiology*, Leicester: Apollos.

Chartres, Richard, 2015, 'Islington 2015', https://www.thinkinganglicans.org.uk/wp-content/uploads/2015/03/20150101-London-Bishops-Council-item-9-Revival-of-The-See-of-Islington-2015.pdf>, accessed 11.09.2025.

Clammer, Tom, 2018, '"Be Born in our Hearts": Being Transported and Transformed by the Liturgy' in Aiden Platten (ed.), *Grasping the Heel of Heaven*, Norwich: Canterbury Press.

Cottrell, Stephen, 2020, 'Church of England Bishops as Pastor and Evangelist' in Roger Standing and Paul Goodliff (eds), *Episkope: The Theory and Practice of Translocal Oversight*, London: SCM Press, pp. 71–80.

Croft, Steven, 2008, *Ministry in Three Dimensions*, second edition, London: Darton, Longman and Todd.

Croft, Steven, 2020, 'The Cure of Souls', *Diocese of Oxford: Bishop Steven's Blog*, <https://blogs.oxford.anglican.org/the-cure-of-souls/>, accessed 21.01.2022.

Croft, Steven, 2022, 'The Cure of Souls', *Diocese of Oxford: Bishop Steven's Blog*, <https://blogs.oxford.anglican.org/the-cure-of-souls/>, accessed 11.09. 2025.

Cross, F. L. and Livingstone, E. A., 2009, *The Oxford Dictionary of the Christian Church*, third edition, Oxford: Oxford University Press.

Dales, Douglas, 2005, 'One Body: The Ecclesiology of Michael Ramsey' in Douglas Dales et al. (eds), *Glory Descending*, Norwich: Canterbury Press.

Davies, Madeleine, 2021, 'Lord Chancellor "likely" to pass names of new C of E bishops to Queen', *Church Times*, <https://www.churchtimes.co.uk/articles/2021/11-june/news/uk/lord-chancellor-likely-to-pass-names-of-new-c-of-e-bishops-to-queen>, accessed 11.09.2025.

Davies, Madeleine, 2021,'Synod to discuss target of 10,000 new lay-led churches in the next ten years', *Church Times*, https://www.churchtimes.co.uk/articles/2021/2-july/news/uk/synod-to-discuss-target-of-10-000-new-lay-led-churches-in-the-next-ten-years, accessed 11.09.2025.

Davies, Madeleine, 2022, 'Fewer dioceses, specialist bishops: Archbishops' confidential paper revealed in detail', *Church Times*, <https://www.churchtimes.co.uk/articles/2022/11-february/news/uk/fewer-dioceses-specialist-bishops-archbishops-confidential-paper-revealed-in-detail>, accessed 11.09.2025.

Doniger, Wendy (ed.), 1999, 'Crosier' in *Merriam-Webster's Encyclopaedia of World Religions*, Springfield, MA: Merriam-Webster, p. 269.

Dowling, Ronald L., 2006, 'The Presentation of Candidates' in Ronald L. Dowling and David R. Holeton (eds), *Equipping the Saints: Ordination in Anglicanism Today*, Blackrock: Columba Press, pp. 135–7.

Fagerberg, David, 1992, *What Is Liturgical Theology?*, Collegeville, MN: The Liturgical Press.

Farrer, Austin, 1991,'Walking Sacraments' in Leslie Houlden, *Austin Farrer: The Essential Sermons*, London: SPCK.

Fraser, Giles, 2022, 'The Church's War on the Clergy', *UnHerd*, <https://unherd.com/2022/02/justin-welbys-war-on-the-parish/>, accessed 11.09.2025.

Galkin, Elliott W., 1998, *A History of Orchestral Conducting in Theory and Practice*, New York: Pendragon Press.

Gardner, Fiona, 2021, *Sex, Power, Control: Responding to Abuse in the Institutional Church*, Cambridge: The Lutterworth Press.

Gibson, Paul A., 2006, 'A Baptismal Ecclesiology: Some Questions' in Ronald L. Dowling and David R. Holeton (eds), *Equipping the Saints: Ordination in Anglicanism Today*, Blackrock: Columba Press, pp. 35–44.

Gittoes, Julie, Green, Brutus, and Head, James, 2013, 'Introduction' in Julie Gittoes, Brutus Green and James Head, *Generous Ecclesiology: Church, World and the Kingdom of God*, London: SCM Press.

Goodliff, Paul, 2020, 'Translocal Ministry and Scholarship' in Roger Standing and Paul Goodliff (eds), *Episkope: The Theory and Practice of Translocal Oversight*, London: SCM Press, pp. 225–31.

Goodliffe, Paul, 2020, 'Contemporary Models of Translocal Ministry: Ecumenical Landscapes' in Roger Standing and Paul Goodliff (eds), *Episkope: The Theory and Practice of Translocal Oversight*, London: SCM Press, pp. 44–60.

Green, C. A. H., 1937, *The Setting of the Constitution of the Church in Wales*, London: Sweet and Maxwell.

Grundy, Malcolm, 2011, *Leadership and Oversight: New Models for Episcopal Ministry*, London: Mowbray.

Hall Jennings, Helen, 1950, *Leadership and Isolation: A Study of Inter-Personal Relationships*, second edition, London: Longmans, Green & Co.

Hanson, R. P. C., 1969, 'The Nature of the Anglican Episcopate' in Michael Ramsey (ed.), *Lambeth Essays on Ministry*, London: SPCK.

Hayward, John, 2022, 'Growth, Decline and Extinction of UK Churches', *Anglican Ink*, <https://anglican.ink/2022/05/21/growth-decline-and-extinction-of-uk-churches/>, accessed 11.09.2025.

Hodgson, Anthony, 2018, 'The Origins and Evolution of Suffragan Bishops in the Church of England', Lambeth PhD Thesis, available from the British Library.

Holloway, David, 2020, *Finance, Centrism and the Quota*, <https://www.churchsociety.org/wp-content/uploads/2021/05/finance_centralism_quota.pdf>, accessed 11.09.2025.

Horsman, Sarah et al, 2021, '"I Was Handed Over to the Dogs": Lived Experience, Clerical Trauma and the Handling of Complaints Against Clergy in the Church of England', <https://www.sheldonhub.org/usercontent/sitecontentuploads/3/1A10E25DCB7DB5E02AB69C0188CF7975/handed%20over%20to%20the%20dogs%20final.pdf>, accessed 11.09.2025.

Hubbard, Julian, 2020, 'Translocal Ministries in the Church of England as Institutional Leadership' in Roger Standing and Paul Goodliff (eds), *Episkope: The Theory and Practice of Translocal Oversight*, London: SCM Press, pp. 93–102.

Irving, Alexander, 2019, 'Baptismal Ecclesiology and the Ordination Rites of the Church of England in the 2005 Common Worship Ordinal', *Churchman*, 133 (3), pp. 203–23.

Jones, James, 2020, 'Church of England Bishops as Religious and Civic Leaders' in Roger Standing and Paul Goodliff (eds), *Episkope: The Theory and Practice of Translocal Oversight*, London: SCM Press, pp. 81–92.

Jones, Simon, 2016, *Celebrating Christian Initiation: Baptism, Confirmation and Rite for the Christian Journey*, London: SPCK.

BIBLIOGRAPHY

Kavanagh, Aidan, 1990, *Elements of Rite*, Collegeville, MN: Liturgical Press.

Kaye, B., 2008, *An Introduction to World Anglicanism*, Cambridge: Cambridge University Press.

Keller, W. Peter, 1970, *A Shepherd Looks at Psalm 23*, Grands Rapids, MI: Zondervan.

Krikorian, Meshach Paul, 1999, 'The Spirit of the Shepherd: An Interpretation of the Psalm Immortal' in Miriam Taylor Wert, *Meshach Paul Krikorian*, Nappanee, IN: Evangel Press.

Leggett, Richard, 2006, 'By Public Prayer and the Imposition of Hands: The Prayer of the People and the Ordination Prayer' in Ronald L. Dowling and David R. Holeton (eds), *Equipping the Saints: Ordination in Anglicanism Today*, Blackrock: Columba Press, pp. 71–84.

Lenski, Noel, 2016, *Constantine and the Cities: Imperial Authority and Civic Politics*, Philadelphia, PA: University of Pennsylvania Press.

Lynch, Gerry, 2024, 'The Failure of Anglican Managerialism', *The Critic*, <https://thecritic.co.uk/the-failure-of-anglican-managerialism/>, accessed 11.09.2025.

Maddela, Tomos S., 2006, 'The Episcopal Church in the Philippines' in Ronald L. Dowling and David R. Holeton (eds), *Equipping the Saints: Ordination in Anglicanism Today*, Blackrock: Columba Press, pp. 153–9.

McCool, Gerald A., 1975, *A Rahner Reader*, London: Darton, Longman and Todd.

McLeod, S. A., 2018, 'Maslow's Hierarchy of Needs', *Simply Psychology*, <https://www.simplypsychology.org/maslow.html>, accessed 11.09.2025.

Middleton, Julia, 2007, *Beyond Authority*, Basingstoke: Palgrave Macmillan.

Miller, Victoria C., 1993, 'Ecclesiology, Scripture, and Tradition in the "Dublin Agreed Statement"', *Harvard Theological Review*, 86 (1), pp. 105–34.

Monroe Barnett, James, 1979, *The Diaconate: A Full and Equal Order*, Harrisburg, PA: Trinity Press International.

Morris, Jeremy, 2013, 'Building Community' in Julie Gittoes, Brutus Green, and James Head, *Generous Ecclesiology: Church, World and the Kingdom of God*, London: SCM Press.

Muller, Valentine, 1944, 'The Prehistory of the "Good Shepherd"', *Journal of Near Eastern Studies*, 3 (2), pp. 87–90.

Munro, Ellen, 2011, *The Munro Review of Child Protection: Final Report*, <https://assets.publishing.service.gov.uk/government/uploads/system/uploads/attachment_data/file/175391/Munro-Review.pdf>, accessed 11.09.2025.

Newbigin, Lesslie, 1977, *The Good Shepherd: Meditations on Christian Ministry in Today's World*, Leighton Buzzard: The Faith Press.

Newman, John Henry, 1877, 'The Restoration of Suffragan Bishops' in *The Via Media of the Anglican Church*, vol. II, London: Basil Montagu Pickering.

Noonan, James, 1996, *The Church Visible*, New York: Viking.

Northcott, Michael, 2011, 'Parochial Ecology on St Briavels Common: Rebalancing the Local and Universal in Anglican Ecclesiology and Practice', *Journal of Anglican Studies*, 10 (10), pp. 68–93.

Pepinster, Catherine, 2021, 'Looking for Radical solutions to Decline, Church of England debates lay-led house churches', *Religion News Service*, <https://religionnews.com/2021/07/09/looking-for-radical-solutions-to-decline-church-of-england-debates-lay-led-house-churches/>, accessed 11.09.2025.

Percy, Martyn, 1998, *Power and the Church: Ecclesiology in an Age of Transition*, London: Cassell.

Percy, Martyn, 2014, 'Are these the leaders that we really want?', *Church Times*, <https://www.churchtimes.co.uk/articles/2014/12-december/comment/opinion/are-these-the-leaders-that-we-really-want>, accessed 11.09.2025.

Percy, Martyn, 2021, '"Nuts and Bolts" Reflecting on the Governance Review Group Report', *Modern Church*, <https://modernchurch.org.uk/martyn-percy-nuts-and-bolts-i-reflecting-on-the-governance-review-group-report>, accessed 11.09.2025.

Percy, Martyn and Bash, Anthony, 1998, 'Wisdom and Weakness in Ministerial Formation: "Ambassadors" as a Paradigm for the Early Church' in Martyn Percy, *Power and the Church: Ecclesiology in an Age of Transition*, London: Cassell, pp. 40–58.

Platten, Stephen, 2007, 'Foreword' in Archbishops' Council, *Common Worship: Ordination Services*, London: Church House Publishing, pp. 2–3.

Plater, Ormonde, 2009, *Deacons in the Liturgy*, second edition, London: Church House Publishing.

Podmore, Colin, 2001, 'The Choosing of Bishops in the Early Church and in the Church of England: An Historical Survey' in Archbishops' Council, *Working with the Spirit: Choosing Diocesan Bishops*, GS 1405, London: Church House Publishing, pp. 113–38.

Podmore, Colin, 2008, 'A Tale of Two Churches: The Ecclesiologies of The Episcopal Church and the Church of England Compared', *Ecclesiastical Law Journal*, 10 (1), pp. 34–70.

Podmore, Colin, 2008, 'A Tale of Two Churches: The Ecclesiologies of the Episcopal Church and the Church of England Compared', *Ecclesiastical Law Journal*, 10, pp. 34–70, reprinted in *International Journal for the Study of the Christian Church*, 8, 2008, pp. 124–54.

Podmore, Colin, 2000, 'Re-telling the Tale', *Theology* 114 (1), pp. 13–22.

Podmore, Colin, 2010, 'The Baptismal Revolution in the American Episcopal Church: Baptismal Ecclesiology and the Baptismal Covenant', *Ecclesiology*, 6, pp. 8–38.

Prior, David, 1983, 'Resource Parishes – An alternative Way Forward' in Graham Dow et al. (eds), *Whose Hand on the Tiller? The Future of the Church's Ministry as a Response to the Tiller Report*, Bramcote, Grove Books, pp. 20–4.

Ramsey, Michael, 1956, *The Gospel and the Catholic Church*, second edition, London: Longmans, Green & Co.

Ramsey, Michael, 2009, *The Christian Priest Today*, reissue, London: SPCK.

Roberts, Vaughan, and Simms, David, 2017, *Leading by Story: Rethinking Church Leadership*, London: SCM Press.

Rohr, Richard, 2023, *Jesus' Alternative Plan*, London: SPCK.

Rohr, Richard, 2024, 'An Attractive Alternative' in Centre for Action and Contemplation, <https://cac.org/daily-meditations/an-attractive-alternative/>, accessed 11.09.2025.

Rumsey, Andrew, 2017, *Parish: An Anglican Theology of Place*, London: SCM Press.

Selwyn, Edward G., 1947, *The First Epistle of St Peter*, London: Macmillan.

Sinclair, J. M. et al, 2000, 'Upon' in *Collins Dictionary and Thesaurus*, Glasgow:

HarperCollins, p. 1313.

Sison, Marites N., 2013, 'The Lord Archbishop of Canterbury', *Anglican Journal*, <https://anglicanjournal.com/the-lord-archbishop-of-canterbury/>, accessed 11.09.2025.

Slocum, Robert Boak, 2015, *The Anglican Imagination: Portraits and Sketches of Modern Anglican Theologians*, Abingdon: Routledge.

Sneddon, Jonathan, 2013, 'Mitres and Maces – The Medieval Clergy at War', *Medieval Warfare*, 3 (2), pp. 6–8.

Staff Reporter, 2021, 'Bishop of Winchester steps back after diocesan rebellion', *Church Times*, <https://www.churchtimes.co.uk/articles/2021/21-may/news/uk/bishop-of-winchester-steps-back-after-diocesan-rebellion>, accessed 11.09.2025.

Stancliffe, David, 2003, *God's Pattern Shaping our Worship, Ministry and Life*, London: SPCK.

Stancliffe, David, 2018, 'Making Common Worship: Securing Some Underlying Theologies' in Aiden Platten (ed.), *Grasping the Heel of Heaven*, Norwich: Canterbury Press.

Stancliffe, David, 2023, 'Ordination in the Church of England: Theology and Practice in the Common Worship Ordinal' in Thomas Pott, James Hawkey and Keith Pecklers (eds), *Malines: Continuing the Conversation*, London: SPCK, pp. 141–52.

Standing, Roger, 2020, 'Episkope, Identity and Personhood' in Roger Standing and Paul Goodliff (eds), *Episkope: The Theory and Practice of Translocal Oversight*, London: SCM Press, pp. 203–12.

Standing, Roger, 2020, 'Theological Issues: Constants in Context' in Roger Standing and Paul Goodliff (eds), *Episkope: The Theory and Practice of Translocal Oversight*, London: SCM Press, pp. 14–43.

Standing, Roger, 2020, 'The Shape of Translocal Oversight' in Roger Standing and Paul Goodliff (eds), *Episkope: The Theory and Practice of Translocal Oversight*, London: SCM Press, pp. 213–24.

Stewart, Alistair C., 2014, *The Original Bishops: Office and Order in the First Christian Community*, Grand Rapids, MI: Baker Academic.

Stewart, Chris, 1999, *Driving Over Lemons: An Optimist in Andalucia*, London: Sort of Books.

Sykes, Stephen, 1994, 'Foundations of Anglican Ecclesiology' in Jeffrey John (ed.), *Living the Mystery: Affirming Catholicism and the Future of Anglicanism*, London: Darton, Longman and Todd, pp. 24–48.

Tam, Sharon, 2015, *The Trinitarian Dance*, Eugene, OR: Wipf and Stock.

Thompson, Emma, 2021, 'Holy Relic: What Will be Left of the Church of England after the Pandemic?', *The Spectator*, <https://www.spectator.co.uk/article/holy-relic-what-will-be-left-of-the-church-of-england-after-the-pandemic/>, accessed 11.09.2025.

Tiller, John, 1983, *A Strategy for the Church's Ministry*, London: CIO Publishing.

Timpson, James, 2024, *The Happy Index*, Manchester: Harper North.

Tims, George et al., 1986, *New English Hymnal: Full Music Edition*, Norwich: Canterbury Press.

Tribe, Shawn, 2018, 'The Pontifical Dalmatic and Tunicle: A Brief History and Consideration', *Liturgical Arts Journal*, <https://www.liturgicalartsjournal.

com/2018/08/the-pontifical-dalmatic-and-tunicle.html>, accessed 11.09.2025.

Vancil, Jack W., 1992, 'Sheep, shepherd' in *Anchor Bible Dictionary*, edited by Noel Freedman, 5, New York: Doubleday, pp. 1187–90.

Ware, Timothy, 1997 [1963], *The Orthodox Church*, new edition, London: Penguin Books.

Weber, Max, 1978 [1922], *Economy and Society*, edited by Guenther Roth and Claus Wittich, Berkeley, CA: University of California Press.

Weil, Louis, 1983, *Sacraments and Liturgy: The Outward Signs*, Oxford: Blackwell.

Weil, Louis, 2002, *A Theology of Worship*, Cambridge, MA: Cowley Publications.

Weil, Louis, 2006, 'Baptismal Ecclesiology: Uncovering a Paradigm' in Ronald L. Dowling and David R. Holeton (eds), *Equipping the Saints: Ordination in Anglicanism Today*, Blackrock: Columba Press, pp. 18–34.

Wheeler, Michael, 2018, 'Much more than nothing at all – Henry Scott Holland', *Church Times*, <https://www.churchtimes.co.uk/articles/2018/8-june/faith/faith-features/much-more-than-nothing-at-all-henry-scott-holland>, accessed 11.09.2025.

Williams, Hattie, 2019, 'Channel Islands to leave the see of Winchester', *Church Times*, <https://www.churchtimes.co.uk/articles/2019/11-october/news/uk/channel-islands-to-leave-the-see-of-winchester>, accessed 11.09.2025.

Williams, Rowan, 1995, *A Ray of Darkness*, Oxford: Coley Publications.

Williams, Rowan, 2020, 'Foreword' in Roger Standing and Paul Goodliff (eds), *Episkope: The Theory and Practice of Translocal Oversight*, London: SCM Press, pp. xxi–xxii.

Wilson, David Harris, 1956, *King James VI & I*, London: Jonathan Cape.

Winter, Sean F., 2020, 'Beyond the Household: The Emergence of Translocal Ministry in the New Testament' in Roger Standing and Paul Goodliff (eds), *Episkope: The Theory and Practice of Translocal Oversight*, London: SCM Press, pp. 3–13.

Wintz, Susan K. and Handzo, George F., 2005, 'Pastoral Care Staffing and Productivity: More than Ratios', *Chaplaincy Today*, 21 (1), pp. 3–10.

Wright, Christopher J. H., 2004, *Old Testament Ethics for the People of God*, Leicester: Inter-Varsity Press.

Wyatt, Tim, 2017, 'Archbishops propose new way forward on sexuality after Synod reject Bishops' report', *Church Times*, <https://www.churchtimes.co.uk/articles/2017/17-february/news/uk/synod-rebuff-for-bishops-report-on-sexuality>, accessed 11.09.2025.

Zizioulas, John D., 2011, *The Eucharistic Community and the World*, edited by Luke Ben, London: T&T Clark.

Websites

Caskey, J. et al., 'Mausoleum of Galla Placidia' in *Art and Architecture of the Middle Ages: Exploring a Connected World*, Ithaca, NY: Cornell University Press <https://artofthemiddleages.com/s/main/item/90>, accessed 05.08.2025.

Church of England, 'Diocese: Our Regional Presence', *Church of England*, <https://www.churchofengland.org/about/diocese-our-regional-presence>, accessed 11.09.2025.

Church of England, 2017, 'Discerning in Obedience: A Theological Review of the Crown Nominations Commission', *Church of England*, <https://www.churchofengland.org/sites/default/files/2018-01/gs-misc-1171-discerning-in-obedience-report-on-the-review-of-the-cnc.pdf>, accessed 11.09.2025.

Church Times, 2015, 'Out of the question', *Church Times*, <https://www.churchtimes.co.uk/articles/2015/9-january/regulars/out-of-the-question/out-of-the-question>, accessed 11.09.2025.

Country Meters, 'South Sudan Population', <https://countrymeters.info/en/South_Sudan>, accessed 11.09.2025.

Cuddesdon, 'Principal', <https://www.rcc.ac.uk/about-us/our-staff/rt-revd-humphrey-southern>, accessed 11.09.2025.

Diocese of Gloucester, 2015, 'Confirmation of Election', <https://www.gloucester.anglican.org/2015/confirmation-of-election/>, accessed 11.09.2025.

Ministry Division, 2014, 'Criteria for Selection for the Ordained Ministry of the Church of England', *Church of England*, <https://www.churchofengland.org/sites/default/files/2017-10/selection_criteria_for_ordained_ministry.pdf>, accessed 11.09.2025.

Royal Navy, 'Chaplain', <https://www.royalnavy.mod.uk/careers/roles-and-specialisations/services/surface-fleet/chaplain, accessed 11.09.2025.

Save the Parish, <https://savetheparish.com/>, accessed 11.09.2025.

The Archbishop of Canterbury, 'The Consecration of the Bishop of St Germans and the Bishop of Horsham, Lambeth Palace Chapel 15th July 2020 11:30am', <https://www.youtube.com/watch?v=r7zIK5ojkgI&feature=youtu.be>, accessed 11.09.2025.

The Archbishop of Canterbury, 'The Consecration of the Bishop of Lewes, Lambeth Palace Chapel 15th July 2020 2:30pm', <https://www.youtube.com/watch?v=NUpxLoJCCWc&feature=youtu.be>, accessed 11.09.2025.

The Archbishop of Canterbury, 2021, 'Bishop Emma Ineson to be Bishop to the Archbishops of Canterbury and York', *The Archbishop of Canterbury*, <https://www.archbishopofcanterbury.org/news/news-and-statements/bishop-emma-ineson-be-bishop-archbishops-canterbury-and-york>, accessed 11.09.2025.

The Archbishop of Canterbury, 2021, 'Bishop Tim Thornton to retire as Bishop of Lambeth', *The Archbishop of Canterbury*, <https://www.archbishopofcanterbury.org/news/news-and-statements/bishop-tim-thornton-retire-bishop-lambeth>, accessed 11.09.2025.

The Catholic Telegraph, 2013, 'Pope Francis: Priests should be "shepherds living with the smell of the sheep"', *The Catholic Telegraph*, <https://www.thecatholictelegraph.com/pope-francis-priests-should-be-shepherds-living-with-the-smell-of-the-sheep/13439>, accessed 11.09.2025.

The Episcopal Church of South Sudan, 'About', <https://southsudan.anglican.org/about/>, accessed 11.09.2025.

The Guardian, 2013, 'Archbishop of Canterbury enthronement – in pictures', *The Guardian*, <https://www.theguardian.com/uk/gallery/2013/mar/21/archbishop-of-canterbury-enthronement-pictures>, accessed 11.09.2025.

The Porvoo Communion, 'Porvoo Communion – A Communion of Churches', <http://porvoocommunion.org/>, accessed 11.09.2025.

UK Population Data, 'Population of England 2022', <https://populationdata.

org.uk/population-of-england/>, accessed 11.09.2025.

York Minster, 'Jonathan Frost Installed as 76th Dean of York', <https://yorkminster.org/latest/jonathan-frost-installed-as-76th-dean-of-york/, accessed 11.09.2025.

Index of Names and Subjects

agent of unity 107, 141, 146–50, 159
al-Miskin, Matta 124
Alternative Service Book 19–20, 41, 44–9, 130
Anglican Communion 13–16, 24–5, 28, 35–6, 133, 157
  Church of Ireland 107, 113–14
  Church in Wales 74, 77–8, 107, 112–14, 147
  Episcopal Church of the Philippines 35–6
  Episcopal Church of Scotland 77–8, 112–15
  Episcopal Church of South Sudan 148
  Episcopal Church of the United States of America 20, 24–37
apostle 2, 17, 44, 58, 61–3, 107–9, 141–6, 159
applied theology 8
Archbishop of Canterbury 21, 50, 56, 78
authority 3–4, 6–7, 12–21, 43–8, 74–5, 82, 85–9, 96, 109–15, 120–2, 132–8, 143–150, 156, 163–5, *see also* power, weighty
Avis, Paul 3, 6, 12, 14, 16–17, 20–1, 24, 55, 68, 82, 84, 131, 142

Bailey, Kenneth E. 118–28, 166

baptism 6–7, 24–37, 41–2, 44–6, 54–9, 53, 162
Barnett, James Munroe 92
Bash, Anthony 57
Bible 7, 18–19, 31, 64, 107–10, 114–15, 118–20, 127, 130, 134, 138, 161, *see also* Scripture
  1 Peter 61–2, 108–11, 118–20, 126
  1 Timothy 22, 61, 98, 143
  Acts 61, 66, 109, 111, 116, 143, 151, 167
  Ephesians 111
  Exodus 110
  Ezekiel 109
  Jeremiah 126
  John, Gospel of 93, 108, 110–15, 118, 124, 138
  Mark 120
  Philippians 31, 61
  Psalms 24, 66, 115, 118–22, 124–5, 146, 166
  Revelation 10, 110
  Timothy 22, 61, 143
  Titus 61, 66
body of Christ 3, 13–17, 21, 25, 31, 34, 36–7, 41–3, 48–51, 54–9, 72, 75–6, 81, 85, 87, 93, 95, 97, 100, 104, 111, 115, 123, 127, 131, 133, 143–5, 153,

155, 158, 160, 162-3, 165-6
Book of Common Prayer 1662 3, 16-18, 30, 41, 44-8, 50-1, 54, 69-71, 113-15, 130, 141-2
Book of Common Prayer 1979 24-7, 30-4, 36-7
Bradshaw, Paul 22, 31, 52
bride 2
Brown, Rosalind 91
bully 126

Caeremoniale Episcoporum 132
calling 2, 6, 14, 18, 45, 48, 97, 99-100, 108, 127, 144, 164, *see also* vocation
candidate 15, 25, 30, 32-3, 35-6, 39, 43, 45-6, 48-53, 57, 59, 79, 85, 91, 96-103, 111, 135, 153, 164
canon law 1-2, 13-14, 50, 63, 69, 72-3, 86, 114, 151, 157
cathedral 35, 76-7, 131-4
catholic 14-16, 28, 36, 51, 58, 80
 catholic order 80
 catholicity 10, 17, 21, 34, 36, *see also* ecumenical
CEO 5, 83, 97-8
Charry, Ellen T. 54-5
child of God 6, 88
Chrism Eucharist 36
Church Commissioners 150
Church of England reports
 Cameron 158-9
 Discerning in Obedience 74-5, 97, 139, 142
 Green 84, 89
 Senior Church Leadership 94
 Setting God's People Free 150
 Tiller 157
Church of God 6, 88

Clergy Discipline Measure 149, 155, 165
coercion 127, 132, 136, 157, 165
collaboration 24, 31-2, 37, 46, 48, 54, 59
collegiality 50, 59
community 13, 17, 19-21, 26-7, 30, 35, 43, 47-51, 55-62, 74, 77, 82-3, 85-9, 94, 97, 102, 115, 124, 142, 149, 153-4, 159-63, 166-7,
conductor 94-5
congregation 32, 35-7, 41-51, 54, 59, 63, 81, 91, 111-12, 133-4, *see also* laity
consecrate 44, 68-72, 131, 167
Constantine, emperor 64
corporate 18, 29, 33-4, 44, 49, 54, 99
corpus permixtum 14, 57, 59
Cottrell, Stephen 83, 137, 142, 144, 160
Croft, Steven 5, 94, 139
Crown Nominations Commission 74-5, 96-7, 103
crozier 83, 130, 132, 134, 138, *see also* pastoral staff
cumulative orders 4-6, 68, 87, 91-4, 108, 161
cursus honorum 6, 30, 86, 93, 122, 144, 149
Common Worship: Ordination Services
 The Declarations 15, 31-2
 The Giving of the Pastoral Staff 111, *see also* pastoral staff
 The Litany 33, 59
 The Peace 33, 53, 59
 The Preface 31
 The Presentation 39

INDEX OF NAMES AND SUBJECTS

The Welcome 32–3, 80, 85, 111, 134
Cyprian of Carthage 156

deacon 1–7, 14, 17, 20, 30–33, 41, 44–51, 60, 68–77, 86–7, 91–105, 107, 109, 123, 141, 144, 147, 149, 159–61
dean, of cathedral 78
dean, rural or area 76
delegation 88
denomination 4, 13, 15–17, 25–6, 58, 63, 68, 163, see also ecumenical
diocese 6, 28–9, 34–6, 43–4, 62–3, 72–7, 80–9, 96–9, 103–4, 111, 126, 133–7, 144–50, 153–9, 163–6
　Diocese of Blackburn 149
　Diocese of Salisbury 153–5
discernment 27, 91, 96–103, 135–7, 163–4
divorce 86

Early Church 61–4
Eastern Orthodox 10, 15, see also denomination
ecclesiology 1–4, 7–8, 12–15, 20–1, 24–37, 41–6, 54–9, 62–4, 76, 81, 84, 97, 102–3, 113–18, 153, 162, 166
　sacramental 1, 15, 21, 41–2, 154–64
　baptismal 7, 24–37, 41, 44–6, 54–5, 153, 162
ecumenical 17, 25–6, 82, 79, 85–6, see also denomination
election 19, 45–6, 135, 147
enslaved liberator 136
enthronement, of a bishop 80, 133, 137
epiclesis 47–8
episcopale iudicium 64
episcopal ring 130
episkope 61, 73, 83, 108
equality of the orders 87, 165
eschatology 92, 102
Eucharist 24–6, 29–30, 34–7, 41–6, 48, 54–9, 82, 130, 144–6, 162–4, 166, see also Holy Communion
Eucharistic assembly 29, 34, 37, 41–2, 46–8, 54, 59, 82, 130, 162, 166
Eucharistic president 26, 82, 144
ex cathedra 47

Fagerberg, David 2, 41–5, 59
fallibility 102
Farrer, Austin 159
Fisher, Geoffrey 157
fishing 125, see also mission
flock 2, 22, 65, 90, 103, 107–15, 118–28, 130–8, 141–50, 155–6, 160–1, 165
focal minister 48
foot washing 91–105
Fraser, Giles 150

Gardener, Fiona 155–6
Gibson, Paul 34, 55
glory 49, 113, 116, 119–21, 126–8, 142, 162, 166
Goodliff, Paul 83–4, 144
governor 28, 87, 114, 118
Gregory the Great 137
guardians of the faith of the Apostles 17, 22, 107, 109, 116, 139, 141–6, 150, 159

habitus 8, 61
Hanson, R. P. C. 149, 156–7
hierarchy 20, 73, 80, 86, 114, 166, *see also cursus honorum*
High Priest 2, 17, 109, 141
historical episcopal succession 16
Holland, Henry Scott 123
Holy Communion 3, 39, 48, 54, 64, *see also* Eucharist
Holy Spirit 6, 14, 16, 20, 25, 27, 30–6, 41–2, 47–51, 55, 59, 86, 97, 101–2, 111, 116, 128, 131, 133, 154
Hooker, Richard 18, 58–9
Hope Hailey, Veronica 154
Horsham, consecration of 62, 74
Hubbard, Julian 81, 87

International Anglican Liturgical Consultation 31
  Berkley Statement 31
Ignatius of Antioch 156
image of God 60
in loco Christi 162, 166
individual 8, 26–7, 30, 42, 46–8, 57, 59–60, 90, 125, 160
inhabit 3, 5, 61, 75, 93, 98, 103–5, 109, 123, 155, 159, 162
institution 6, 12–15, 20–1, 58, 73, 80–9, 94, 97–104, 126, 136, 146, 148, 153–66
integrated 1, 6, 12, 19–20, 31, 34, 37, 42, 48, 50, 54, 58, 60, 76, 95, 153, 157, 166
Irving, Alexander 39, 44–6
Islington, see of 73

Jones, James 81, 144
Jones, Simon 134
judge 86, 100, 149

jurisdiction 75, 88, 132–3, 136
kabod 124, *see also* glory
Keller, W. Phillip 121
kingdom 7–9, 12–13, 19–21, 30–1, 42–3, 59, 72, 81–2, 88, 92, 116, 144, 160, 165–6
koinonia 54, 56
Krikorian, Meshach Paul 119

laity 1–6, 17–19, 24–36, 42–3, 59–60, 72, 82, 93, 95, 112, 132, 135–6, 147–50, 153, 157–8, 160–1, *see also* baptized
Lambeth Quadrilateral 19, *see also* Anglican
laying on of hands 31, 46–8, 56, 69, 94, 160
Leggett, Richard Geoffrey 33, 43
leitourgia 41–5, 50, 153, 159, 162, 166
Lewes, consecration of 41, 53
lex credendi 2
lex orandi 2
lifelong orders 4, 60, 62, 76, 85–6, 105, 137
Liturgical Commission 4, 17–19, 32, 35, 59, 65
love 6–7, 14, 31, 48, 72, 82–4, 92, 99, 110–12, 119, 123–8, 137, 145, 149, 160

managerialism 5, 76, 83–4, 97–8, 147
mandate 62, 97, 133, 136, 147
  Royal Mandate 97, 147
Mandela, Nelson 90
marriage 22, 42, 63, 66, 85–6, 105, 137, *see also* wedding
Middleton, Julia 148
mission 17–19, 54–5, 59–61, 81,

INDEX OF NAMES AND SUBJECTS

100, 107–11, 115, 125, 136–7, 142–5, 156, 159, 167
mitre 130, 134
monarch 13–14, 28–9, 47, 59, 114, 119–21, 126, 146–7
monepiscopacy 62, 74, 158
Muller, Valentine 126

Newman, John Henry 158
Nicea, Council of 63
Northcott, Michael 29

oath of allegiance 15, 147
ontology 1–7, 12–14, 21, 54–7, 60–4, 68–72, 76, 80–3, 86–8, 96–9, 102–3, 107–15, 122, 136, 142, 153, 160–4
ordination of women 56, 145, *see also* traditionalist
oversight 5, 35, 61–4, 70–6, 82, 85, 88, 95, 99, 113, 145–6, 158, 161

parish 34–6, 43, 50, 73–6, 81–2, 98, 131, 134, 147, 157–8, 161
participation 36, 41–51, 155, 161–2
pastor 30–2, 72, 86–9, 113–15, 125, 146, 149, 161
pastoral cycle 8
pectoral cross 130
Percy, Martin 24, 28, 57–8, 84, 98–100
pistis 142
Plater, Ormond 135
Platten, Stephen 1–3
Podmore, Colin 24–37, 66–7, 136
porrectio instrumentorum 134
Porvoo agreement 17, *see also* ecumenical
power 6–7, 32, 48–50, 63–4, 75, 80–9, 91–104, 111, 120–3, 127–8, 137–9, 146, 150, 155–6, 159–66, *see also* authority
praxis 1, 7–9, 13, 19, 33, 64, 77, 83, 91, 107, 133–4, 137, 146, 159, 164–5
Preface to the Declaration of Assent 12–21
presbyter 5–6, 16, 32, 69–71, 78, 91, 94, 113, 157–9, 163, *see also* priest
priest 1–7, 14–17, 27–33, 44–51, 60, 68–70, 73–5, 83, 87, 93, 101, 108–11, 114–15, 123, 136, 141, 144, 147–9, 160–1, *see also* presbyter
primus inter pares 114
Prior, David 157, 167
privilege 6, 93, 96
prophetic ministry 93
proselytizing 125, 143, 167

quinquesecularism 19, 156

Ramsey, Michael 58, 79, 152, 167
recruitment 96
redemption 14, 43, 50, 57, 60, 111, 114, 125–6
relational ontology 57, 60, 68, 76, 107, 253, 162
resurrection 17, 42, 60–2, 124, 143–4
Revision Committee 69–70, 115, *see also Common Worship: Ordination Services*
ritual 18, 91–2, 95, 105, 159
Roberts, Vaughan S. 148
rod of iron 115, 119

Rohr, Richard 7, 165
Roman Catholic 10, 34, 63, 132–3, 147, *see also* denominations
Roy, Andrew 125
royal priesthood 2, 76, 116
royal we 44, 51

sacrament 1, 6, 8, 12–21, 24, 27, 34, 37, 41–2, 47, 50, 54–64, 75–6, 91, 97–8, 107, 137, 145–8, 153, 159, 162–6
safeguarding 7, 10
Save the Parish 150
Scripture, 3, 8, 14–21, 35, 58, 61–3, 68, 120, *see also* Bible
selection 92–104, *see also* discernment
senior clergy 70, 73, 86, 149, 164
sentinel 137, 144
servant 38, 44, 48, 89, 100, 105, 107, 109, 161
shared episcopacy 69, 76
sheep 86, 108–15, 118–28, 136–38, 143, 146, 149–50, 154, 160, 165
Sheldon Community 149, 154–5
shepherd 1, 2, 22, 33, 61, 81–2, 86–8, 107–15, 118–28, 130–8, 141–50, 153–66
   Good Shepherd 108, 111–12, 118–21, 126–8, 137–8, 161
sign 12, 21, 34, 54, 58–60, 63, 92, 131–2, 162
Simms, David 148
St Germans, consecration of 41, 49
Stancliffe, David 4, 8, 20, 57, 80, 92, 131–4, 149, 159
Standing, Roger 62–3, 68, 81–2, 84–8, 136, 143

status 6, 16, 27, 75, 83, 91–2, 108, 119, 147, 150, *see also cursus honorum*
Stewart, Chris 149
successive ordinations 4, 6, 87, *see also* cumulative orders
suffragan or area bishop 39, 74, 76, 82, 96, 158
Sykes, Stephen 4
synod 4, 14, 19, 28–9, 69–70, 115, 136, 145–6, 163–4
   General Synod 10, 14, 19, 69–70, 115, 136, 145, 163–4

teacher 22, 155, 161
traditio instrumentorum 18, 130, 135
traditionalist 50, 151, *see also* ordination of women
translocal 62, 73, 76, 78–9, 82–3, 85, 87–8, 164
Trinity 47, 54, 60, 94
trust 82, 85–6, 102–4, 109–10, 115, 120–7, 132, 135–8, 142–50, 154, 160–6
Tutu, Desmond 123

ubi caritas, chant 92
unity 3, 5, 14–16, 24–6, 30, 35, 56–8, 60, 63, 74, 87, 94, 103, 107, 111–14, 134, 141–2, 145–50, 159–60, 164

veni creator, chant 4
via media 4, 20, 58
vicarious ministry 93
vocation 6, 20, 27, 45, 62, 83, 101–2, 112, 135–7, 142, 166, *see also* calling
vulnerability 7, 88

Weber, Max 87, 163
wedding, 9, 36, 45, 60, 137, 162, *see also* marriage
weighty 124, *see also* authority
Weil, Louis 24–7, 50
Whalon, Pierre 24, 28
Williams, Rowan, 63, 77, 90, 136
Winter, Sean F. 61–2
wisdom 84, 99, 103, 120, 124, 163
world 6–7, 14–16, 29, 32–34, 43, 54–60, 75, 81–3, 86, 92, 99, 103, 108, 110–12, 123–4, 156, 160, 163–6
Wright, Christopher J. 118

Zizioulas, John 56

www.ingramcontent.com/pod-product-compliance
Lightning Source LLC
Chambersburg PA
CBHW022056290426
44109CB00014B/1124